TIPS
from
the
TOP

TIPS
from
the
TOP

EDITED BY EDIE MILLIGAN

ALPHA

A Pearson Education Company

International Standard Book Number: 0-02-864413-1
Library of Congress Catalog Card Number: 2002115295

04 03 02   8 7 6 5 4 3 2 1

Interpretation of the printing code: The rightmost number of the first series of numbers is the year of the book's printing; the rightmost number of the second series of numbers is the number of the book's printing. For example, a printing code of 02-1 shows that the first printing occurred in 2002.

Printed in the United States of America

For marketing and publicity, please call: 317-581-3722

The publisher offers discounts on this book when ordered in quantity for bulk purchases and special sales.

For sales within the United States, please contact: Corporate and Government Sales, 1-800-382-3419 or corpsales@pearsontechgroup.com

Outside the United States, please contact: International Sales, 317-581-3793 or international@pearsontechgroup.com

Publisher: *Marie Butler-Knight*
Product Manager: *Phil Kitchel*
Managing Editor: *Jennifer Chisholm*
Senior Acquisitions Editor: *Mike Sanders*
Development Editor: *Ginny Bess Munroe*
Production Editor: *Katherin Bidwell*
Copy Editor: *Cari Luna*
Cover Designer: *Doug Wilkins*
Book Designer: *Trina Wurst*
Indexer: *Brad Herriman*
Layout/Proofreading: *Angela Calvert, John Etchison*

To my father, William W. Milligan, who very early in my life taught me to recognize, respect, and aspire to true professionalism. Everyone who has contributed to this book has exceeded even his standards.

CONTENTS

INTRODUCTION

On the personal finance shelf at your local bookstore there are only two kinds of authors: experts who stepped away from their professions long enough to write, and writers who researched the subject long enough time to become experts. When you buy a personal finance book it may not be immediately obvious which type you are reading. Because the longer experts step away from their profession, the more they look like writers; and the longer writers research the topic, the more they look like experts.

Writing a book is a major effort. Time, talent, and tolerance are required in massive quantities. People who are working as professionals in demanding areas such as accounting, law, financial planning, insurance, credit counseling, and investments rarely have time to shoot off an e-mail to their mother, let alone craft an entire manuscript. So those people who do find the time have necessarily pulled away, if only temporarily, from their core profession. It is the nature of personal finance books that the information is likely to change quickly, depending upon the economy, the tax laws, and other forces, so deadlines are usually impossible and the work overshadows their normal activities of their profession. This leaves the reader with the choice of purchasing books from authors who are no longer spending all day in the trenches of personal finance battles being fought across the country.

Nothing is more revealing than how a specific family was confronted with a specific decision that significantly impacted their future. All the factors that impact this decision are revealed in the personal relationship the professional shares with that client. Sure, the SEC rules and the tax laws and the insurance regulations are important, but the more important issue is how that complicated landscape is perceived by the client and what the client would like to achieve.

The farther away an author gets from these relationships, the less the author can communicate to a reader on the pages of a book. They can quote facts, consequences, strategies, and outcomes, but to build a sense of how those factors impact a real person, they have to know real people. The contributors in this book do. They are practicing their crafts and have brought their knowledge to you in the most difficult format. It was nothing short of torture for most of them to "get to the point." They are relationship builders, hand-holders, educators, and counselors. They want to know you before they help you. They are trained and even regulated to not give advice before they are sure it is appropriate for you.

But they did get to the point. Actually, they made hundreds of points that are relevant to you. This book is what you get when you ask over a hundred professionals to tell you the most important thing that they know about their craft, or the least understood strategy, or the simplest tactic for managing their finances that no one seems to use. When you read a traditional personal finance book by one author you need to sift through a whole chapter to find the one or two points that you can personally use. You throw out all the buildup to that piece of information and you tend to remember the punch line. This book gathers all of those punch lines (you know, the important stuff) into one place. There's no filler here to make the book look like it says more than it does. Just tip after tip of great advice, little-known facts, and powerful strategies that have been proven to work for people just like you, the clients.

Personal finance is a field that draws professionals from many educational backgrounds, professional licensures, and accreditations. Many of these professions do battle over what is probably merely marketing turf. Who is most qualified to give tax, estate planning, investment, or insurance advice? Is it the one with the highest level of education or the most letters after their name or the most years in practice? Does it matter how they receive their compensation? Is it better if they work for themselves or for an international conglomerate? These are hard questions for consumers to answer. One thing does seem clear: No one person seems to have all of the expertise or all of the answers.

Whether these distinctions are relevant or not, they have resulted in the fact that many professionals across these fields now tend to shy away from publishing all together. Until now. This book brings you a rare collection of the many voices of personal finance. What you might find is that even though the experts' specific knowledge may differ and occasionally their perspectives clash, one thing is ultimately clear: They care about their clients immensely. Their profiles speak not of degrees and accolades, but of their true passion for helping people.

Many times professionals who work with personal finance issues carry the label "bean counter." This implies a focus on numbers and away from people. You will find that the Top Money Minds selected for this text have not left people out of the equation. In fact, for them, people and their personal circumstances make up the equation.

HOW TO USE THIS BOOK
From the complete novice to the compulsive personal finance reader, this book has something for everyone. If you are just getting started making your way through the personal finance forest, just open the book to a section that sounds interesting and read a few tips. Look for one that seems like it might solve a problem or open up an opportunity for you and try it! If you love reading the latest scoop in personal finance strategies, this book will be a gold mine for you. Make it a game: See how many tips in each chapter you already know and how many are brand new to you. Rank the new ones by their possible usefulness to you and then get to work! The Top Money Minds will probably keep you busy for months, learning, growing, and improving your financial position.

EXTRAS
Throughout the book I have sprinkled helpful and interesting sidebars to compliment the tips supplied by our Top Money Minds. "In Money Words" are common household phrases that are translated into their meaning in your money life, giving you great food for thought. "Mind Over Money" are tips that help you see the psychological impact that money has in your life and give you some strategies for designing better money attitudes that lead to financial security. I have also included favorite websites of our contributors that can take you to new levels of understanding or ongoing information regarding your financial decisions. And finally, in several chapters you will find a Point/ Counterpoint Section where we have highlighted advice where our experts disagree. You may have sensed some disagreement on these topics and now you can see some of the specific arguments on both sides.

Acknowledgments

Tips from the Top was the brainchild of Mike Sanders, acquisitions editor at Alpha Books. As he came to me with this idea, he was intending for me to write it. After getting over the shock of listening to a writer turn down an invitation to write, he embraced the idea of inviting a variety of professionals to come together in one binding to bring readers the most relevant collection of financial tips ever compiled. Thank you, Mike, for your willingness to champion this new idea through the hurdles of the publishing world.

Without a doubt, this book never would have happened without the tireless enthusiasm of the public relations executives at the financial service associations around the country. They not only identified and recruited the Top Money Minds, they gave me the initial enthusiasm for the project that sustained me through all the deadlines and editing passes! I would like to sincerely thank the following for their trust and support: Joel Allegretti (American Institute of Certified Public Accountants), Ellen Turf (National Association of Personal Financial Advisors), Lydia Sermons-Ward (National Foundation for Credit Counseling), Doug Nogami (CFP Board of Standards), Sharon Burns (Association for Financial Counseling and Planning Education), Heather Almand (Financial Planning Association), Betsy Bott (National Assocation of Insurance and Financial Advisors), Kallie Guimond (American Association of Debt Management Organizations), Rich Wyler (Association for Investment Management and Research), David Tittsworth (Investment Counsel of America), Rachel Rich (International Foundation of Employee Benefit Plans), Ade Schreiber (Registered Financial Planners Institute), and Michelle Connor (Society of Financial Service Professionals).

As the project took shape, several people on my team made my job a delight: Julie Dowrey, who coordinated the administrative and marketing functions; Will Delphia, Preston Powell and Joe DelMedico, who designed and supported the website; and Angie Hollerich, who is always there to help me brainstorm and focus.

A special thanks goes to my good friend Jordan Goodman at www.moneyanswers.com for the glossary terms from *Barron's Dictionary of Finance and Investment Terms* (Sixth Edition, 2003). The "In Money

Words" sidebars were contributed by Melody Carlsen from the International Foundation for Employee Benefits. The money websites were gathered by my crack sidebar squad of Steve Wightman, Phyllis Bernstein, Cathie E. Cobe, Jennifer Delcamp, Raj Pillai, Michael Eisenberg, Pat Hanratty, and Angie Hollerich.

The great team at Alpha Books has definitely exceeded all expectations once again: Marie Butler-Knight, Phil Kitchel, Jennifer Chisholm, Mike Sanders, Ginny Bess Munroe, Katherin Bidwell, Cari Luna, Trina Wurst, Angela Calvert, and John Etchison. They are able to stay focused on quality while remaining calm in the face of torturous deadlines. Thank you guys!

For a writer to be without words is a rare moment indeed, but I can't imagine what I could say to thank these 110 unique individuals for their special place in my life over the last six months. The Top Money Minds are not only tops in their understanding of personal financial concepts, they are all top human beings, with vision and insight into how to make something happen that didn't exist before. They made it truly delightful to get up each morning and look for the next great tip to bring to you. I feel blessed to have come to know each of them and have learned valuable lessons from all of them, not just about money. It is no wonder that they have risen to the top of their professions.

TRADEMARKS

All terms mentioned in this book that are known to be or are suspected of being trademarks or service marks have been appropriately capitalized. Alpha Books and Pearson Education, Inc., cannot attest to the accuracy of this information. Use of a term in this book should not be regarded as affecting the validity of any trademark or service mark.

TOP MONEY MINDS

To be included in this group of accomplished financial practitioners, each of these professionals has demonstrated a dedication to their profession, their clients, and their interest in continually helping people everywhere to raise their level of financial security. They have volunteered their time to prepare tips for this volume. Complete information about their approach to their work, their credentials, and education is listed in Appendix A. Please write them and thank them for the wonderful information they have shared with you.

Harvey Aaron	Canton, Massachusetts
Kathy Adams-Smith	Hamilton, Ohio
Michael Alberts	East Woodstock, Connecticut
Kent Anthony	Sterling, Kansas
Frank Arnold	San Antonio, Texas
Carolyn Baker	Farmington, Minnesota
Reg Baker	Las Vegas, Nevada
Elaine Bedel	Indianapolis, Indiana
Kristofor Behn	Boston, Massachusetts
Phyllis Bernstein	New York, New York
Clark Blackman II	Houston, Texas
Sidney Blum	Northbrook, Illinois
Lesley Brey	Honolulu, Hawaii
Connie Brezik	Scottsdale, Arizona
Susan Bruno	Rowayton, Connecticut
Jack Capron	Syracuse, New York
Cary Carbonaro	Clermont, Florida
Melody Carlsen	Brookfield, Wisconsin
Jon Chernila	Irvine, California
Christine Cobb	Houston, Texas
Cathie Cobe	Columbus, Ohio
Preston Cochrane	Salt Lake City, Utah
John Connell	Denver, Colorado

James Conrad	Wexford, Pennsylvania
Charles Copeland	Redlands, California
Brad Cougill	Indianapolis, Indiana
Joan Coullahan	Sterling, Virginia
William Cratty	Hingham, Massachusetts
Donna Cygan	Albuquerque, New Mexico
Jennifer Delcamp	Bethany, Oklahoma
Jonathan Dinkins	Owings Mills, Maryland
Peg Downey	Silver Spring, Maryland
Stephen Drake	Prescott, Arizona
Sandra Dunaway	Mobile, Alabama
Michael Eisenberg	Los Angeles, California
Gregory Fenton	Sandwich, Massachusetts
John Feyche	Torrance, California
Mitchell Freedman	Sherman Oaks, California
Jill Gianola	Columbus, Ohio
Don Gomez	Atlanta, Georgia
John Grable	Manhattan, Kansas
Sherman Hanna	Columbus, Ohio
Patrick Hanratty	Cleveland, Ohio
Joe Harper	Columbus, Ohio
Timothy Hayes	Pittsford, New York
Bruce Heling	Brookfield, Wisconsin
David Hogan	Tulsa, Oklahoma
Angie Hollerich	Gahanna, Ohio
Dennis Houlihan	Fort Wayne, Indiana
Bonnie Hughes	Rome, Georgia
Henrietta Humphreys	San Francisco, California
Alexis Jensen	Torrance, California
Ann Jevne	Norwalk, Connecticut
Steve Johnson	Metairie, Louisiana

Raymond Julian	Newton, Massachusetts
William Kaiser	Dallas, Texas
James Kantowski	Bethesda, Maryland
Stuart Kessler	New York, New York
Paul Knott	Wilmington, North Carolina
Randall Kratz	Houston, Texas
Marsha LePhew	Rock Hill, South Carolina
Randall Leshin	Delray Beach, Florida
Deborah Levine	Los Angeles, California
John Henry and	
Constanza Low	Pine Plains, New York
Judith Ludwig	Canton, Massachusetts
Paul Lyons	Dallas, Texas
Suzi Marsh	Stone Mountain, Georgia
Judi Martindale	San Luis Obispo, California
Jeffrey Mehler	Centerbrook, Connecticut
Jeff Michael	Riverside, California
Helen Modly	Middleburg, Virginia
Steven Morris	Norcross, Georgia
Cheryl Moss	De Pere, Wisconsin
Barbara O'Neill	Newton, New Jersey
Craig Olson	Portland, Oregon
Lloyd Painter	Louisville, Kentucky
Raj Pillai	Solon, Ohio
William Pomeroy	Baton Rouge, Louisiana
Barbara Raasch	New York, New York
Gregory Railsback	Vancouver, Washington
Kathleen Rehl	Lutz, Florida
Paul Richard	San Diego, California
Howard Safer	Nashville, Tennessee
Samuel Sanders, Jr.	Baton Rouge, Louisiana

Michael Schulman	Central Valley, New York
Robert Schumann	New Albany, Ohio
Joseph Sedita	Plant City, Florida
Robert Seltzer	Beverly Hills, California
John Sestina	Columbus, Ohio
Martin Sickles	Atlanta, Georgia
Louis Stanasolovich	Pittsburgh, Pennsylvania
Loyd Stegent	Houston, Texas
Judy Stewart	Carlsbad, California
Parke Teal	DeLand, Florida
Timothy Thaney	Rochester, New York
Lindsey Torbett	Alexandria, Louisiana
Chad Tramp	Des Moines, Iowa
Linda Tucker	North Little Rock, Arkansas
Richard Vera	Atlantic Highlands, New Jersey
Jim Wagenmann	Bethesda, Maryland
Robert Walsh	Jersey City, New Jersey
Frank Washelesky	Chicago, Illinois
Nate Wenner	Minneapolis, Minnesota
Steven Wightman	Lexington, Massachusetts
Mark Wilson	Newport Beach, California
Leonard Wright	Los Angeles, California
John Wyckoff	Portland, Oregon
Susan Zimmerman	Apple Valley, Minnesota

1

FINANCIAL PLANNING GOAL SETTING

Wealth is not his that has it,
but his that enjoys it.

—Benjamin Franklin

Terms from the Top

correlation   Statistical measure of the degree to which the movements of two variables are related.

diversification   Spreading of risk by putting assets in several categories of investments—stocks, bonds, money market instruments, and precious metals, for instance, or several industries, or a mutual fund, with its broad range of stocks in one portfolio.

fair market value   Price at which an asset or service passes from a willing seller to a willing buyer. It is assumed that both buyer and seller are rational and have a reasonable knowledge of relevant facts.

liquid asset   Cash or easily convertible into cash. Some examples include money-market fund shares, U.S. Treasury bills, and bank deposits.

modified adjusted gross income   Determined by subtracting from gross income allowable adjustments, such as IRA payments and alimony payments; modified for specific eligibility calculations, such as Roth IRA, Hope credit, and Coverdell accounts by adding back certain adjustments.

risk averse   Term referring to the assumption that, given the same return and different risk alternatives, a rational investor will seek the security offering the least risk—or put another way, the higher the degree of risk, the greater the return that a rational investor will demand.

statement of net worth (balance sheet)   Financial report showing the status of an individual's assets, liabilities, and equity on a given date.

Source: reprinted by permission of Jordan Goodman, Dictionary of Finance and Investment Terms *(Barron's, 5th Edition)*

When you're looking for financial security, how can you even begin to know where to start? This is a great place—right here at the beginning of this outstanding collection of tips from the country's top financial experts. Money is complicated, elusive, frustrating, and often boring. When your money life is working well, all other challenges seem a little easier. When your money life is upset, it may not seem to matter how well the rest of your life is put together.

Setting goals is not something humans do by nature. We work toward goals, we dream about goals, but we don't often actually *set* them, *monitor* them, and *reach* them. That takes discipline, focus, and usually a team effort between family and professionals who can help streamline the process. The tips in this chapter should spark a desire to begin thinking and dreaming. Find the one that makes you pause and think about where you will be in 10, 20, or 50 years and what positive impact you can have on that outcome today.

All tips in this chapter are intended for informational purposes only. Should you find one potentially helpful to your situation, you should consult with your legal, tax, or investment professional familiar with your individual situation to determine its suitability prior to taking any action or investing any money.

GETTING MOTIVATED

We've all heard ourselves begin a sentence with, "Someday when I have enough money, I'll …" Goal setting is merely turning that phrase around to mean, "I've decided that I'll have the money someday to …" Pick the day, pick the goal, and put into motion the mechanisms that will make it happen. It can be one of the scariest things we do, because it reminds us that we may have more control over our financial security than we would like to believe. Failure is no longer something we can blame on others when we plan with intent and information.

◆◆◆

The power of your dreams is the key to the success of your financial plan. Powerful dreams equate to a powerful plan. Be specific and descriptive as you answer these questions about each of your dreams. What is the dream? Why is this dream important? When will I need the financial resources for this dream? How much will I need? Do I see myself attaining this dream? The clarity and intensity of your responses to these questions will give you the passion and focus you need to stay true to your plan when stumbling blocks appear in your path. Got it? Now do it!

Joseph E. Sedita, CPA/PFS, CFP®
Owner, Joseph E. Sedita and Co. Certified Public Accountants

If you are a woman, you have an estimated 9 out of 10 chance that you will manage your finances alone during at least one point in your life. If you never marry or lose your spouse to death or divorce, it will be all up to you. It is important for you to get educated about money and accept responsibility for your financial future. The following quote says it all: If it is to be, it is up to me. For information about personal finance topics, contact your local Cooperative Extension office or the Women's Institute for a Secure Retirement (www.wiser.heinz.org).

Barbara O'Neill, Ph.D., CFP®, AFC, CHC
Author of Saving on a Shoestring

All you really need to know about financial planning is right at your fingertips … more is better than less and sooner is better than later. Whether you are a young and successful person whose future plans stop at forecasting your weekend or a parent whose children have flown the coop, you should start planning for your family's financial future now. The best strategy is to develop a plan early, then build on that plan as time progresses. Remember, financial planning is a process, not a one-time event. As your life changes, so, too, will your financial needs.

Howard Safer, M.B.A., CPA/PFS
EVP, Regions Morgan Keegan Trust Co.

Paying attention to the basics as a young adult will serve you financially later in life. Generally it takes a big dose of common sense. Good health equals low lifetime medical costs, so eat moderately, sleep well, and exercise a lot. Good humor helps weather the bumps in life, so seek and maintain good friends. Passion is a great motivator, so find out what work you like to do and then do it with all your heart. Most of the good stuff is still measured in commitment, not dollars.

Bonnie A. Hughes, CFP®
President, A&H Financial Planning and Education, Inc.

When setting financial goals, remember to make them SMART: Specific, Measurable, Achievable, Realistic and Tangible. Write them down, and track your progress regularly.

Clark M. Blackman II, CPA/PFS, CFP®, ChFC, CFA®, CIMA, AAMS®
Managing Director and Chief Investment Officer, Post Oak Capital

---

IN MONEY WORDS

Know thyself … Goals, time horizon, risk tolerance, discipline

---

Everyone's heard the saying: "You can't take it with you." The flip side of this is: "The only reason to make money is to spend it." Surprised? Consider that there are only three ways to spend money: for your own needs and wants; for the needs and wants of your family or other loved ones; and for the needs of society, either through your taxes or your contributions to charity. Taking this further, the only reason to save a part of the money you make is to spend it later. Therefore, build a plan that balances today's spending with your future hopes and dreams in these three areas.

Cheryl A. Moss, CPA/PFS, CFP®, CLU, CDP
Tax Advisor

If you are about to tie the knot, make sure to discuss financial planning before getting married. Discussing financial matters and establishing a joint financial plan can help to ensure that matrimonial bliss carries over to your finances.

Steve Johnson, CPA/PFS, CFP®
Owner, Johnson Financial

Pigs get fed and hogs get slaughtered. Set reasonable goals and don't get greedy along the way.

J. Victor Conrad, CPA/PFS, CFP®, ChFC
Financial Advisor, The MONY Group

Build a dream retirement. Dreams do come true if you set goals and chart out action plans. Start now by writing down your age to retire, where you will live, how much you want to spend, and what you will do. This is your dream retirement and your incentive to build an action plan to make it come true.

Connie Brezik, CPA/PFS
Investment Advisor, Asset Strategies, Inc.

Only a few paths to real wealth have ever existed: earnings, investing, inheritance, theft, fraud, and lotteries. Set your sights on earning and investing. It feels better than inheritance, theft, or fraud and it is infinitely more attainable than winning the lottery. Spend less than you earn and invest thoughtfully over a long time horizon. Staying off the consumption treadmill allows energy for pursuing true passions. Investing thoughtfully keeps economic power with you. Quiet wealth is within the reach of every motivated person.

Bonnie A. Hughes, CFP®
President, A&H Financial Planning and Education, Inc.

Money Answers (www.moneyanswers.com). Fun ideas and great strategies for everyday money decisions.

Having a dream is not the same as living a dream. The bridge between having and living is a plan. To create your plan, first answer three questions. Why do I want to achieve this dream? What knowledge, resources, and assistance will I need to achieve this dream? What fears will keep me from this dream? Next, do three things. Commit your dream to writing. Specify a completion date. Identify the actions necessary for success. Now, take some action toward your dream today, be persistent, and review your plan periodically. That's it. Have fun on your journey!

Joseph E. Sedita, CPA/PFS, CFP®
Joseph E. Sedita and Co. Certified Public Accountants

PICKING A PLANNER

Financial Planning, as a profession, is about 30 years old. It might actually be "The World's Youngest Profession." Prior to this short existence, financial advice came from relatives, friends, employers, ministers, insurance salespeople, and tax preparers. Attorneys and accountants certainly touched these areas in their practices, but none would have identified "financial planning" as a service they provided a quarter-century ago.

Now, you have your pick of a terrific range of professionals from different educational backgrounds and different licensing/accrediting programs to help you with your planning. About the Credentials in the appendix will help you evaluate the differences in these credentials for your own needs. The following tips will also help you begin to decide if and where you should seek the guidance of a professional.

♦ ♦ ♦

Do it yourself or hire a financial professional? Consider the same three issues you would in any other area of life, (car repair, house cleaning, or brain surgery, for example.) Namely, do you have the time, interest, and ability to do the job yourself well? If one or more of these elements is lacking, you risk a poor result. Dust bunnies under the bed may be annoying but are rarely deadly. However, in the complex world of money, missteps are often costly and can be financially fatal. Honestly evaluate yourself in terms of time available, interest, and ability in each of the various areas of finance. Then supplement your skills with the services of competent and caring professionals.

Cheryl A. Moss, CPA/PFS, CFP®, CLU, CDP
Tax Advisor

Would you ask your neighbor or friend if you needed heart surgery to do the deed? Most likely not. Asked a little differently, would you ask your neighbor or friend to get you to retirement with your future $1,000,000, $2,000,000, or $5,000,000? Most likely so. Take time, more than the eight hours that the average American takes during a lifetime, to look for those with expertise that is measured by CPA/PFS, CFA®, CFP®, CLU, or ChFC. Spend time up front. Interview, decide, and take action. This person will be gold to you and your family over the years.

Leonard C. Wright, CPA/PFS, CFP®, CLU, ChFC
Principal, Strategic Financial Group

Choosing a financial planner may be the single most important financial decision you make. Here are a few places to call to check them out:

- Certified Financial Planner Board of Standards: 888-CFP-MARK
- American Institute of Certified Public Accountants: 888-777-7077, ext2
- National Association of Securities Dealers: 800-289-9999
- North American Securities Administrators Association: 202-737-0900
- National Fraud Exchange: 800-822-0416 ($39 fee)

Ask to confirm that the advisor is in good standing and whether there are any complaints or regulatory/disciplinary black marks on their record.

Clark M. Blackman II, CPA/PFS, CFP®, ChFC, CFA®, CIMA, AAMS®
Managing Director, Post Oak Capital

When you interview a financial advisor, know the tough questions to ask:

1. What is your educational background?
2. How long have you been offering financial planning services?
3. What continuing education in financial planning do you pursue?
4. Are you a member of any professional financial planning associations?
5. Have you ever been cited by a professional or regulatory governing body for disciplinary reasons?
6. Will you or an associate work for me?
7. How is your firm compensated?

For more details, check out www.NAPFA.org.

Cary Carbonaro, M.B.A., CFP®
President, Family Financial

In choosing a financial planner, be sure their product solutions include real estate, owning your own business, equities, bonds, and life insurance. It is only through a broad selection of products that true diversification can take place.

Craig Olson, CPA/PFS
Partner, Parrott Partnership

IN MONEY WORDS

Patience is a virtue ... Invest for the long term

Don't be afraid to ask exactly how the advisor is compensated and how much he or she will make as a result of working with you.

Don A. Gomez, CFP®
President, Momentum Financial Advisors

Why should you select a fee-only advisor? They work solely for their clients and are compensated only by a previously agreed on fee. Fee-only advisors may charge a retainer fee, hourly fee, assets under management fee, net worth fee, or a combination of these fees. You need to decide if you are willing to pay out of pocket for objective advice or go to a commissioned salesperson who will offer their products that may or may not be the best for you. You might perceive their services to be free, but best products (in most cases) are the ones with the lowest cost that fee-only advisors have access to.

Cary Carbonaro, M.B.A., CFP®
President, Family Financial

POINT ⦚▶

When you are evaluating financial advisors, make sure you understand how they get paid. You may consider choosing an advisor that is not influenced by commissions, but rather works on a fee basis. Be sure you distinguish between fee-only and fee-based. Fee-based advisors might still earn commissions on products such as insurance and annuities. The National Association of Personal Financial Advisors (NAPFA) defines a fee-only advisor as one who is "compensated solely by the client with neither the advisor nor any related party receiving compensation that is contingent on the purchase or sale of a financial product." By working with a fee-only advisor, there are no commissions involved which helps your advisor remain totally objective, resulting in a better recommendation for you.

William K. Kaiser, CPA/PFS
Financial Advisor, Howard Financial Services, Inc.

◀⦚ COUNTERPOINT

Much journalistic ink has been spilled over the issue of whether it is better to hire a fee-only or a commission-oriented financial professional. How do you decide? Competence, trustworthiness, and caring (or the lack thereof) exist on both sides of the compensation divide. Therefore, focus your efforts on locating a professional who is competent (knows the right things), trustworthy (does the right things) and who you feel truly cares about your needs ahead of their own. Any advisor who passes these tests will be quite willing to discuss and help you feel comfortable with how they are compensated.

Susan Zimmerman, M.A., LMFT, ChFC, CLU
Author of The Power in Your Money Personality

MIND OVER MONEY

A positive attitude is an important resource to achieving your financial goals. Believe in yourself and your ability to take actions that will improve your financial future. No one cares as much about the quality of your life as you do.

Barbara O'Neill, Ph.D., CFP®, AFC, CHC
Author of Saving on a Shoestring

GOAL-SETTING STRATEGIES

Whether you embark on this process by yourself or with the help of a professional, there are a variety of strategies that can work for you. The tips in this section give you an overview of some of the strategies that you may want to consider. Later chapters will cover in greater depth the specific actions to take to watch your goals become reality.

♦ ♦ ♦

Prepare a statement of net worth twice a year. I recommend that this statement be prepared after the June 30th and December 31st investment statements are received. You should include the estimated fair market value of any real estate that you own and any mortgage amounts. Personal property (automobiles, jewelry, etc.) should not be included unless it is substantial such as an art collection. The net worth statement should separate accounts according to ownership (i.e., husband, wife, joint) and it should be totaled. Remember, it's not what you earn that will make you wealthy, it's what you keep. You can be a high wage earner, but if you are also a high spender you may never be able to retire because you will be in the class of the working rich.

Judy Ludwig, CPA/PFS, CFP®, ChFC, AEP
Advisor, Tandem Financial Services, Inc.

If you want to be financially independent, you will need to build assets. These assets need to be things that can make you money, such as stocks, rental property, and land. Boats, cars, houses, or campers do not count. They cost you money.

H. Lindsey Torbett, CPA/PFS, CFP®
President, Wealth Development Group

Be careful not to put all of your eggs in one basket. An important aspect of investment management is diversification. Studies have determined that how you divide money among fixed income, growth, and other investments often is more important in determining overall portfolio performance than in selecting specific investments. This is called asset allocation. Using specific investment policies that identify your appropriate asset allocation is a key. So how do you do this? Since no one can predict with accuracy an investment that will perform the best in any given time, funds should be allocated among different asset classes having low correlation. By having assets with low correlation, losses incurred by one class will hopefully be offset by gains in another.

Phyllis Bernstein, CPA/PFS
President, Phyllis Bernstein Consulting

Save at least 10 percent of each paycheck. Most wage earners should accumulate 10 percent of their annual income into a primary cash reserve and another 10 percent into a secondary reserve. (Treasury Bonds, Municipal Bonds). The outcome of this strategy is that you live within your means, you don't spend more than you make. Spending more than you make is a fast way to the poorhouse. Self-employed and retired individuals should build their cash reserves to an even greater level. Once you have achieved this level of liquid savings, future deposits should be directed toward balancing and building your portfolio according to your goals.

Robert B. Walsh, CPA/PFS, CFP®
President, Lighthouse Financial Advisors, Inc.

According to the legendary football coach Vince Lombardi, the difference between success and failure is not the lack of knowledge or strength, but the lack of will. To win at finances, you will need a healthy dose of discipline in addition to all the knowledge you can gain through books, websites, seminars, and working with financial coaches. So map out a strategy to reach your financial goals, and remain patient but flexible. Do not tinker with the starting lineup every day!

Raj Pillai, Ph.D., CFP®
NAPFA-Registered Advisor, Financial Fitness Network of Solon

Establish benchmarks at regular intervals for financial goals to measure your progress. If you want to save $5,000 in two years, for example, toward a new car, you should save $2,500 after a year and $1,250 in six months. Even small amounts of savings can grow to significant sums over time through the power of compound interest. For example, $100 a month earning 8% will grow to $18,420 in 10 years. Time + Money = Magic.

Barbara O'Neill, Ph.D., CFP®, AFC, CHC
Author of Saving on a Shoestring

Ever wonder if a particular "rule of thumb" applies to you? To tell, you first need to figure out your dreams! If you know where you are going, you're in a better position to figure out if a strategy works for you. For instance, taking every advantage to put aside retirement savings may not be your choice, if you instead want to wipe out your credit card debt. With that as a goal, the tax deferral has less appeal than the improved cash flow. Ask yourself, "What does this strategy accomplish? Is that what I am trying to do?"

Peg Downey, M.A., CFP®
Partner, Money Plans

IN MONEY WORDS

Your direction is as crucial as your speed ... Having a financial plan

---

To accumulate wealth, focus on saving first and investing second. The single best financial move that you can make is to save regularly. Adding to your investment portfolio monthly or quarterly is a surefire way to achieve wealth. For example, assume you have a $100,000 portfolio that earns 10 percent per year. After 25 years that portfolio will grow to over $1,200,000. Add only $1,000 per month and that same portfolio would grow to over $2,200,000. You end up with an additional $1,000,000 in savings, thanks to the magic of compounding!

Constanza Low, M.I.M., and John Henry Low, M.B.A.
Vice President and President, Knickerbocker Advisors Inc.

Here are four goals to set in divorce to ensure a foundation for your future financial success:

1. Suitable housing—this means either buying out your spouse's equity in your present home, renting, or buying a new residence after the divorce.
2. No debt—a mortgage is fine and a car payment is okay too. If possible, pay off any credit card debt.
3. Retirement assets—these are usually tax-deferred and are a foundation for future wealth.
4. Liquid assets—savings accounts, CDs, and money market accounts all offer flexibility to pay for those unexpected expenses.

Joan Coullahan, M.B.A., CDP
Co-author of Financial Custody: You, Your Money, and Divorce

As you begin to build your investment portfolio, ask yourself, "Would I rather eat more or sleep more?" When working with a planner, the key to successful investing is to understand how much risk you are really willing to take. Your planner should provide you with a client questionnaire that will help determine your risk tolerance level.

Michael M. Eisenberg, CPA/PFS
Michael M. Eisenberg, An Accountancy Corporation

Your family money goals look great on your refrigerator alongside the kids' pictures! After a family conference to discuss the family financial goals for the vacation, new furniture, TV, or other items, place the goal on a piece of paper and chart the savings. A bar graph can be used and let the kids color each $10.00 saved. This is a great way to help your kids learn about goals, money, savings, and graph skills.

Kathy Adams-Smith, M.P.A.
Director of Credit Counseling Services, LifeSpan, Inc.

If tight finances forced you to accept a job instead of pursuing your dream of going to graduate school, consider taking courses on a part-time basis. If the coursework will enhance your job skills, chances are your employer will be happy to pick up the tab. You may also be eligible for the Lifetime Learning Credit on your federal income tax return (Form 8863) if your modified adjusted gross income (MAGI) is below $80,000 (joint filers) or below $40,000 (single). The credit is phased out for incomes above $100,000 (joint) and $50,000 (single).

Raj Pillai, Ph.D., CFP®
NAPFA-Registered Advisor, Financial Fitness Network of Solon

The best way to reduce your debt quickly is to put yourself on a credit diet. Resolve to avoid any new borrowing until you have slimmed down your debt load.

Steve Johnson, CPA/PFS, CFP®
Owner, Johnson Financial

MIND OVER MONEY

Developing and keeping a plan for your finances is one of the best investments in yourself that you can make.

Constanza Low, M.I.M., and John Henry Low, M.B.A.
Vice President and President, Knickerbocker Advisors Inc.

By using a simple program on your computer, you can estimate the average annual return of your investments. Include a number of years and, if possible, both up and down markets. For example, more than 4 years ago, you started investing. Year 1 you invested $100,000; year 2 you added $20,000 and withdrew $2,000 for a net $18,000; year 3 you withdrew $5,000; and at the end of year 4 you had a total of $150,000 in the account. Okay, how well did you do? Using Microsoft's Excel program:

1. Input into cell A-1 **-100,000.**
2. Input into cell A-2 **-18,000.**
3. Input into cell A-3 **+5,000.**
4. Input into cell A-4 **+150,000.**

5. In cell A-5, go to the Insert menu located at the top of the spreadsheet.
6. Click on Insert.
7. Then, click on Function.
8. Select IRR from the Financial menu.
9. Click OK.
10. Input into cell Values A1:A4.
11. Click OK.

The answer: 10 percent Average Annual Return. Compare your average annual performance to those of the various market indices for the same period.

Deborah O. Levine, M.B.A, M.S.T., CPA/PFS, CFP®
Financial Planner, AFP Group

If you tithe or have substantial recurring annual charitable contributions, you can reduce your gift tax by up to two thirds by using a Charitable Lead Trust. Annual giving of $100,000 can reduce $2,000,000 of an estate to $670,000 for gift tax purposes. With the new gift tax exclusion limits now $1,000,000, you might find this tool very effective. You will need both an estate planning CPA and an attorney to design the trust to your specific needs. Expect set-up costs around $2,000 and annual costs averaging $500.

Charles P. Copeland, CPA/PFS
President, The Copeland Group

If you're like most small business owners, you may be planning that the proceeds from the sale of your business will fund your retirement. Unfortunately, you may find that when you are ready to sell the business it does not have the market value to support your retirement lifestyle. A better plan is for the sale to be the icing on the cake—with other investments outside the business taking care of your financial independence. With secure investments in place as the layers of the cake, it takes the pressure off the business to provide for your retirement.

Craig Olson, CPA/PFS
Partner, Parrott Partnership

If all you have just done is set a goal to begin setting goals, you are on your way. You have taken the biggest step on your journey toward financial security. Take others along with you and it will be more rewarding. Communicate with family, consult with professionals, and don't forget to congratulate yourself!

2

INVESTMENT FUNDAMENTALS

'Tis easy to see, hard to foresee.

—*Benjamin Franklin*

TERMS FROM THE TOP

dollar cost averaging (constant dollar plans)   Method of accumulating assets by investing a fixed amount of dollars in securities at set intervals. The investor buys more shares when the price is low and fewer shares when the price is high; the overall cost is lower than it would be if a constant number of shares were bought at set intervals.

fixed-income investment   Security that pays a fixed rate of return. This usually refers to government, corporate, or municipal bonds, which pay a fixed rate of interest until the bonds mature and to preferred stock, paying a fixed dividend.

hedge fund   Private investment partnership in which the general partner has made a substantial personal investment and often takes large risks on speculative strategies.

hybrid investment (derivative)   Investment vehicle that combines two different kinds of underlying investments. For example, a structured note, which is a form of a bond, may have the interest rate it pays tied to the rise and fall of a commodity's price.

long-term capital gains assets   Assets with a holding period of 12 months or longer and applicable in calculating the advantageous capital gains tax.

ordinary income assets   Assets whose gain at sale is taxed as the income from the normal activities of an individual, as distinguished from those taxed under capital gains tax rates, which have historically been lower than ordinary tax rates.

REIT (Real Estate Investment Trust)   Company, usually traded publicly, that manages a portfolio of real estate to earn profits for shareholders. It will pay significant dividend income—90 percent of its cash flow, by law.

small capitalization stocks (small cap)   Usually have a market capitalization (number of shares outstanding multiplied by the stock price) of $500 million or less.

Source: reprinted by permission of Jordan Goodman, Dictionary of Finance and Investment Terms *(Barron's, 5th Edition)*

The hunt for the best investment strategy is joined every day by new investors who are sure that everyone else knows something that they don't. There has to be a trick or a system that is sure to work and make them a lot of money—fast. A lot of money is spent on stock-picking newsletters and eyes are glued to stock tickers on computer screens across the country. Our experts were united in their advice that this effort is wasted. Instead, a steady path based on solid principals, combined with a resistance to emotion-based decision-making seems to be the secret.

The tips throughout this chapter give you a rare peek at the type of decision-making models the experts use to help their clients form good investment strategies. Much of it you may have heard before, but ask yourself if you are really following that strategy or just thinking that you are. Use this chapter to challenge your assumptions about your own investment choices.

All tips in this chapter are intended for informational purposes only. Should you find one potentially helpful to your situation, you should consult with your legal, tax, or investment professional familiar with your individual situation to determine its suitability prior to taking any action or investing any money.

RISK VS. RETURN

An old adage advised to take as much risk as you could and still be able to sleep at night. This assumes that the only way to pick investments that are good for you is some pre-programmed subconscious mechanism that allows you to get a good night's sleep. Planners have become a little more sophisticated than that to help you understand your personal risk tolerance and its impact on your investment results. These tips can help you understand how to manage your need for returns against your need for sleep.

◆ ◆ ◆

Best hot stock tip—there are no hot stock tips!

William K. Kaiser, CPA/PFS
Financial Advisor, Howard Financial Services, Inc.

If you are timing the market, remember that the economy, like the weather, is unpredictable; and no one has yet figured out what the future holds. Therefore, stay diversified with your investment strategy to take advantage of whatever market conditions lie ahead. Frequent changes in your investment strategy will cause you to incur significant costs that are difficult to recoup.

Clark M. Blackman II, CPA/PFS, CFP®, ChFC, CFA®, CIMA, AAMS®
Managing Director, Post Oak Capital

MIND OVER MONEY

As you look for ways to improve your investment success, remember that investors tend to seek out information that confirms their investment decisions. As a result, many investors have a tendency to underestimate the probability that they will lose money and overestimate their ability to choose moneymaking investments. During bull markets this can lead to investor overconfidence. If overconfidence persists in a bear market the result can lead to significant portfolio losses. If you want to reduce this bias you should consider how past investment decisions—those that led to success or failure—might have turned out differently.

John Grable, Ph.D., CFP®, RFC
Director, Institute of Personal Financial Planning

Just when investing feels the worst is probably the best time to add to your portfolio. Remember that since World War II, there has never been a 10-year period during which the investment markets lost money. Those 60 years included four wars, eight international crises, and 10 domestic crises. Remember all the events that caused the market to correct: the Korean and Vietnam wars, the Cuban Missile Crisis, JFK's assassination, the oil shocks of 1973–74, 18 percent inflation rates, Watergate and Richard Nixon's resignation, the collapse of the Russian and Mexican financial markets, the World Trade Center bombing, the Asian market crises, Clinton's impeachment hearings, and U.S. banking crises.

Constanza Low, M.I.M., and John Henry Low, M.B.A.
Vice President and President, Knickerbocker Advisors Inc.

IN MONEY WORDS

What do I have to lose? ... Understanding investment risk and loss

---

Join the club! Or start your own. Visit www.better-investing.org. Becoming a member of an investment club is a fun, nonthreatening way to stake out your position in the stock market. You'll become so educated about how and why to buy and sell stocks, you will never fall for a stock sales pitch again.

Bonnie A. Hughes, CFP®
President, A&H Financial Planning and Education, Inc.

Next time you want to take a risk and buy a stock on some hot tip, go to Vegas instead. You will probably lose less money and have a heck of a better time!!

William K. Kaiser, CPA/PFS
Financial Advisor, Howard Financial Services, Inc.

Focus on investment factors you can control, because you'll never be able to control the market. Your investments' performance depends on several factors, including:

• How much you spend.
• How much you save.
• How long your money will be invested.
• How diversified your portfolio is.

- The return "the market" gives you.
- How much of that return you surrender to fees and expenses.
- Your use of tax-reduction strategies.
- The extent to which you make informed life decisions that impact your investments.

You have lots of control over everything *except* what the market gives you.

Kathleen M. Rehl, Ph.D., CFP®
Owner, Rehl Financial Advisors

Invest based upon risk. Keep score based on return. As you begin to develop your financial plan be sure to differentiate between these two important terms risk and return. First, determine the level of risk, or the percentage of your portfolio's value, you are willing to lose. Calculate an expected portfolio return based on those characteristics. Base your financial plan on the risk (or downside) characteristics of your investments as opposed to the return (or upside) characteristics of the investments. This will increase the chances of achieving your financial planning goals and allow you to sleep more comfortably along the way.

Patrick T. Hanratty, M.B.A., CPA/PFS, CFP®
Managing Director, Capital Advisors, Ltd.

Making an investment by looking in the rearview mirror is a sure way to come up short if you only look at yesterday's winners. Look at what industries have been out of favor for the last few years and consider whether any of those industries has a future. If yes, then buy either the best fund or individual companies in that industry. A good example is REITS (real estate investment trusts), which were out of favor in the late nineties because nobody wanted to own real estate. Smart people realized there would be a need for real estate in the future so they bought these investments when others only wanted technology stocks. They were looking down the road, not in their rearview mirror.

Sid Blum, CPA/PFS, CFP®, ChFC, ATP
President, Successful Financial Solutions, Inc.

If you do not need to take risk, do not take it.

James Kantowski, CPA, CFP®
Wealth Management Advisor, RSM McGladrey

When the stock market falls, don't sell. Remember those average annual stock market returns that are frequently quoted? You've heard them: since 1925 the S&P 500 has earned 10 percent per year on average, small capitalization stocks 12 percent, and long-term bonds 5 percent. Guess what? Those average returns include bear markets, lots of them, on average one every three to five years.

Constanza Low, M.I.M., and John Henry Low, M.B.A.
Vice President and President, Knickerbocker Advisors Inc.

Famous last words: This time the market is different!

Steven B. Morris, M.B.A., CPA/PFS, CLU
Principal, Steven B. Morris CPA

American Association of Individual Investors (www.AAII.com). They publish monthly general and special journals covering every topic of personal finance in depth.

Understanding Alpha is one of the basics that will help you be successful in your investment strategy. It shows you where you get extra value relative to the risk undertaken in your investments. Alpha is the absolute measure of the performance of a managed portfolio compared to the returns on an unmanaged portfolio of equal risk. You can find out an investment's Alpha through *Morningstar* or Thomson's CDA Weisenberger. Over a 20-year period, most investments will range between –2 and 2. Positive is good, negative not so good. The higher the Alpha, the more reward you are getting for assuming the risk of the investment.

Leonard C. Wright, CPA/PFS, CFP®, CLU, ChFC
Principal, Strategic Financial Group

Knowing the impact of taxes on your long-term financial plan will go a long way to helping you reach your goals. Consider all of your assets together and develop a tax minimization strategy. A top tax bracket earner in some states can pay up to 45 percent in taxes on ordinary income. Decide where to place your diversified assets collectively, not independently. Qualified plans may be a good place to store your ordinary income assets with long-term capital gain assets held outside of tax advantaged plans. Work with your CPA to help develop an effective strategy.

Leonard C. Wright, CPA/PFS, CFP®, CLU, ChFC
Principal, Strategic Financial Group

So you want high return and zero risk! I am here to tell you it doesn't exist. If the market return rate of an investment is three percent and you see an advertisement for 15 percent, you might want to jump on it. You send a check and start receiving your 15 percent. Then one day, the checks stop coming and you are out all of your money. That is the time you decide to figure out what happened or call in a professional. My advice is to do this checking before you invest. You need to know who you are buying from, what type of investment it is, and if it is legitimate. We all know that if something sounds too good to be true, it probably is.

Cary Carbonaro, M.B.A., CFP®
President, Family Financial

Investments that might be considered nonstandard, such as oil and gas programs, real estate limited partnerships, hedge funds, venture capital, pre-IPO investments, and private mortgages, carry certain risks by their very nature but can be very rewarding if successful. The key is to be involved only with those opportunities that are above board and follow certain basic rules. Rule 1: Perform your own review. Don't just rely on your golf partner. Rule 2: All checks should be to an escrow agent or directly to a recognized corporate entity, not to a commissioned salesperson. Rule 3: Review your statements and updates. Make sure that reports come directly from management and make sense to you from a tax and accounting standpoint.

Joe Harper, CFP®
President, Harper Associates, Inc.

ASSET ALLOCATION AND DIVERSIFICATION

Most people have been on a diet or are planning to start one—tomorrow. The easiest way to understand the concepts of asset allocation and diversification is to think about how we eat. Our bodies need different categories of nutrients: protein, carbohydrates, fats, water, vitamins, etc. Our financial bodies are no different. They can't live on just one type of asset any more than our bodies could survive just on water. How much of each asset class you own relative to the others is the process of asset allocation.

Back to our diet, once we decide we need 25 percent fat, 35 percent carbohydrates, and 40 percent protein, we have to determine where we will get those nutrients. We know that eating a variety of foods ensures our health. It is the same with investments. Diversification of our assets within each class ensures that we are taking less risk to earn our desired return. Our experts have offered their encouragement and direction in using these and other basic principles of sound investing.

◆◆◆

Be disciplined! Make a plan and stick to it, save regularly (even if it is just a little), sell high and buy low and cut expenses. Always practice being and staying focused. Never stop trying to stay focused even if you need to remind yourself over and over again. Funny as it may sound, you need to practice discipline to be disciplined.

Reg Baker, CPA/PFS
Owner, Reg Baker CPA, LLC

When the stock market falls, don't sell—buy! If your favorite can of soup normally sells for $1.50 per can, and today it is marked down to $0.75, wouldn't you stock up? Do the same with your investments. Think of stock market downturns as "sales" of stocks and load up. With patience and a long-term investment outlook (10 years plus), you are sure to be rewarded.

Constanza Low, M.I.M., and John Henry Low, M.B.A.
Vice President and President, Knickerbocker Advisors Inc.

Studies have shown that up to 90 percent of portfolio performance is based on your asset allocation.

Paul D. Lyons, CPA/PFS, CFP®
Manager, KPMG Personal Financial Planning

Don't forget to include the investment allocation in your permanent life insurance with investment options when considering your overall asset allocation. Policies such as variable universal contracts are often overlooked when calculating asset allocation percentages. It's also a good idea to review your overall asset allocation at least annually.

Susan J. Bruno, CPA/PFS, CFP®
Principal, Winged Keel Financial Advisors, LLC

Diversification is like driving your car down the freeway. There are always investments in the carpool lane and several stuck in traffic. The trick is to be in many different investments so that when your investment enters the carpool lane, you will enjoy the increase in value. Many investors are tempted to jump in an investment after it has been on the autobahn. The trouble is, we tend to jump in at the time when the investment is merging off of the autobahn and back on the surface streets, leaving us wondering why the performance of our portfolio is in the pits.

Leonard C. Wright, CPA/PFS, CFP®, CLU, ChFC
Principal, Strategic Financial Group

MIND OVER MONEY

Don't get caught playing the competitive spectator sport of the returns game. Many people like to boast about how much they earned on a particular investment. Don't listen. It is not how much you earn on one investment but whether or not you can retire!

Constanza Low, M.I.M., and John Henry Low, M.B.A.
Vice President and President, Knickerbocker Advisors Inc.

Need any better example than the stock market decline in 2000/2001 to see why the periodic rebalancing of your asset allocation is important?

If the run-up in equities and technology stocks in the late '90s had expanded the percentage of your portfolio in these assets to a point beyond their original allocation, then rebalancing them annually would have saved you lots of trouble and eased the pain of this bear market.

Paul D. Lyons, CPA/PFS, CFP®
Manager, KPMG Personal Financial Planning

MIND OVER MONEY

During a tough market, remember, it is not a loss unless you sell.

Constanza Low, M.I.M., and John Henry Low, M.B.A.
Vice President and President, Knickerbocker Advisors Inc.

POINT ⅢⅢ▶

Given the volatility in today's stock markets, your portfolio needs to have over 25 individual stocks to be properly diversified. If you do not have the time, interest, or aptitude to research and track this many stocks, use a broadly diversified index fund (like a total market fund) as a core position in your portfolio. Once the core has been built, pick individual stocks in small chunks to complement the portfolio.

Mark Wilson, CFP®, APA
Vice President, Tarbox Equity, Inc.

◀ⅢⅢ COUNTERPOINT

Did you know that the latest research on diversification indicates that you need as many as 60 stocks in a portfolio to effectively eliminate "specific stock" risk, not 20 stocks as was previously believed by many investors?

Clark M. Blackman II, CPA/PFS, CFP®,
ChFC, CFA®, CIMA, AAMS®
Managing Director and Chief Investment Officer, Post Oak Cap

Learn from the employees who have lost it all. Diversify away from company stock whenever possible. While it is good to be confident in your company, remember that your paycheck and benefits are already dependent upon the performance of your company. Don't allow your investments to have that same dependence. Within your company's retirement plan, you may have more diversification options than you realize. In fact, all plans must allow you to begin diversification for longer-term employees after age 55. Find out exactly what your options are and diversify accordingly.

Mark Wilson, CFP®, APA
Vice President, Tarbox Equity, Inc.

INVESTMENT VEHICLES

It's one thing to know what might work to help you reach your investment goals. It's quite another to put it into action and select specific vehicles that meet the criteria you have selected. Our experts offer you some more specific strategies for knowing when you are making a good decision. Here's help to filter out the "noise" that sometimes drowns out the core concepts that are ready to work for you.

♦ ♦ ♦

When dealing with most professionals (e.g., physicians, accountants, lawyers), a second opinion confirming the first is a reassuring thing. However, if you get the same buy or sell recommendation from several investment advisors, you probably should ignore the advice.

Chris Cobb, CPA/PFS
Portfolio Manager, Lighthouse Capital Management

Compound interest is like the increasing prize levels on the game show *Who Wants To Be A Millionaire?* In the beginning of both the game show and your time as an investor, money doubles slowly. After several decades of compound interest, however, you are doubling larger amounts, like the final questions on the game show. Just like the game, however, you have to play the early rounds to get to the big money.

Barbara O'Neill, Ph.D., CFP®, AFC, CHC
Author of Saving on a Shoestring

Remember that in distressed equity markets you have dollar cost averaging at work for you. If you systematically invest the same amount every month, then you are actually buying more shares at lower costs with the same money. This will do wonders for your portfolio over the long run.

Paul D. Lyons, CPA/PFS, CFP®
Manager, KPMG Personal Financial Planning

Don't invest in the stock market just because everyone tells you that it has earned an average of 10 percent a year for a long, long time. Remember Milton Friedman's warning not to try to cross a river on foot just because someone tells you it has an average depth of only four feet!

Raj Pillai, Ph.D., CFP®
NAPFA-Registered Advisor, Financial Fitness Network of Solon

Is it any surprise that reading a fund prospectus is boring? How much is it worth to be a little bored? Lately, it has cost clients dearly, sometimes $15,000 or more per hour for allowing someone else to fully captain their financial ship. By taking only a couple hours out of your time you can discover how the fund has performed over the prior 10 years; how much it charges in fees; whether A, B, C, or F shares will put more dollars in your pocket; what kind of taxes the fund distributes over the years; whether the fund manager is trying to make a quick buck by market timing or if they are picking solid long-term investments; and which countries and the industry sectors they invest in and their largest holdings. Get excited, take the voyage! It's your duty to challenge your advisor.

Leonard C. Wright, CPA/PFS, CFP®, CLU, ChFC
Principal, Strategic Financial Group

MIND OVER MONEY

Common sense is needed when markets are at their tops and things are going "too" well. Faith and trust is needed when markets are at their bottoms and things are looking bleak.

J. Victor Conrad, CPA/PFS, CFP®, ChFC
Financial Advisor, The MONY Group

Motley Fool (www.motleyfool.com)   This site has daily market reports and analysis. You can do comparisons and research before making your investment decisions.

To see how fast it takes for money to double, use The Rule of 72. Divide the expected interest rate into 72 to determine how long it takes for a sum of money to double. For example, 72 divided by 8 percent interest (average annual return) = 9 years. The Rule of 72 and other investment fundamentals are explained in the Cooperative Extension "Investing For Your Future" course for beginning investors. The course is available online at www.investing.rutgers.edu.

Barbara O'Neill, Ph.D., CFP®, AFC, CHC
Author of Saving on a Shoestring

Trading range is calculated by doubling the standard deviation, then adding and subtracting the result from the average investment performance over a 15- or 20-year period. You can have a high level of confidence that the investment will be between these two numbers 95 percent of the time. If an average return of 16 percent is achieved over a 20-year period with a standard deviation at 14 percent, then the trading range is –12 percent (16 – 28) to 44 percent (16 + 28). Two resources for investment performance and standard deviation are *Morningstar* or *CDA Weisenberger.*

Leonard C. Wright, CPA/PFS, CFP®, CLU, ChFC
Principal, Strategic Financial Group

Confused by the latest economic report on the nightly news? Intuitively we know that a strong economy makes for appreciating values and vice versa. Why then, doesn't your portfolio move in lock step patterns with the economic news? That is because the markets are forward-looking (10 to 18 months) while economic reports are compiled from events that have already occurred. Economic forecasts are projections derived from the historical record and the fuel for most investment strategies. Don't panic. Consult with a financial professional who can design a disciplined risk-adjusted plan to diversify your portfolio holdings.

Jonathan S. Dinkins, CPA/PFS, CIMA, CMFC®
Senior Consultant, Glass Jacobson Investment Advisors LLC

How much should you contribute to your retirement plan at work? First decide how much you can afford to miss from your paycheck. Then take that amount and gross it up for taxes. For example, let's say you can miss $75 from your biweekly paycheck. If you divide this amount by your marginal tax bracket subtracted from one, the result is the amount you can contribute to your retirement plan. If your tax bracket is 27 percent, you can contribute $102.74 ($75 divided by 0.73), rather than the original $75. Over a fifteen-year period at 9 percent, this extra $27.74 per paycheck could add up to an additional $22,194.

Cathie E. Cobe, CPA/PFS, CFP®, CLU, ChFC
Retirement Management Spec., Nationwide Retirement Solutions

To protect against taking on more investment risk than you can afford, first determine how much you expect to withdraw from your portfolio over the next five to seven years. Withdrawals in the next 12 months should be allocated to cash or ultra-short term bonds. Amounts you expect to withdraw over the following four to six years should be invested in short and intermediate-term investment grade bonds and bond funds. Any remaining funds in your portfolio can be considered long-term and eligible for growth-oriented stock investing up to your emotional risk tolerance. Review your expected withdrawals at least annually and adjust accordingly.

Bruce R. Heling, CPA/PFS, CFP®
President, Heling Associates, Inc.

To figure the percentage of your portfolio to put in equity investments, first build a safety net with fixed-income investments. Then invest the remainder in equities to provide for long-term growth. If you are retired, the allocation to fixed-income investments should be sufficient to cover five to seven years of your net cash outflow, which is the excess of living expenses over pension income and Social Security. During a bear market, you would fund net cash outflow from interest income and the sale of fixed-income investments, avoiding the need to sell equities at depressed prices.

John Henry Wyckoff, M.B.A., M.S.T., CPA/PFS, CFP®
Advisor, Ron McCallister Financial Advisors, Inc.

Are you wrestling about when to sell your company stock options? Options that are substantially appreciated behave similarly to holding the stock outright, becoming merely a tax-deferral mechanism. The real risk is if the stock price decreases in value. Keep in mind your options are leveraged, so a decrease in the stock price will diminish your option equity on a higher magnitude and at an increasing rate, quickly evaporating your gains. Once your option portfolio realizes a significant level of appreciation, you may wish to consider diversifying your portfolio and selling your options.

Jonathan S. Dinkins, CPA/PFS, CIMA, CMFC®
Senior Consultant, Glass Jacobson Investment Advisors LLC

Stock options are utilized by a great many companies to provide incentive to their employees. As the options vest and accumulate, they can become a substantial part of your investment portfolio. You must decide between developing a long-term strategy of diversification, with a tax cost, or rolling the dice with a concentrated portfolio. There are employees of many companies (i.e., Enron, Worldcom) who now wish they had chosen the former strategy. Learn from the mistakes of others and own the options you worked so hard to earn—don't let them own you.

Patrick T. Hanratty, M.B.A., CPA/PFS, CFP®
Managing Director, Capital Advisors, Ltd.

IN MONEY WORDS

What goes up must come down ... High double-digit stock market returns will eventually fall

---

Thinking about investing in municipal bonds and taking advantage of the tax benefits? Try this before you decide: Divide the return of the municipal bond by your marginal tax bracket subtracted from one. For example, if your marginal tax bracket is 35 percent and you're looking at a 6 percent municipal bond, your return would have to be 9.2 percent on a taxable bond to be a comparable investment (6 divided by .65). There could be additional state tax benefits, depending on who issued the municipal bond and what the tax treatment is in your state.

Cathie E. Cobe, CPA/PFS, CFP®, CLU, ChFC
Retirement Management Spec., Nationwide Retirement Solutions

Don't make a long-term commitment to stocks with more money than you will be willing to leave invested if market trends take a turn for the worse. If you have more "long-term" money than emotional risk tolerance, consider investing the difference in hybrid investments like convertible and high-yield bond funds, where the risk is less than the risk posed by stocks but the potential for growth greater than with investment-grade bonds.

Bruce R. Heling, CPA/PFS, CFP®
President, Heling Associates, Inc.

Are you looking for that long-term investment in your IRA that can keep pace with inflation and avoid the risks of the stock market? Since commission-based advisors might not recommend them, you might not have heard about TIPS (Treasury Inflation-Protection Securities). TIPS are Treasury notes and bonds that provide an inflation-adjusted return. They might be appropriate for that part of your portfolio that you want to protect from the risk inherent in the stock market. TIPS can be purchased online at www.publicdebt.treas.gov.

Alexis M. Jensen, CPA, CFP®
President, Z&W Wealth Management

You can purchase TIPS (Treasury Inflation-protected Securities) upon original issuance by making a noncompetitive bid via the government's Treasury Direct program. This requires filling out a "Treasury Bill, Note, & Bond Tender" application form and making arrangements for payment of the purchase price and subsequent receipt of interest and principal payments. The form can be downloaded and printed out from www.publicdebt.treas.gov.

Phyllis Bernstein, CPA/PFS
President, Phyllis Bernstein Consulting

Still confused? It is a lot to absorb. Investment strategies may be the most anxiety-producing area of personal finance. Do yourself a favor and don't try to understand it all at once. Go back and find the tip that intrigued you the most and try it. Follow your progress and watch your feelings of mastery of the topic develop more every day. If you already feel fairly solid with the information in this chapter, read on—Chapters 3 and 4 are full of exciting information.

3

MUTUAL FUNDS

*If you would be wealthy, think of saving
as well as getting.*

—Benjamin Franklin

Terms from the Top

capital gain   Difference between an asset's adjusted purchase price and selling price when the difference is positive.

cost basis   Original price of an asset, used in determining capital gains. It usually is the purchase price, but in the case of an inheritance it is the appraised value of the asset at the time of the donor's death.

dividend   Distribution of earnings to shareholders, prorated by class of security and paid in the form of money, stock, scrip, or rarely, company products or property.

growth fund   Mutual fund that invests in stocks of corporations that have exhibited faster-than-average gains in earnings over the last few years and are expected to continue to show high levels of profit growth.

index fund   Mutual fund that has a portfolio matching that of a broad-based portfolio, such as the Dow Jones Industrial Index or the Standard & Poor's 500 Index, and indices of the small- and mid-capitalization stocks.

preferred stocks   Class of capital stock that pays dividends at a specified rate and that has preference over common stock in the payment of dividends and the liquidation of assets. Preferred stock does not ordinarily carry voting rights.

reinvested dividends   Distributed earnings from a stock or mutual fund that are automatically used to buy more shares of the same investment, usually at no additional sales charge.

security overlap analysis   Process of determining the extent of the common investments held by two or more different mutual funds.

Source: reprinted by permission of Jordan Goodman, Dictionary of Finance and Investment Terms *(Barron's, 5th Edition)*

A mutual fund is a great deal of money, collected from a large group of investors, invested in a variety of investments that follow some strategy or philosophy. When you match your needs with that philosophy, the fund should perform optimally for you. So it is important to know your needs and then to investigate the purpose of the fund.

Mutual funds have shown a great ability to stay in business over the years that they have grown in popularity. They have added numerous customer service options and created "products" with different fee structures and investment strategies. They have packaged themselves inside of retirement plans and insurance products. They're everywhere!

All tips in this chapter are intended for informational purposes only. Should you find one potentially helpful to your situation, you should consult with your legal, tax, or investment professional familiar with your individual situation to determine its suitability prior to taking any action or investing any money.

FUND PICKING

More than any other single force in the economy, the mutual fund industry has brought equity investing to within the reach of every worker in the country. Mutual funds don't only help us diversify our risk, they allow us to contribute small amounts of money into the stock market and other investment venues.

As great as this opportunity is, we now have a new problem. Which fund do you pick? The combinations are endless. Each prospectus is more confusing than the next. Who do you believe? Our experts give you some basics to use in this sometimes frustrating process.

♦ ♦ ♦

You might find that investing in individual stocks makes exciting cocktail party conversation, but it remains a risky proposition. If you are looking to maximize your investment dollars, you need to look no further than the ordinary mutual fund—a safer, more diversified instrument, and with more leverage, to boot. Whereas individual stocks can only earn their returns through a combination of dividends and appreciation, mutual funds provide possible returns from five distinct sources: interest payments, dividends, short- and long-term capital gains, and share price appreciation.

Timothy M. Hayes, M.B.A., RFC, CMFC®
President, Landmark Financial Advisory Services, LLC

Consider using the "lifestyle" funds (look for the key phrases: "life," "target," "strategy," or "allocation.") that may be available as an option within your company's retirement plan (i.e., your 401[k]). These are pre-allocated funds-of-funds that are logically built and well diversified and are usually available in Aggressive, Growth, and Conservative flavors. These portfolios are almost always a more reasonable mix than the typical investor would select for himself. For the more informed investor, they still make a solid core holding.

Mark Wilson, CFP®, APA
Vice President, Tarbox Equity, Inc.

Morningstar (www.morningstar.com).   You can do comparisons of mutual funds, get research reports, 10Ks, and so on.

As you look at various mutual funds, consider a balanced fund. Balanced funds have a mix of assets consisting of common stocks, preferred stocks, and bonds. By combining this mix of assets in one fund, you obtain diversification of income and long-term growth. A list of balanced funds can be obtained from Morningstar Reports. Remember, mutual fund investment returns and principal values will fluctuate so that their value upon redemption may be worth more or less than their original value. Read the mutual fund's prospectus carefully before you invest or send money.

Kent E. Anthony, CIC, CFP®, CMFC®
President, First Group Insurance

Do you want an investment that has low expenses, is tax efficient, has consistent management, and is very likely to outperform its peers? Buy a low-cost index fund!

Mark Wilson, CFP®, APA
Vice President, Tarbox Equity, Inc.

Using a diverse group of index mutual funds is a great way to structure a portfolio. When selecting non-index mutual funds, make sure that you compare their risk and return to the proper benchmark or index. A fund that invests in small-capitalization growth stocks, for example, should be analyzed against a small-capitalization growth benchmark such as the Barra or Wilshire Small Growth Index. Many investors make the mistake of comparing every fund's performance against that of the popular S&P 500 Index. By so doing, you would overlook wonderful funds while possibly concentrating your portfolios in investments that are too similar.

Constanza Low, M.I.M., and John Henry Low, M.B.A.
Vice President and President, Knickerbocker Advisors Inc.

IN MONEY WORDS

Don't be a copycat ... Be a contrarian

Consider finding mutual funds that use more than one money manager per fund. Some mutual fund families use portfolio counselors where each takes a percentage of the fund. By having more than one or two money managers the fund can offer better continuity of management if one of the managers leaves the fund. The prospectus will give you the number of fund managers and how long each has been with the fund. Ask your financial advisor to recommend funds with multiple fund managers.

Kent E. Anthony, CIC, CFP®, CMFC®
President, First Group Insurance

Do your own research and invest in no-load mutual funds rather than pay a commission. Morningstar gathers information on mutual funds and provides free web-based tools to help you sift through the 14,000 funds available to find the funds that meet your requirements. Go to www.Morningstar.com. After registering, select "Funds" on the top tool bar. Next, choose "Fund Selector" under Morningstar Tools (right-hand side of page). Several search criteria will appear on the screen, which can be used to filter out all the load or commission funds, focus on a particular segment of the market, exclude funds with new managers, and much more.

Jill Gianola, CFP®, MBA
Owner, Gianola Financial Planning

Are you concerned that your money in a mutual fund might be going to buy stock in a business you feel is harmful to society?

Socially responsible investing (SRI) is a field that encourages investors to check out their investments to make sure they are consistent with their values. Socially responsible mutual funds do not invest in companies that have a majority of interest in tobacco or alcohol. There are other criteria that are important to many investors such as environmental responsibility, treatment of employees, and advertising policies. These funds are a good choice for those wanting to control where their money is going! Find them through your financial advisor or mutual fund rating services.

Kent E. Anthony, CIC, CFP®, CMFC®
President, First Group Insurance

When you purchase mutual funds, remember to examine all of the fund's costs, not only the initial sales charge (i.e., the load). This is particularly true for funds to be held for many years. Often, the reduced annual charges of loaded funds will provide superior returns when compared to no-load funds with higher annual costs. The cost information will be found in the fund's prospectus. Here is an example:

- Fund 1 has a 4.25 percent initial sales charge (load) and annual charges of 1.41 percent.
- Fund 2 has no up-front load and annual charges of 2.31 percent.

Assuming a $10,000 investment into each fund and 5 percent growth, the following chart gives the total fund expenses for each fund:

	Fund 1	Fund 2
After 1 year	$562	$216
After 5 years	$1,163	$1,144
After 10 years	$2,044	$2,462

Michael David Schulman, M.B.A., M.A., CPA/PFS
Principal, Schulman Co. CPA P.C.

For those of you who really enjoy analyzing ways to save money, here is a detailed example to help you learn how to calculate the difference in the fees associated with different fund classes:

	Class A	Class B	Class C	Class P
Maximum Sales Charge on Purchases as a % of Offering Price	5.75%	none	none	none
Maximum Deferred Sales Charge	none	5.00%	1.00%	none
Annual Fund Operating Expenses (expenses deducted from fund assets) (as a % of average net assets)				
Management Fees	0.31%	0.31%	0.31%	0.31%
Distribution and Service (12b-1) Fees	0.39	1.00%	1.00%	0.45%
Other Expenses	0.12%	0.12%	0.12%	0.12%
Total Operating Expenses	0.82%	1.43%	1.43%	0.88%

This example is intended to help you compare the cost of investing in the fund with the cost of investing in other mutual funds. This example, like that in other funds' prospectuses, assumes that you invest

$10,000 in the fund at maximum sales charge, if any, for the time periods indicated and then redeem all of your shares at the end of those periods. The example also assumes that your investment has a 5 percent return each year and that the fund's operating expenses remain the same. Although your actual costs may be higher or lower, based on these assumptions your costs (including any applicable contingent deferred sales charges) would be:

Share Class	1 Year	3 Years	5 Years	10 Years
Class A shares	$654	$822	$1,004	$1,530
Class B shares	$646	$752	$982	$1,547
Class C shares	$246	$452	$782	$1,713
Class P shares	$90	$281	$488	$1,084

You would have paid the following expenses if you did not redeem your shares:

Share Class	1 Year	3 Years	5 Years	10 Years
Class A shares	$654	$822	$1,004	$1,530
Class B shares	$146	$452	$782	$1,547
Class C shares	$146	$452	$782	$1,713
Class P shares	$90	$281	$488	$1,804

Cary Carbonaro, M.B.A., CFP®
President, Family Financial

If you have limited money to invest right now, and you want broad diversification at a relatively low cost, purchase a stock index fund that tracks the Wilshire 5000 Index and a bond index fund that tracks the Lehman Brother Aggregate Bond Index.

Many of these funds have the words "total stock market" or "total bond market" in their names. There are also three situations where you can invest with smaller amounts than are typically required to open mutual fund accounts: accounts for minors, IRAs and other types of retirement accounts, and automatic investment programs where shareholders' bank accounts are regularly debited for mutual fund deposits.

Barbara O'Neill, Ph.D., CFP®, AFC, CHC
Author of Saving on a Shoestring

Once you settle on an asset allocation, stick with it. One way to take the emotions out of investing is to "rebalance" periodically. Rebalancing is based on logic and forces you to sell high and buy low.

Angie Hollerich, CEP, CCA
Author of Grab the Brass Ring of Financial Security

IN MONEY WORDS

A penny a day ... The power of dollar cost averaging

When choosing a mutual fund, don't chase the highest recent returns. Instead, look at the Sharpe ratio to determine how much risk a fund took to get the returns it earned. The higher the Sharpe, the better, meaning the mutual fund took lower risk for higher returns. For example: Fund A may have a three-year average return of 10 percent with a Sharpe ratio of -.15, and fund B may have a three-year average return of nine percent, yet have a Sharpe ratio of +.10. This means fund A probably took on greater risk, to only get a one percent better return, so fund B may give the investor more "bang for the buck" or "return for the risk." Sharpe ratios can be looked up by your financial advisor or found on a website such as www.morningstar.com by clicking on "MPT Stats" for each fund.

Randall Kratz, CFP®
Owner, Kratz Investment Advisory Network

Don't assume that owning a mixture of different mutual funds equals a diversified portfolio. Visit one of the mutual fund research sites on the web to perform a security overlap analysis of your mutual funds. You will be surprised to see how many of your funds actually own the same securities! Go to www.morningstar.com and register as a premium user with a 14-day free trial. Select portfolio, and build a portfolio of the funds you are considering. Select X-ray: stock overlap and you will see which funds own the same stocks. By selecting a basket of funds that have the least amount of overlap, you can build a better diversified portfolio.

Helen L. Modly, CFP®, ChFC, CLU
Vice President, Focus Financial Consultants, Ltd.

WORDS TO THE WISE MUTUAL FUND INVESTOR

As much as most of our experts like mutual funds for many of their clients, they did have some cautions for you. There are some common mistakes and tax hits that they see frequently, and they wanted you to know about them.

♦ ♦ ♦

Ignore the lists of mutual funds with the best recent performance. The best performing funds for the last three-month or one-year period are likely the ones that will be future underperformers. Instead, choose a mix of funds that cover a variety of market segments (i.e., large companies, small companies, international companies, and fixed income) and buy consistently good performers within each of those segments.

Mark Wilson, CFP®, APA
Vice President, Tarbox Equity, Inc.

Choose your mutual funds carefully, and then stick with them! If you dump the funds you own to buy "the best funds" on someone's list, it can be a recipe for failure. That's because funds usually make these lists based on their past performance, which has little to do with how they perform in the future. After all, if you own a baseball team, you aren't likely to win the World Series by firing your manager every year and hiring last year's Manager of the Year!

Raj Pillai, Ph.D., CFP®
NAPFA-Registered Advisor, Financial Fitness Network of Solon

In Money Words

Tomorrow's a new day ... Past returns are not indicative of future performance

---

You want to buy a mutual fund at $30 a share in a taxable account, and the fund has announced a $2 per share distribution. If you buy the fund before the distribution, you will pay $30, then receive the $2 distribution, and pay tax on the $2. If you wait until after the distribution, you can buy the fund at $28 without paying tax on the $2. To avoid "buying the dividend," check with the mutual fund company or its web-site to determine when the fund will pay its distribution, particularly near year-end, when many funds make distributions.

John J. Feyche, M.S., M.B.T., CPA/PFS
Manager, Z&W Wealth Management

Ask why your advisor uses mutual funds; are they compensated by a third party for placing your money in the funds; and, do they have their money invested in these funds? You should be skeptical of their response. You have made your money, they are now trying to make theirs.

Parke Stratford Teal, CPA/PFS
Principal, Dreggors, Rigsby, and Teal, P.A.

Mind Over Money

Don't be fooled by recent trends in the markets. Investors tend to focus exclusively on specific information or trends and project the recent past into the future. This common human bias does not take into account the tendency for the markets to revert to their long-term average return. Extreme performance returns tend to be followed by more average returns. Now may be the time to take a look at how your projections of market trends are being influenced by recent events.

John Grable, Ph.D., CFP®, RFC
Director, Institute of Personal Financial Planning

No-load mutual funds will put more of your money to work for you. Loads (euphemism for commissions) can take a big bite out of your money. For example, $10,000 invested in a no-load fund means that your entire $10,000 is invested and begins to work for you. Put that same $10,000 in a fund that has a 5 percent load, and $500 gets deducted as a commission so only $9,500 goes to work for you. Stay away from mutual funds followed by "B shares," "C shares," or "D shares," etc. These funds charge some sort of commission, whether up-front, upon sale, or ongoing, or a combination of these.

Constanza Low, M.I.M., and John Henry Low, M.B.A.
Vice President and President, Knickerbocker Advisors Inc.

Max Funds (www.maxfunds.com). The advice is irreverent and cuts through all of the "Wall Street hype" surrounding mutual funds.

You have already taken the first step in helping make a bad investment work for you by deciding to sell a mutual fund, held in a taxable account, at a loss. Your job is not finished yet, however, if you are going to sell only part of the position. The IRS allows you to use several methods for deciding which shares will be sold. To get the most benefit, use the "Specific Identification" method and then select the shares with the highest cost. Inform the mutual fund company and they will guide you.

Patrick T. Hanratty, M.B.A., CPA/PFS, CFP®
Managing Director, Capital Advisors, Ltd.

Make sure you understand the cost of purchasing mutual funds with contingent sales charges (so-called B shares). B shares have additional annual expenses. Their total cost can even exceed the cost of buying the funds with up front sales charges.

Don't be misled into believing that B shares are the same as no-load funds!

Raj Pillai, Ph.D., CFP®
NAPFA-Registered Advisor, Financial Fitness Network of Solon

Don't forget to add your reinvested dividends and capital gains to your cost basis calculation when you sell mutual fund shares.

Your cost of the shares is not just the amount you originally invested. It also includes all of the reinvested dividends and capital gain distributions included in taxable income over the years. Look for mutual fund families that will track your average share cost, including reinvested dividends and capital gain distributions, and provide the information to you when you sell.

Steven B. Morris, M.B.A., CPA/PFS, CLU
Principal, Steven B. Morris CPA

Steele (www.steele.com). The most comprehensive in-depth source for analyzing mutual funds and exchange traded funds.

For folks in high tax brackets: Be careful of purchasing mutual funds outside of retirement plans that have high capital gains and dividend distributions in the last quarter of the year. You may find yourself paying taxes at ordinary rates as high as 39.6% for income that was reinvested in your account.

Steve Wightman, CFP®
Life Advisor Specializing in Money, Lexington Financial Mgmt

Mutual funds that offer check-writing privileges are a great convenience for investors. You can access your investment principal with a simple stroke of the pen. However, you may have triggered a capital gain or loss in your portfolio without even realizing it. You may not be aware that each time you write a check (on a nonmoney market fund) it is considered a sale of shares for tax purposes and may result in a taxable event. It is important to remember to report these sales on your tax return. Use your Form 1099 to assist you.

Patrick T. Hanratty, M.B.A., CPA/PFS, CFP®
Managing Director, Capital Advisors, Ltd.

Mutual funds have become the way most of us invest as individuals. Like many great ideas, they have grown dozens of arms and legs that make them difficult to keep up with sometimes. Reading a prospectus or a quarterly statement may not seem like it sheds much light on the specific questions you have. Keep learning and asking questions of your mutual fund company. Very soon you'll be a confident mutual fund investor.

4
PORTFOLIO MANAGEMENT

Be ashamed to catch yourself idle.

—Benjamin Franklin

Terms from the Top

arbitrage   Profiting from differences in price when the same security, currency, or commodity is traded on two or more markets.

downside risk   Estimate that a security will decline in value and the extent of the decline, taking into account the total range of factors affecting market price.

hedge   Strategy used to offset investment risk. A perfect hedge is one eliminating the possibility of future gain or loss.

interest rate risk   Risk that changes in interest rates will adversely affect the value of an investor's securities portfolio.

low basis   Original cost plus out-of-pocket expenses that must be used in calculating capital gains or losses. A basis is considered low if the asset has appreciated significantly above the basis amount.

market risk (systematic risk)   That part of a security's risk that is common to all securities of the same general class (stocks and bonds) and thus cannot be eliminated by diversification. The measure of systematic risk in stocks is the Beta Coefficient.

stop loss order   Order to a securities broker to buy or sell at the market price once the security has traded at a specified price called the stop price, to protect profits or prevent further losses. A stop order may be a day order, a good-till-canceled-order, or any other form of time-limit order.

wash sale   Purchase and sale of a security either simultaneously or within a short period of time. Wash sales taking place within 30 days of the underlying purchase do not qualify as tax losses under IRS rules.

Source: reprinted by permission of Jordan Goodman, Dictionary of Finance and Investment Terms *(Barron's, 5th Edition)*

We all know that the first step in solving a problem is to admit we have one. The same holds true for portfolio management. Before you can begin to manage your portfolio, you have to admit you have one. Even if you only have a 401(k) account, a small IRA, and some bonds your grandpa gave you, you have a portfolio. When you begin to see all your investments as part of a portfolio and you make decisions with that reality in clear sight, good things begin to happen.

As your portfolio grows, which it will, the decisions get harder but you have more options available to you. Both investment choices and tax strategies become ways to grow your net worth even more. Whether or not you are using financial advisors, it is imperative for you to see your combined assets as one portfolio for a critical phase of your strategic planning.

All tips in this chapter are intended for informational purposes only. Should you find one potentially helpful to your situation, you should consult with your legal, tax, or investment professional familiar with your individual situation to determine its suitability prior to taking any action or investing any money.

THINKING LIKE A PORTFOLIO MANAGER

Stockbrokers are the most busy on the days that the stock market loses ground. Those with more evolved clientele are executing buy orders on those days, taking advantage of the "sale" prices of the day. Those with less evolved clientele are taking calls from clients wanting to know if they should sell to cut their losses. Think about which kind of client you are (or would be with more assets). Making the switch from a panic seller to a sale buyer is the most critical change you can make. Use the tips that follow to begin your journey toward thinking like a portfolio manager.

◆ ◆ ◆

Portfolio management doesn't have to be rocket science. Keep it simple by maintaining the following relationship between your assets: 34 percent in cash or bonds, 33 percent in an index fund of the total U.S. stock market and 33 percent in real estate, including your residence. The most important factor? Save regularly to keep increasing your total net worth.

> *Judi Martindale, M.Ed., CFP®, EA*
> *Author of* No More Baglady Fears

As you begin constructing your investment portfolio, build it like a football coach would build a team. Start by establishing your overall philosophy (goals, objectives, risk tolerance). Next, incorporate your offensive and defensive schemes (asset allocation model). Make sure you build a solid foundation with sound blocking and tackling techniques (core equities, index funds, core bonds). Then, add your vertical passing game and a few gadget plays for extra punch (active managers, hedge funds, private equity). Finally, review your team's performance regularly, making adjustments as warranted (monitor portfolio, compare managers against peers, and rebalance as needed).

> *Patrick T. Hanratty, M.B.A., CPA/PFS, CFP®*
> *Managing Director, Capital Advisors, Ltd.*

MIND OVER MONEY

Here is a thought that should help you get through the bad times *and* the good times. Common sense is needed when markets are up. Faith and trust are needed when markets are down. Keeping a level head during both the lows and the highs should help you succeed in reaching your goals.

> *J. Victor Conrad, CPA/PFS, CFP®, ChFC*
> *Financial Advisor, The MONY Group*

The stock market is an auction, where buyers and sellers come together to agree on a price. You cannot buy a stock at a discount if it is popular and attracting many buyers. The market is never "different this time." Don't blindly follow the crowd. The best opportunities are usually found where most investors are not looking.

Chris Cobb, CPA/PFS
Portfolio Manager, Lighthouse Capital Management

Market Watch (cbs.marketwatch.com). Great strategies for the average mutual fund investor.

When you sell a stock is a very important part of portfolio management. Your portfolio management criteria for selling stocks should include a downside risk factor, an annualized rate of return factor, a holding period, and consideration of minimizing income taxes (if in a taxable account). Having criteria in place prior to purchasing stocks can help to achieve the desired rate of return over a reasonable time frame. For example, you might decide when you purchase a stock to place a stop loss order at a price 20 to 25 percent below the purchase price and a sell order at a predetermined price above the purchase price.

David O. Hogan, CPA/PFS, CFP®
Principal, Hogan & Slovacek, PC

IN MONEY WORDS

Definition of insanity ... Timing the market and expecting to come out ahead

---

Are you sure you are diversified? Even with all the work to maintain a large number of accounts, are you noticing that your investments all go up at the same time and down at the same time? This is likely an indication that you are not truly diversified. A high number of accounts or funds in your portfolio does not necessarily mean you are diversified. Many times, upon further research, you will find that your different funds all own similar types of stocks. Be sure you have exposure to all segments of the market, large cap, large value, small cap, small value, international large, international small, emerging markets, bonds, and periodically rebalance.

Chad P. Tramp, PFS, CFP®
Wealth Management Advisor, RSM McGladrey

Diversification is back in style. Betcha didn't know that. Actually, it never went out of style. It was just ignored while the technology bubble was being produced. If you drifted away from a diversified portfolio, rebalance and own large-cap growth and value stocks, small-cap growth and value stocks, real estate, international investments, and fixed-income securities.

Connie Brezik, CPA/PFS
Investment Advisor, Asset Strategies, Inc.

CNN Financial News (www.cnnfn.com). Ongoing financial market information and analysis.

If you would like better returns on your investment portfolio, try to truly diversify among asset classes that perform differently from all other asset classes. Investing in just large domestic stocks or mutual funds that only invest in large stocks doesn't get the job done anymore. Split the investments equally among the following seven asset classes via mutual funds:

- Domestic equities (50 percent large domestic stocks, 25 percent small value stocks and 25 percent small growth stocks)
- REITS
- Long/short equity
- Announced merge arbitrage
- Tactical asset allocation
- High-quality bonds
- Bank loan mutual funds

This portfolio will provide equity-like returns with bond-like risk. Rebalance equally at least annually.

Louis P. Stanasolovich, CFP®
CEO and President, Legend Financial Advisors, Inc.

IN MONEY WORDS

In need of an attitude adjustment ... Time to rebalance your portfolio

Ever wonder how all those fancy asset allocation software programs work? They simply try to find the most efficient portfolio of differing assets that will fit your risk tolerance. Efficiency means that for any given level of risk, there is no other portfolio that will earn a higher return. It also means that for a certain level of return needed, there is no other portfolio that has less risk. The blend of assets that fit all these variables the best will be your recommended asset allocation. Good thing we have software!

Paul D. Lyons, CPA/PFS, CFP®
Manager, KPMG Personal Financial Planning

SPECIFIC STRATEGIES

Once you are thinking like a portfolio manager, you still need to learn some proven strategies for getting the best return you can for the risk you can tolerate. In this section, our experts will give you their best advice for following what they have seen work in their own practices. Pick one or two and begin implementing the strategy. See what happens!

◆ ◆ ◆

Periodic portfolio rebalancing lets you benefit from the principle of "sell high and buy low." If you designed your portfolio using target percentages for each asset class, over time it will become overweighted in some asset classes and underweighted in others. To bring each asset class back to its assigned percentage requires sell assets in the overweighted categories and buy assets in the underweighted categories. This helps you overcome the tendency to want to hold on to "winners." The result will be that you sell asset classes that have appreciated, "selling high," and purchase other asset classes, "buying low."

John Henry Wyckoff, M.B.A., M.S.T., CPA/PFS, CFP®
Advisor, Ron McCallister Financial Advisors, Inc.

You can keep more of the money your portfolio earns if you minimize the income taxes generated by your investment portfolio. Account allocation is an important factor in minimizing the taxes your portfolio generates. Account allocation is the strategic matching of the tax characteristics of the investment product with the taxability of the account. The optimal strategy would place tax-free and passive investments in taxable accounts and actively managed growth and taxable income investments in tax-deferred accounts. This strategy will decrease the income taxes generated by your investment portfolio and allow you to keep more of what your portfolio earns.

Patrick T. Hanratty, M.B.A., CPA/PFS, CFP®
Managing Director, Capital Advisors, Ltd.

Betcha didn't know that you can do something special with all that company stock that is in your retirement plan. Call your benefits department and ask them about something called NUA. That stands for net unrealized appreciation. You may be able to get capital gains treatment on a large portion of your company stock when you sell it (which could save you up to 18.6 percent of your investment).

Paul D. Lyons, CPA/PFS, CFP®
Manager, KPMG Personal Financial Planning

IN MONEY WORDS

All good things must come to an end ... The technology wave

When "stuff" happens in your life, take time to revisit your asset allocation. Throughout your life there will be events that involve changes in your circumstances as an investor, such as divorce, death of a loved one, or loss of a job. These changes, more than not, would lead to the modification of policies, objectives and/or risk tolerances in the asset allocation in your portfolio. The process of Dynamic Asset Allocation is intended to maintain equilibrium between your objectives and the asset allocation process.

Angie Hollerich, CEP, CCA
Author of Grab the Brass Ring of Financial Security

You don't want to take any risks in retirement with your hard-earned money. Therefore, to avoid risk you are investing 100 percent of your retirement funds in bonds and CDs. However, what you may not realize is that unless you are so wealthy that you are spending significantly less than four percent of your net worth each year, you are increasing your odds of running out of money before you die. You may be avoiding market risk, but you are incurring significant risk in the form of inflation, interest rate risk, and re-investment rate risk. Consider adding some equity exposure (20 to 25 percent) to your portfolio to increase your odds of your money lasting throughout your retirement.

Chad P. Tramp, PFS, CFP®
Wealth Management Advisor, RSM McGladrey

Specific identification allows you to determine the exact shares you wish to sell and puts you in the driver's seat concerning the deferral of tax liabilities. For example, if you own 10 shares of ABC Company (five shares purchased at $5 per share and five purchased at $10 per share) your average cost is $7.50 per share. If ABC is currently trading at $10 per share and you were to sell five shares, and assume an average cost basis of $7.50 per share, you would be generating a taxable capital gain of $2.50 per share. However, by utilizing "specific identification," it is possible to designate the five shares you sell as those that were originally purchased at $10. By doing so, there is no taxable gain on the transaction!

Richard A. Vera II, M.B.A., CPA/PFS, CDP, CSA
CEO, CPA & Financial Services, LLC

MIND OVER MONEY

When the markets go down and you wonder if you should get out, just keep asking yourself one thing: Ten years from now, do I believe that American companies will earn more or less money than they do today? If the answer is more (and it should be), stay invested!

Constanza Low, M.I.M., and John Henry Low, M.B.A.
Vice President and President, Knickerbocker Advisors Inc.

It is often said, "It's not what you make but what you keep." With this in mind, in general, it's best to defer paying income taxes as long as possible. Assuming you want some bonds in your overall asset allocation mix, consider positioning your taxable bonds in IRAs, 401(k)s, and other tax-deferred accounts. By deferring the tax payment on your taxable bond interest, your account can grow larger; and since you pay the higher "ordinary income" rates on taxable bonds (and IRA distributions) anyway, why not defer it?

J. Victor Conrad, CPA/PFS, CFP®, ChFC
Financial Advisor, The MONY Group

Always remember to include tax-deferred retirement plans in your portfolio risk allocation. Your tax-deferred plans should always have the safest taxable portion of your total portfolio. Your higher-risk investments (i.e., tech stocks) should be held outside of your tax-deferred retirement plans. Someday you might need to use the tax write-off!

Parke Stratford Teal, CPA/PFS
Principal, Dreggors, Rigsby, and Teal, P.A.

IN MONEY WORDS

Life has its ups and downs ... Beauty of a balanced portfolio

---

Do you have tax-free bonds in your IRA? If so, switching to taxable bonds can increase your nest egg. Why? When you take money out of an IRA, the interest earned on your bonds will be taxed, even if the bonds are normally tax-free. In effect, tax-free bonds lose their tax-free status when put into an IRA. Since a taxable bond of the same quality and maturity as a tax-free bond will pay you more interest, you can increase your IRA balance by investing in taxable bonds. Increasing your interest rate from 4 percent to 5 percent each year on a $100,000 IRA gives you about $72,000 extra income over 25 years.

John J. Feyche, M.S., M.B.T., CPA/PFS
Manager, Z&W Wealth Management

If you would like to sell a mutual fund for tax-loss purposes, but want to stay fully invested in the market, there's a way around the IRS 30-day wash sale rule. Simply switch your current investment for one with a similar objective. For example, switch your position in an index fund for a position in an Exchange Traded Fund. This way you get to deduct the loss and you won't miss any gains made by the market in the meantime. To get back into the original fund, wait 31 days, and then switch to the original investment.

Patrick T. Hanratty, M.B.A., CPA/PFS, CFP®
Managing Director, Capital Advisors, Ltd.

You might think that because you're in the highest federal income tax bracket, tax-free municipal bonds must be the best choice for your bond portion of your asset allocation strategy, but you'd be wrong. Consider owning taxable bonds in your tax-deferred accounts (IRAs, 401[k], variable annuities, etc.), where you get a higher rate of interest that will permit your money to grow to a larger value over time. Follow the money: $10,000 earning 3 percent tax-free is worth $10,300 after 12 months, but that same $10,000 earning 6 percent tax-deferred is worth $10,600 after 12 months.

Angie Hollerich, CEP, CAC
Author of Grab the Brass Ring of Financial Security

CBS MarketWatch (bigcharts.marketwatch.com). Historical quotes, and of course, as the name implies, great charting capabilities.

Diversification is the key to a successful investment portfolio. Invest in domestic and international stocks; in large-, mid-, and small-size companies; in value and growth stocks, and in a diversified bond portfolio. Make sure that no single stock represents more than 5 percent of your portfolio (2 percent or less is even better). That way, you avoid the devastating impact of the next Enron. To accomplish this level of diversification with individual stocks, you would need a portfolio of over $50,000,000! Low-cost mutual funds are the best way to diversify your portfolios and reduce your investment risk.

Constanza Low, M.I.M., and John Henry Low, M.B.A.
Vice President and President, Knickerbocker Advisors Inc.

Do you rely on income earned from your bonds as a hedge against portfolio volatility? If so, you may be exposed to more risk than you first considered. Bond values can erode overnight. Three factors affect valuation:

- Credit rating
- Changing interest rates
- Time to maturity

A credit downgrade or rising interest rates can cause a 10 to 20 percent loss of value. Avoid exposure to junk bonds or bonds with maturities greater than five years if you cannot assume this level of risk. Invest in a money market fund when substantial interest rate increases are expected in the next 12 months.

Jonathan S. Dinkins, CPA/PFS, CIMA, CMFC
Senior Consultant, Glass Jacobson Investment Advisors LLC

You can invest in real estate directly by owning rental properties and/or raw land. You can also invest in real estate indirectly by purchasing units of a real estate investment trust or REIT (pronounced reet). REITs invest in commercial real estate such as office buildings and apartment complexes. They are bought and sold like shares of stock and, like mutual funds, provide professional management and diversification. For more information about REITs, visit www.nareit.com.

Barbara O'Neill, Ph.D., CFP®, AFC, CHC
Author of Saving on a Shoestring

ADVANCED STRATEGIES

You are not done. As you build your net worth, you will have new challenges and new opportunities to minimize taxes and increase your returns. You may have scoffed at the notion of how "the rich get richer." But now is your turn to take advantage of these proven tactics.

◆ ◆ ◆

A better way to buy a stock than just submitting a market or limit order is to sell a put option below the current market. You will collect an option premium in return for your patience. For example: Company XYZ is currently at $30 per share but you only want to pay $25. Sell a put option of 2–3 months at a strike price of $25. In return, you will be paid $250 per 100 shares to wait. So instead of paying $25 (if it drops to that price), you only pay $22.50 per share ($25 – $2.50 premium received). Much better deal!

Angie Hollerich, CEP, CAC
Author of Grab the Brass Ring of Financial Security

IN MONEY WORDS

Always chasing rainbows ... Last year's stock market winners

How would you like to buy and sell an entire portfolio of stocks as easily as buying and selling one share? Similar to an index mutual fund, an exchange traded fund ("etf") can be bought and sold throughout the day, even sold short and bought on margin. You can get instant exposure to everything from a broad-based market index to a specific industry sector or an international sector. No sales loads. No high management fees. Ability to minimize taxable capital gains. Diversification. Use a broker of your choice.

Peg Downey, M.A., CFP®
Partner, Money Plans

Do you own rental or investment property that you would like to sell but don't want to pay the large capital gains? Consider completing a Section 1031 exchange to transfer your equity in one property to a new replacement property without a tax hit.

You can trade a property you wish to sell for other real estate that has better cash flow, less management responsibility, or simply a more favorable location. The rules are complex, so make sure you have good tax advice prior to selling the first property.

Frank L. Washelesky, J.D., CPA/PFS, CVA
Director, Ostrow Resin Berk & Abrams, Ltd.

Are you an investor finding yourself concentrated in a single or few stocks because you have low basis? Consider an equity collar. This strategy may have some tax consequences so it's best to work with someone knowledgeable in this area. First, you buy a put option on the stock, which will protect you from the stock going below a certain price. If the stock does fall you can put or sell it to the issuer of the put option. To make the transaction as cost neutral as possible you would also sell a call option, which has the effect of giving up some of the potential appreciation. This strategy will help you minimize the risk of your single company exposure.

Chad P. Tramp, PFS, CFP®
Wealth Management Advisor, RSM McGladrey

Demutualization is a process where savings depositors of community banks are first in line for private share offerings before banks go public. Community banks were established under federal charter to serve the financial needs of depositors. Changes in the law in the nineties allow banks to convert to stock companies. The value of stock before public trading is equal to the bank's assets, but on the first day of trading, shares equal the value of all assets, plus the value of all shares—effectively doubling stock value. Lucky savings depositors receive a letter offering shares at $10. Buy 1563 shares and keep for 366 days. Repeat the process seven times for a cool million. See list at www.cash-planner.com.

Steve Wightman, CFP®
Life Advisor Specializing in Money, Lexington Financial Mgmt.

If you are considering investing in hedge funds, consider using managers that use an absolute return strategy or market neutral strategy. While there is still risk involved, these strategies typically have a much lower standard deviation (3 to 6 percent) and yet maintain consistent attractive returns, usually ranging from 8 to 12 percent. More importantly though, you must know the manager with whom you are investing. Investing in hedge funds can be more qualitative than it is quantitative. Because it can be difficult to conduct due diligence on the underlying manager, consider using a fund of funds in order to diversify in strategy and reduce your risk. While you may be paying an extra fee for the fund of funds manager, you are getting their expertise in conducting the due diligence on the underlying managers.

William K. Kaiser, CPA/PFS
Financial Advisor, Howard Financial Services, Inc.

Wall Street Journal (http://online.wsj.com/public/us). *Wall Street Journal* online for anything you want to know about Wall Street and so much more. Here you can track your investments, research anyone or anything from options to equities to mutual funds.

A foreign asset protection trust offers tremendous protection from future malpractice claims, judgments, liens, and misplaced lawsuits. You can still indirectly control your assets and use income from the assets for living expenses in the U.S. The foreign asset protection trust is not a device to avoid U.S. taxes but a device to be sure your hard-earned assets remain in your control. Some offshore jurisdictions make it next to impossible for a creditor to obtain a judgment against those assets. This allows the trustee, if desired, to structure a greatly reduced settlement, or no settlement at all, with the creditor. The key is to plan now before litigation becomes an issue.

Stephen A. Drake, Ph.D., CPA/PFS, CFP®
President, Optima Financial Resources

Diversify through a professional, and then do this: Sell rolling covered calls on your equities. If you purchased equity shares at 25, sell a call at, say, 30. You'll receive an immediate cash premium for each contract (representing 100 shares of stock). You always win! If prices remain flat or descend, you keep rolling calls month to month and collect premiums. If share prices increase, you may be forced to sell your shares (mercy me, at higher prices) and find new ones. This strategy adds double digits to your returns in any market and it works well with stocks or exchange-traded-funds—especially inside an IRA where you won't be taxed. To learn more, contact Chicago Board Options Exchange (CBOE) at 312-786-5600, your broker, or any stock exchange.

Steve Wightman, CFP®
Life Advisor Specializing in Money, Lexington Financial Mgmt.

If you didn't know you have a portfolio, you do now. Many of these tips will apply to things you'll need to think about in the future, but many are ripe for the picking right now. Grab 'em and go! The sooner you begin acting as if you have these issues to consider, the sooner you will.

5

MANAGING TAXES

Pray, Father Abraham, what think you of the times? Won't these heavy taxes quite ruin the country? How shall we be ever able to pay them? What would you advise us to?

Benjamin Franklin (Poor Richard's Almanack)

Terms from The Top

alternative minimum tax (AMT)   Federal tax aimed at ensuring that wealthy individuals, trusts, estates, and corporations pay at least some income tax.

capital gains tax   Tax on profits from the sale of capital assets; after a minimum holding period the tax rate is traditionally more favorable than ordinary income tax.

itemize   Using an item that allows a taxpayer to reduce adjusted gross income; such as mortgage interest, charitable contributions, state and local income and property taxes, IRA contributions, and unreimbursed business expenses.

marginal tax bracket   Point on the income-tax rate schedules where taxable income falls. It is expressed as a percentage applied to each additional dollar earned over the base amount for that bracket.

prospectus   Formal written offer to sell securities that sets forth the plan for a proposed business enterprise.

qualified plans   Tax-deferred plan set up by an employer for employees under 1954 Internal Revenue Service rules. Such plans usually provide for employer contributions—for example, a profit-sharing or pension plan—and may also allow employee contributions. They build up savings, which are paid out at retirement or on termination of employment.

taxable distribution   Payout of realized capital gains on securities in the portfolio of the fund with tax consequences.

turnover ratio   Volume of shares traded as a percentage of total shares in a portfolio at a given time.

Source: reprinted by permission of Jordan Goodman, Dictionary of Finance and Investment Terms *(Barron's, 5th Edition)*

We all pay them. We all hate them. And over the years more and more "loopholes" have been closed. But there are very deliberate things you can do to minimize the tax hits you take over your earning and investing lifetime. Some will pay off over the long run and some will have an impact on your tax bill this year.

It is your obligation to pay income taxes, but not a penny more than you owe. The problem is that sometimes it is difficult to know how much that is. Even experts will disagree. You may find that one tax advisor finds a deduction that another missed. It's not easy. The more you know the fewer potential mistakes you will make. Read on.

All tips in this chapter are intended for informational purposes only. Should you find one potentially helpful to your situation, you should consult with your legal, tax, or investment professional familiar with your individual situation to determine its suitability prior to taking any action or investing any money.

TAX CONCEPTS

Let's start with a variety of tax concepts that you may not know. It's one thing to be able to read a tax form, and another to understand how your investment decisions will impact the bottom line on that form.

♦ ♦ ♦

First, learn how much you pay in taxes and to which government. Add up the taxes from your school district, property, car tags, gasoline, phone bill, groceries, occupational tax, local, state, and federal income tax, special assessment taxes, capital gains, luxury tax, and travel (hotel/airline) taxes. Did

I miss any? If you earned $36,579 in a single income family or $68,605 in a two-income family in 1998, you may have paid more than 37.6 percent of that single income and 39 percent of that two-income amount back in federal, state, and local taxes, according to the Tax Foundation. Although federal taxes have been decreasing, state, local, and payroll taxes have been increasing at a rate fast enough to increase the overall percentage of income. Still want to sit at home and not vote?

Bonnie A. Hughes, CFP®
President, A&H Financial Planning and Education, Inc.

Always know the current tax effects (and annual cumulative effects) prior to selling investments. If your broker has trading authority, does not know the effect, and sells anyway, then fire him.

Parke Stratford Teal, CPA/PFS
Principal, Dreggors, Rigsby, and Teal, P.A.

IN MONEY WORDS

Look before you leap ... Overly risky investments

Interest payments on amounts borrowed from a 401(k) plan are not deductible because the 401(k) plan does not secure a mortgage on the loan. Because of this, it is not usually advantageous from a tax standpoint to borrow from your 401(k) plan for your house purchase. On top of that, you will owe income tax on that interest you have paid into the fund when you withdraw from your 401(k) plan for retirement.

Barbara J. Raasch, CFA®, CPA/PFS, ChFC
Partner-in-charge of Wealth Management Solutions, Ernst & Young

Consider holding fixed-income instruments in your retirement plan. Income from fixed-income investments are taxed annually at your marginal tax rate where as equities are taxed at reduced capital gains rates only at the time of sale. If fixed-income instruments are held in your retirement plan you can defer all taxes until the time of distribution or sale of equity and save the difference between the marginal tax rate and capital gains rate.

James Kantowski, CPA, CFP®
Wealth Management Advisor, RSM McGladrey

When you pay foreign taxes on an investment, you may claim a foreign tax credit against your income tax obligation to Uncle Sam. However, foreign investments held in tax-deferred accounts (401[k], IRA) do not qualify for the foreign tax credit. Therefore, if you structure your portfolio so that all investments subject to foreign taxes are held in your taxable accounts, you will not lose this valuable dollar-for-dollar tax credit. You can check the section of a mutual fund's prospectus that discusses dividends, capital gains, and taxes in order to find out if a fund is likely to be subject to foreign taxes.

Loyd J. Stegent, CPA/PFS, CFP®
Director of Financial Planning, Cornelius, Stegent & Price

SAVING TAXES

Our experts spend a great deal of their days looking for ways for their clients to save money on their taxes. You don't have to spend that much time, but only read carefully through this section. Chances are several of these tips will apply to your situation and save you a good deal of money next year.

♦ ♦ ♦

Following is a list of commonly overlooked tax deductions that can help you minimize your tax liability:

- Accounting fees for tax preparation
- Appreciation on property donated to charity
- Casualty or theft losses
- Contraceptives, if bought with a prescription
- Employee moving expenses
- Gambling losses to the extent of gambling winnings
- Investment advisory fees
- Labor union dues
- Lead paint removal
- Legal or accounting fees to collect or determine taxable income (including alimony)
- Penalty for early withdrawal of savings

- Protective clothing required at work
- Separately billed IRA trustee administration fees
- Subscriptions to professional journals
- Worthless stock or securities

Richard A. Vera II, M.B.A., CPA/PFS, CDP, CSA
CEO, CPA & Financial Services, LLC

Since interest on loans is paid in arrears, if your mortgage payment is due on the first day of the month, you can accelerate your mortgage interest deduction for the month of December by paying your January 1st mortgage payment on December 31st each year. By paying one day early, you get to deduct interest one year early. If the interest on your January 1 payment is $10,000, that could reduce this year's taxes by $4,000.

Barbara J. Raasch, CFA®, CPA/PFS, ChFC
Partner-in-charge of Wealth Management Solutions, Ernst & Young

Can't collect on a debt? You may be able to save some taxes, at least. If you have loaned someone money, you need to make sure you take steps to collect the debt. If you are unable to collect it, you may want to deduct a nonbusiness debt in the year it, becomes totally worthless. Your efforts to collect the debt should include evidence that there was debt, which has now become worthless.

Phyllis Bernstein, CPA/PFS
President, Phyllis Bernstein Consulting

A smart way to keep more cash while contributing to charity is to donate investments that have performed well since you bought them instead of writing a check. If you've owned that investment for over a year, when you donate it to the charity, you can deduct the gifted value on your taxes. The charity can then sell that investment and receive the cash. By doing this, the charity gets its money and you keep more money in your pocket since you don't have to pay capital gains taxes on the increased value of that investment.

Don A. Gomez, CFP®
President, Momentum Financial Advisors

Contributions to a Roth IRA are nondeductible, but withdrawals are generally tax-free. It is still possible for you to convert your traditional IRA to a Roth IRA to take advantage of future tax-free growth. The tax-deferred amount in the traditional IRA will be subject to income taxes in the year of conversion. However, if you have a low earnings year or have a traditional IRA that was funded with after-tax dollars, converting some or all of the account could be very beneficial. Check with your broker to see if you qualify, income-wise, for this provision. Then have them roll over the traditional IRA to a Roth IRA in the year that you are willing to pay the tax.

Frank L. Washelesky, J.D., CPA/PFS, CVA
Director, Ostrow Resin Berk & Abrams, Ltd.

Be sure that you don't pay more income taxes on inherited IRA distributions than necessary. If you have inherited an IRA from an estate where estate taxes have been paid, be sure to find out the amount of taxes attributable to the IRA so you as beneficiary can claim an income tax deduction on your income tax return when you take a taxable distribution. The deduction is taken by the beneficiary on Form 1040 Schedule A in the year a distribution is taken from the inherited IRA. The amount of the deduction claimed depends on the estate tax paid on the IRA (calculated using a method referred to as the "with/without" method.)

Susan J. Bruno, CPA/PFS, CFP®
Principal, Winged Keel Financial Advisors, LLC

That tech stock you bought a few years ago has dropped 60 percent. Now you'd like to give it to your child. But gifting it outright to your child can cost you tax dollars. Instead, sell the stock, and you will be able to take a tax loss. Then give the sales proceeds to your child; these funds can then be used or reinvested as appropriate.

John J. Feyche, M.S., M.B.T., CPA/PFS
Manager, Z&W Wealth Management

If you itemize your deductions, you can get a tax deduction while helping others. Assemble your old clothes and household items. Forget the yard sale. What a waste of time! Instead, make a list of what you will donate. Obtain the Salvation Army's Valuation Guide for Donated Items (check www.salvationarmy.org for nearest location or call 404-873-3101). Value every item. Total the list. Get a receipt. File both the list and the receipt in your current year tax file. It's important to do the list up front! I can assure you that you won't make the list after you donate. When you see how much you save in taxes you'll be glad you did!

Martin J. Sickles, CPA/PFS, CFP®
President, Financial Planning Partners

IN MONEY WORDS

Like selling a car to a used car salesman ... Consider the source of tax and investment advice

---

Remember that the wash sale rule does not apply when you sell a stock at a gain. So if you have a bunch of dogs in your portfolio, sell them and offset the resulting loss by selling and buying back some of your winners. Here's how: Suppose you own 1,000 shares of LOSER, Inc. that you paid $10/share for and that is now worth $6/share. You also own 300 shares of MONEYMAKER, Inc. that you paid $15/share for and are now worth $35/share. Sell all of the LOSER, Inc. shares. You will have a loss of $4,000. To offset this loss, sell 200 shares of MONEYMAKER at a $4,000 gain. Take the $11,000 ($4,000 from LOSER and $7,000 from MONEYMAKER) and purchase 314 new shares of MONEYMAKER. You now have converted the low basis ($15/share) shares into high basis ($35/share) shares at no tax cost to you.

Michael David Schulman, M.B.A., M.A., CPA/PFS
Principal, Schulman Co. CPA P.C.

You can get more bang for the buck by using the winners in your investment portfolio to make your annual charitable gifts. For example, suppose more than a year ago you bought XYZ stock for $1,000 and it is now worth $10,000. By gifting this stock to your chosen charity instead of $10,000 cash, you will forever avoid the capital gains tax on the $9,000 gain. Your tax deduction will be $10,000 either way. And if you still want to own XYZ stock, use the $10,000 cash you would have otherwise have given to charity and buy more XYZ stock. You'll now have a $10,000 cost basis in the XYZ stock instead of $1,000.

Cheryl A. Moss, CPA/PFS, CFP®, CLU
Tax Advisor

If your kids are under 18 and work in your unincorporated business, put them on the payroll. Their wages are not subject to Social Security, Medicare, or unemployment taxes when they work for you. It reduces your self-employment tax, and you can shift income to their lower tax bracket. For example, assuming you earn all of your income ($70,000) from your business, and take a standard deduction, your total self-employment and federal income taxes will be $16,912. Pay your child a $5,000 salary, and your taxes will go down to $14,968. Your child's tax bill will be only $30. This is over $1,900 in tax savings. Even if this is only a side business and you've already paid the maximum Social Security taxes on your salary, you can still save taxes with this strategy.

Steven B. Morris, M.B.A., CPA/PFS, CLU
Sole practitioner, Steven B. Morris CPA

The older you are ... the better it gets! If you're unhappy with low CD interest rates, consider putting some of your money in a gift annuity. Depending on your age, you can earn healthy guaranteed rates for as long as you live. For example, at age 65 a competitive payout is currently 6.7 percent. In addition, part of the income is tax-free, which raises your effective earning rate. The money left in your annuity when you die goes to benefit your designated charity. You can feel good about that. Ask your favorite charitable organization for more information.

Kathleen M. Rehl, Ph.D., CFP®
Owner, Rehl Financial Advisors

MIND OVER MONEY

If you are considering leaving assets to your grandchildren, you should discuss your intentions with your children. You might find that they feel you have undermined their authority by this using tax savings strategy. Even with the best intentions, you may not know all the real life issues.

Susan J. Bruno, CPA/PFS, CFP®
Principal, Winged Keel Financial Advisors, LLC

For a really large tax deduction in a year when you have substantial income, consider forming a Section 419A or 412(i) benefit plan. Under these plans, your tax deduction will often be 2 to 10 times larger than the amount you would normally be allowed to deduct from a regular pension contribution. These plans can be combined with traditional pension plans for a compound tax deduction for a single year or for many years, whichever you need. Sometimes the 419A plan can be combined with an employee leasing arrangement to reduce coverage to "other" employees. Thus, more of the contribution stays with the owners.

Stephen A. Drake, Ph.D., CPA/PFS, CFP®
President, Optima Financial Resources

If you and your spouse work and are paying child-care costs, you may be able to pay for up to $5,000 through a dependent care assistance program at your employer. This program allows you to exclude up to $5,000 from your taxable income if used to pay for a babysitter, nanny, day care, or other eligible expenses. For an average taxpayer, this can add up to $1,900 in tax savings per year (27 percent federal, 5 percent state, and 6.2 percent Social Security). It beats the tax savings of $240 for one child or $480 for two children the same taxpayers would get if they took the tax credit instead.

Jill Gianola, M.S., M.B.A., CFP®
Owner, Gianola Financial Planning

Try to match income tax deductions with income. If you are earning or receiving an extraordinarily high level of income in any one year (due to a bonus, exercise of stock options, etc.) and are charitably inclined, you should consider making several year's worth of charitable contributions to a Donor Advised Fund. This step will allow you to get a current income tax deduction, subject to federal Adjusted Gross Income limitations. Then you make your contributions, other than pledges, out of this fund in future years.

Susan J. Bruno, CPA/PFS, CFP®
Principal, Winged Keel Financial Advisors, LLC

There are a number of ways you can reduce your tax bite on Social Security, such as deferring the receipt of other income, which reduces the amount of benefit that will be taxed. For example, a retiree may have a choice of receiving periodic pension payments or one lump-sum payment. By choosing the lump-sum and rolling it over into an IRA, the IRA grows tax-free. Another way to reduce the tax bite is to switch funds to EE bonds, which permit the deferral of interest until the bonds are redeemed, and hold off on selling appreciated assets until losses from other sales will become available to offset the gains.

Phyllis Bernstein, CPA/PFS
President, Phyllis Bernstein Consulting

Reduce your taxes by implementing a passive (indexed) investment strategy. Passively managed mutual funds don't buy and sell as often, which leads to usually having a lower turnover ratio, which in turn leads to lower capital gains distributions, which in turn leads to you paying less capital gains tax. Turnover ratios should range from approximately 5 percent to 40 percent depending on the asset class. A small-cap portfolio would be expected to have a higher turnover ratio than a large-cap portfolio. Turnover ratios and tax-adjusted returns can be found at morningstar.com or the finance link on yahoo.com.

James Kantowski, CPA, CFP®
Wealth Management Advisor, RSM McGladrey

Did you know that in some cases, you might qualify for a tax credit for alternative minimum tax (AMT) paid in previous years? AMT adjustments come in two flavors: deferrals and exclusions. If you paid AMT because of deferral items, a dollar-for-dollar tax credit may be available in the future. The most common AMT deferral adjustments result from incentive stock options and depreciation. Review Form 6251 to help determine if you may be entitled to a tax credit in the future.

Jon S. Chernila, CPA/PFS, CFP®, ChFC
Principal, Corbin & Wertz

You can sell a variable annuity at a loss and take an ordinary income loss against ordinary income and avoid the 10 percent pre-59$\frac{1}{2}$ penalty as well. For example, if you purchased a variable annuity in 1999 for $100,000 and it is currently worth $75,000, you can terminate it and take a $25,000 loss against ordinary income. One of the many opportunities this would allow would be to take a like amount out of an IRA (depends on your tax bracket) and shelter the tax due on it—so it could allow you to roll over to a ROTH IRA without any tax impact.

Bill Pomeroy, M.S., CFP®, CRC
Executive Vice President, The Shobe Financial Group

If you have a large capital gain of $500,000 or more from real estate, consider selling the real estate to a Nevada corporation in exchange for a private annuity. A private annuity is a promise to pay by the corporation. The Nevada corporation then sells the real estate for cash to a third party with no tax due. Later, the Nevada corporation and an offshore corporation combined with your newly formed offshore irrevocable trust enter into an agreement whereby the offshore corporation assumes the annuity to you and the cash is transferred to the offshore trust.

Stephen A. Drake, Ph.D., CPA/PFS, CFP®
President, Optima Financial Resources

There is no investment rule that says you have to wait until your investment gets back to even losing value before you can sell it. Harvesting tax losses is a way to actually take advantage of an opportunity when markets dip. These losses can be used to offset any gains you have. In fact, if your capital losses for the year exceed your capital gains, you can deduct up to $3,000 of losses on your federal tax return. An individual taxpayer can even carry forward any unused losses in one year to future years.

J. Victor Conrad, CPA/PFS, CFP®, ChFC
Financial Advisor, The MONY Group

You have managed to invest well, but your buy-and-hold strategy has created large unrealized capital gains. Now, at retirement, you need income from these investments. Rather than pay a large capital gains tax to convert your portfolio to income-generating investments, consider contributing to a Charitable Remainder Trust (CRT). This type of trust can provide you with a fixed return, avoid the capital gains tax, and provide a charitable deduction in the year of the contribution. After a set term of years or your death, the selected charities will receive the assets remaining.

Frank L. Washelesky, J.D., CPA/PFS, CVA
Director, Ostrow Resin Berk & Abrams, Ltd.

Are you an investor finding yourself concentrated in a single or few stocks because you have low basis? There is a solution, but you generally need a minimum of $500,000 to $1,000,000 to do it. An exchange fund is an investment vehicle created by large financial institutions that allows you to contribute your low-basis stock for units of this vehicle invested in stocks of hundreds of different companies. It allows you to diversify without current tax consequences. The downside is that you have locked up your money for typically seven years and you have no say about where the money is invested.

Chad P. Tramp, PFS, CFP®
Wealth Management Advisor, RSM McGladrey

SYSTEMS AND STRATEGIES

Effective tax management includes learning as much as you can about different long-term strategies that can minimize taxes. Some are obvious but difficult to put into place. Others are easy but not so obvious. Our experts have given you tips to get the most out of these strategies.

♦ ♦ ♦

In order to calculate the true cost basis of a mutual fund, make sure to add in all of the capital gains and dividend distributions that were automatically reinvested into the fund. Let's say you originally invested

$1,000 in your favorite mutual fund and sold it five years later for $2,000. Over the years, the fund paid a total of $1,000 in distributions, which were automatically reinvested. If you don't include the reinvested distributions, you'll pay tax on $1,000. However, if you include the distributions, your cost basis will be $2,000. Thus, you won't owe any tax when you sell, because you were already taxed on the earnings at the time they were reinvested.

Brad R. Cougill, CFP®, CMFC®
Partner, Deerfield Financial Advisors, Inc.

Do you never have quite enough deductions to itemize? Try clustering your deductible payments into alternate years. For instance, pay your real estate taxes in January for the previous year and then pay the present year's taxes in December. And make your charitable contributions once every other year—in the year you pay the real estate tax twice.

Peg Downey, M.A., CFP®
Partner, Money Plans

Municipal bonds are often purchased by tax-sensitive investors, but they are not as simple as they seem. First consider that if your marginal tax rate isn't at least 33 percent, you are probably not making as much after taxes as you would from taxable Treasury bonds. Second, many municipal bonds can generate some amount of taxable income. Third, bonds from a high income tax rate state that you don't live in will cost more than you should be willing to pay. Fourth, you should *never* put a municipal bond in your IRA. And lastly, don't forget that municipal bonds are not as safe as U.S. Government bonds because the issuer can default.

Clark M. Blackman II, CPA/PFS, CFP®, ChFC, CFA®, CIMA, AAMS®
Managing Director, Post Oak Capital

Be aware of the potential taxes on assets you receive as part of a divorce settlement. Internal Revenue Code Section 1041 provides that neither you nor your ex-spouse will recognize a gain or a loss on a transfer of property. If the transfer meets the §1041 test, it will be treated as a nontaxable event, and the original cost basis will follow the asset. The effect of this cost basis transfer is to shift to you any tax liability (upon disposition) for the appreciation of the asset. For this reason, it is imperative that you are fully aware of the cost basis and thereby the tax liability that may be associated with the disposition of assets awarded you as part of the divorce settlement process.

Richard A. Vera II, M.B.A., CPA/PFS, CDP, CSA
CEO, CPA & Financial Services, LLC

Store your tax records in a safe place. You should keep all your records available for at least three years (five is even better) in case your return is selected for audit. Keep a copy of your actual return forever.

Steve Johnson, CPA/PFS, CFP®
Owner, Johnson Financial

Did you know you have until April 15th of the following year to make a contribution to your retirement accounts? If you're looking for a deduction while completing your tax return, it's not too late to set aside funds for your future and take the deduction. As of 2002, the general contribution limit is $3,000, or $3,500 if you're over 50. However, if your modified Adjusted Gross Income is above a certain amount, your contribution limit may be reduced. Visit www.irs.gov to order a free copy of Publication 17, the "Tax Guide for Individuals." This will help you find your true contribution limit.

Jeff Michael, Director of Education
Springboard Non-Profit Consumer Credit Counseling

Be aware of the hidden tax implications of incentive stock options. Although you may not have regular income tax when you exercise your options, you may be subject to something called the alternative minimum tax. Know what kind you have before you exercise! If you're not sure, call your benefits department. If you do have these type of options, be sure and ask your accountant if the AMT will apply to you.

Paul D. Lyons, CPA/PFS, CFP®
Manager, KPMG Personal Financial Planning

If you're using a Dependent Care Assistance Program at work, there's another way you can sweeten the deal. If one spouse earns more than the Social Security limit ($84,900 in 2002) and one earns less, have the lower-paid spouse participate in the dependent care plan so you can save the 6.2 percent Social Security tax—an extra $310—on the $5,000 exclusion. And be careful—the limit is $2,500 for a married taxpayer filing separately.

Jill Gianola, M.S., M.B.A., CFP®
Owner, Gianola Financial Planning

Are you a veteran? Many states provide fantastic benefits to men and women who once served in the armed forces. In some states you can receive valuable discounts on local property taxes. To claim these discounts, you'll probably need to provide state and municipal agencies with a copy of your DD Form 214 (Separation Papers).

Michael L. Alberts, M.B.A., CFP®
President, Woodstock Financial Group, LLC

Did you know that your state tax refund might not be taxable for federal purposes? Generally, taxpayers who itemize their deductions must include state tax refunds as income in the following year. This is because they receive a federal tax deduction (on Schedule A) for paying those state taxes. If you are subject to alternative minimum tax (AMT) or are in a loss position, you may not have received full benefit for your state tax deduction. By carefully reviewing your returns, you can determine if the tax benefit rule applies to you.

Jon S. Chernila, CPA/PFS, CFP®, ChFC
Principal, Corbin & Wertz

Internal Revenue Service (www.irs.gov). Visit the Internal Revenue Service for forms and much more.

Do a midyear tax projection in June or July to check if your tax withholding is in line with your projected tax bill. By midyear, you should have a pretty good idea of your income prospects for the rest of the year. Figure out how much tax will be withheld for the rest of the year and add it to your year-to-date withholding. Run these numbers through your tax software or give your tax preparer a call. This will give you a rough estimate. If your withholding needs to be changed, you still have half a year for these changes to take effect. Contact your employer for form W-4 to make tax-withholding changes. If you find that you need to withhold less from your paycheck, use this "found" money to save or reduce debt.

Barbara O'Neill, Ph.D., CFP®, AFC, CHC
Author of Saving on a Shoestring

If you're divorcing and you have children, give some thought to your tax situation. When a divorced couple has children, the spouse who is granted custody is usually the person who is able to take the child deduction on his or her tax return. You should establish in your divorce proceedings that each of you is able to deduct at least one child on your return. The purpose of this is to allow each of you to use the head of household filing status on your tax return and take a dependent deduction.

Jeff Michael, Director of Education
Springboard Non-Profit Consumer Credit Counseling

Real estate tax payments are not deductible for individuals subject to alternative minimum tax (AMT). Therefore, if an unusual event (e.g., exercise of incentive stock options) causes you to be subject to AMT in the current year, you should pay your real estate taxes in January of the following year if you can do so without incurring a penalty of more than 25 percent.

Barbara J. Raasch, CFA®, CPA/PFS, ChFC
Partner-in-charge of Wealth Management Solutions, Ernst & Young

When a child turns 14, all income is taxed at the child's tax rate. You can change your investment strategy to include more income-generating investments, which you may have avoided to minimize the kiddie tax. (The kiddie tax could have taxed some of this income at your highest rate.) Now if you sell any appreciated assets, the income from the sale would be taxed at the child's lower rate. Income from any income-oriented investments would also be taxed at the child's lower rate.

Alexis M. Jensen
President, Z&W Wealth Management

You may take a long-term or short-term capital loss for securities that collapsed this year, buy them back after 31 days has transpired to avoid the "wash sale rules," and take a $3,000 tax loss each year until your loss is exhausted.

Steve Wightman, CFP®
Life Advisor Specializing in Money, Lexington Financial Mgmt.

Before May 7, 1997, taxpayers were generally allowed to defer the gain on the sale of their principal residence if they purchased a more expensive home. If you have previously taken advantage of this tax deferral, the cost basis of your current home must be reduced by the amount of that deferred gain. To determine the cost basis of your home, you will need the information included on Form 2119 for the year you purchased your home.

Barbara J. Raasch, CFA®, CPA/PFS, ChFC
Partner-in-charge of Wealth Management Solutions, Ernst & Young

Even knowing a few basic tax strategies can save you thousands of dollars over your lifetime. The tax code is an overwhelming document, but the tax advisors that study it can create opportunities for you as soon as you open yourself up to the possibilities. If you aren't using all the tips in this chapter, write down a few that you can try this year and watch your savings add up!

6

INSURANCE DECISIONS

*Work while it is called today, for
you know not how much you may be
hindered tomorrow.*

Benjamin Franklin (Poor Richard's Almanack)

Terms from the Top

cash value   The amount the insurer will return to a policyholder on cancellation of the policy.

convertible   The right to switch from one type of insurance policy to another, usually from term to permanent life insurance coverage.

disclosure   Release by companies of all information, positive or negative, that might bear on an investment decision, as required by the Securities and Exchange Commission and the stock exchanges.

illustration   A projected financial description of the expected performance of a life insurance contract.

level premium term   Life insurance contract that covers a specific period of time and carries a cost that remains constant during that period of time.

surplus (retained earnings)   Net profits kept to accumulate in a business after dividends are paid.

surrender charges   Fees charged when an annuity contract is cancelled, usually early in the contract.

variable annuities   Life insurance annuity contract whose value fluctuates with that of an underlying securities portfolio or other index of performance.

waiver of premium   Clause in an insurance policy providing that all policy premiums will be waived if the policyholder becomes seriously ill or disabled and therefore unable to pay the premiums.

Source: reprinted by permission of Jordan Goodman, Dictionary of Finance and Investment Terms *(Barron's, 5th Edition)*

Insurance is the financial product we love to hate, until we have a claim. Whether it is car insurance or health insurance or disability insurance, sometimes it seems that we are just throwing our money to the wind. It is so important to be an informed consumer with all our insurance needs so that our money is spent where it will make the most impact on our financial security.

Insurance is also a complicated product. Reading insurance policies has not become a national pastime. They are not written so that you can easily understand them, so you find yourself relying on your agent to interpret the provisions for you. This means it is important that your agent is well trained and trustworthy.

All tips in this chapter are intended for informational purposes only. Should you find one potentially helpful to your situation, you should consult with your legal, tax, or investment professional familiar with your individual situation to determine its suitability prior to taking any action or investing any money.

LIFE INSURANCE

Term or whole life? Universal or variable? Beneficiary designations? Ownership? Trusts? There are an awful lot of decisions for a contract that only has one claim ever, if that. It has long been determined that life insurance is a product that is *sold*, not *bought*. Buying life insurance can be painful because it helps us confront our own mortality or that of a loved one. Not fun.

Life insurance is one of the most powerful pieces of your financial plan and the dollars spent on it are just as important to spend wisely as any purchase you make. The industry has changed totally in the last 25 years, as tax laws and investment options evolved. It's time to learn the new landscape. The following tips will certainly help.

♦ ♦ ♦

When shopping for insurance products such as life, health, annuities, or disability, examine the insurance company like a mechanic examines a car. Look under the hood to check the company's financial strength. Use one of the rating services (www.moodys.com, www.ambest.com, or www.standardandpoors.com) to help you understand the company's investment practices, the adequacy and liquidity of their surplus, and their earnings history. Don't forget, the strength of the insurance company is a major determinant in whether the company will be able to pay your benefits, your income stream, and the guarantees in your policy.

Patrick T. Hanratty, M.B.A., CPA/PFS, CFP®
Managing Director, Capital Advisors, Ltd.

Term insurance is as great as a plug in a dam, but not so good as a 40-year plan.

Leonard C. Wright, CPA/PFS, CFP®, CLU, ChFC
Principal, Strategic Financial Group

Life insurance planning is actually quite simple. If you have a temporary financial problem (children, personal debt, business loans, etc.), use a temporary solution (term insurance) to protect yourself. If you have a permanent or long-term problem (replacing lost income, business ownership buyout, estate settlement costs, etc.), use a permanent solution (whole life or universal life). In most situations, life insurance is not about savings or cash value; it's about matching the time frame of your problem with the time frame of the solution.

J. Victor Conrad, CPA/PFS, CFP®, ChFC
Financial Advisor, The MONY Group

Don't fall in love with the future cash value of permanent life insurance, and end up buying less than adequate coverage, because you can't afford more. Focus on adequately protecting your family, and purchase enough of (the cheaper) term insurance instead. After all, when you are very hungry, with only a couple of dollars in your pocket, you'd buy a burger instead of a tiny serving of lobster—even if lobster is your favorite.

Raj Pillai, Ph.D., CFP®
NAPFA-Registered Advisor, Financial Fitness Network of Solon

Life insurance is a needed and critical component of sound financial planning. There has never been a death benefit that was not paid nor a beneficiary that felt a death benefit was too high. The key, then, is to buy what you need and try to avoid excessive costs. My bias is to reduce or eliminate commissions. However, if a good product exists that effectively competes, it should certainly be considered. I also think a professional can provide great assistance in obtaining proper and cost-effective coverage. How to reconcile the lot? Hire a professional to help evaluate the need for coverage and explain the choices available.

Joe Harper, CFP®
President, Harper Associates, Inc.

National Association of Insurance Commissioners (www.naic.org). This links to state agencies, companies, and other resources for all your insurance questions.

Consider your life insurance needs as bridge financing, with the ultimate goal to be self-insured. Usually a level premium term policy is the way to go. You may be trying to combine savings with insurance through use of whole life or universal life policies. The problem is that as you get older, the underlying cost of insurance continues to rise even though your premium remains the same. Your need for insurance diminishes as you build wealth. By not separating your savings need from your insurance need, you end up with an increasing cost for insurance you really don't need.

William K. Kaiser, CPA/PFS
Financial Advisor, Howard Financial Services, Inc.

Carrying adequate life insurance coverage on both parents is essential to make sure there will be adequate funds to support your children should either of you die prematurely. Total all costs you would provide for your children and subtract from that amount the income you can reasonably expect the other parent to be able to contribute to the household after paying all his or her costs. As a rule of thumb, it takes assets equal to 20 to 30 times living expenses to be financially independent. Therefore if your family's budget is $100,000 this year, your family probably needs $2 million or $3 million to meet their needs in the future. If you have financial assets equal to $200,000, you can subtract $200,000 from your $2 to $3 million need when determining how much life insurance to purchase.

Barbara J. Raasch, CFA®, CPA/PFS, ChFC
Partner-in-charge of Wealth Management Solutions, Ernst & Young

You might anticipate that your need for life insurance 20 years from now will be about 50 percent of your current needs. In 20 years, however, you might find out that 50 percent is really equal to 100 percent. Why? It seems that it is easy to dismiss inflation. A modest inflation factor over a 20-year period will double the cost of your standard of living. So the coverage you are planning at 50 percent today really becomes 100 percent 20 years in the future.

Leonard C. Wright, CPA/PFS, CFP®, CLU, ChFC
Principal, Strategic Financial Group

Consider the use of term insurance in your pre-retirement years. The premium rates for level premium term policies are extremely low. Even if you are well off, you may want to consider life insurance for career protection if you are close to retirement and counting on those final high-income years. Add the convertible feature if you later want to convert it to a permanent policy for estate planning purposes.

Susan J. Bruno, CPA/PFS, CFP®
Principal, Winged Keel Financial Advisors, LLC

In Money Words

Nothing ventured, nothing gained ... Overly conservative investments

---

If you are a "stay-at-home" spouse, don't think that you do not have a life insurance need just because you don't bring home a paycheck. Don't forget the economic benefits you provide (e.g., cleaning, cooking, child care)! You'll want to quantify how much your spouse would need to pay others to perform these services so he or she would have sufficient funds in the event of your death. In addition, if your spouse would need to change jobs to be sufficiently available for the children, the present value of the reduction in his or her compensation should be covered by the life insurance policy amount carried on your life.

Barbara J. Raasch, CFA®, CPA/PFS, ChFC
Partner-in-charge of Wealth Management Solutions, Ernst & Young

When buying life insurance, if you can find someone who works for a fee and suggests no-commission coverage, you could possibly pay more in fees but have a no-conflict suggestion as a result. In some states, the life insurance lobby has attempted to prohibit knowledgeable fee-oriented advisors from providing this service, but there is a wealth of information available on the Internet as well as direct quotes from some companies. Whatever your decision, don't let the hassle of the process deter you from making a purchase. Even a bad decision can be overturned, but in the meantime your family is being protected.

Joe Harper, CFP®
President, Harper Associates, Inc.

Term insurance can now be purchased in 10-, 20-, and 30-year policies with premiums that are fixed throughout the period. Consider the amount of time for which you need protection, and then try to match up that time frame with the appropriate length of term insurance protection. Many companies will let you reduce the amount of life coverage as long as it does not fall below their minimum requirement. In the future, if you no longer need the larger amount, you can reduce your coverage and reduce your premium at the same time!

Kent E. Anthony, CIC, CFP®, CMFC®
President, First Group Insurance

It is important to exercise caution when replacing a whole life insurance policy with what appears to be an inexpensive universal life insurance policy. Why? If not appropriately funded, a universal life insurance policy will not accumulate adequate cash value over time. The insurance costs that are charged to typical insurance policies increase each year as the insured individual grows older. What this means to the policy owner is that the insurance costs filtering through the policy when the insured is older will escalate and increase in cost beyond what could be afford-able, leaving the policy owner without cash value or insurance on the insured.

Leonard C. Wright, CPA/PFS, CFP®, CLU, ChFC
Principal, Strategic Financial Group

If you own a variable life insurance policy, be sure to ask your agent for an "in-force" illustration every year or two. This is the only way to tell for certain whether your policy's cash value is growing at the rate at which you and your agent assumed it would when you bought it. If it is, you'll enjoy the benefits of the policy as illustrated. If it isn't, chances are you'll have time to make any necessary changes before your cash value erodes and/or your premiums unexpectedly increase.

Timothy M. Hayes, M.B.A., RFC, CMFC®
President, Landmark Financial Advisory Services, LLC

Remember to periodically review the beneficiary designations on all of your life insurance policies and annuities, including employer-paid policies. This is particularly important after a change of marital status (or spouse) or after the birth of new children. For example, if you have your two children listed by name as your life insurance beneficiaries (as opposed to naming "my children"), upon your death only the two named children will receive the insurance proceeds even if additional children were born.

Michael David Schulman, M.B.A., M.A., CPA/PFS
Principal, Schulman Co. CPA P.C.

Confirm the ownership on life insurance policies held by a trust to avoid unintended estate tax consequences. If you have established a life insurance trust, confirm with the carrier that the insurance is owned by the trust and that the beneficiary designations have been correctly filed. If a Form 712 is issued to the deceased as owner instead of the trust, your trustee will be embroiled in an unnecessary estate battle!

Susan J. Bruno, CPA/PFS, CFP®
Principal, Winged Keel Financial Advisors, LLC

Protect yourself against the life insurance time bomb by adding some relatively inexpensive protective features to your term insurance. Add a whole life conversion option for the length of the life insurance term and a waiver of premium option should you become disabled. Depending on the company and age, a convertibility feature can add as little as 9 percent to the premium. The waiver of premium is generally a little more expensive, adding about 20 percent to the overall premium. At one company, adding a waiver of premium feature increases a $28 monthly premium to about $33.

Leonard C. Wright, CPA/PFS, CFP®, CLU, ChFC
Principal, Strategic Financial Group

ANNUITIES

Annuities are probably the most contentious area of financial planning in the country today. Our experts are divided on the best way to use annuities, especially variable annuities. You may have heard the arguments on both sides of this issue and felt very confused. What they *may* agree on is that everyone's situation is different and no financial product is a one-size-fits-all solution. As you read these tips, think about whether your situation fits into the problem being solved by the product recommended.

♦ ♦ ♦

If you want a safe investment and don't want to put your money in the markets, consider fixed annuities. The principal is guaranteed by an insurance company! You can never receive less than your premium payment minus any previous monies received. Because they give you tax-deferred growth, there is the standard penalty for withdrawal before age 59½. Annuities are not subject to probate, either, if you would die before taking all the money out. Fixed annuities (unlike variable annuities) have no annual expenses or upfront costs. They do have surrender charges, which usually disappear after the annuity has been in force for several years.

Kent E. Anthony, CIC, CFP®, CMFC®
President, First Group Insurance

You can transfer the cash value from a life insurance policy to an annuity contract using a 1035 transfer. Under this tax rule, if the premiums you have paid on the life insurance policy are greater than its cash value, the annuity will grow tax-free until its value exceeds the original premiums paid. This can be very useful when you want to end a life insurance policy and are planning to save the cash value. A 1035 exchange requires no special tax filings. The annuity company provides the application and 1035 transfer form. Follow up to make sure the cost basis has been transferred and recorded properly.

Jeff Mehler, M.B.A., CFP®
Principal, Jeffrey N. Mehler, CFP®

Terminally ill patients and those in poor health have investment opportunities that can pay off big—with no risk—for their families. My good friend Roger was terminally ill with cancer last year and wanted some advice to help his family. A new twist to an old investment helped do the trick. He bought a variable annuity for $250,000, which paid a four percent bonus ($10,000), and he purchased an extended benefit rider. This rider paid an extra 40 percent on all of the contract's appreciation upon death. Roger died four months later with the annuity valued at $300,000—allowing for another $20,000 bonus.

Bill Pomeroy, M.S., CFP®, CRC
Executive Vice President, The Shobe Financial Group

If you find you're paying too many taxes on interest earned from CDs, money markets, or savings accounts and you don't currently need the interest income, consider investing these balances in an annuity. Not only will you avoid paying taxes on income you don't need, you will also benefit from deferring taxes on any interest or growth in the investment until you draw it out. Another tax bonus: If you are receiving Social Security benefits, this strategy could lower the amount of your Social Security benefits subject to income tax.

Cathie E. Cobe, CPA/PFS, CFP®, CLU, ChFC
Retirement Management Spec., Nationwide Retirement Solutions

MIND OVER MONEY

The majority of all scams originate with life agents and brokers who have conditioned the client to not be concerned with disclosure—which is why it is important to never let your guard down.

Joe Harper, CFP®
President, Harper Associates, Inc.

Most insurance companies now offer annuities with fixed interest rates ranging from 1 to 10 years. Annuities also have surrender charges for taking out your money early. Consider locking in your interest rate for the same number of years as your annuity has surrender charges. In this way, you never have a surprise about what you are earning. Most companies will let you withdraw the interest at any time without penalty. It is also a good idea to make sure your insurance company guaranteeing the annuity is rated either an A, A+, or A++ by A.M. Best.

Kent E. Anthony, CIC, CFP®, CMFC®
President, First Group Insurance

Here's an alternative to equity-indexed annuities (EIA), which are hybrid investments that promise both a market rate and a guaranteed rate of return. Put half of your money in a variable annuity and the other half in a fixed annuity. An EIA caps your market return to some percentage of its index—70 percent, for example. Splitting the money in half allows you to keep all of the appreciation in the variable annuity, while still protecting the other half of your investment in the fixed annuity and increasing your overall return.

Timothy M. Hayes, M.B.A., RFC, CMFC®
President, Landmark Financial Advisory Services, LLC

Here's a great idea if your variable annuity contract has lost value. If you surrender the contract, the loss is deductible as an ordinary loss, not subject to the $3,000 capital loss limitation. After tax, you might wind up with more cash (which you can now reinvest) than is currently in the policy. For example, the $100,000 that you put into your variable annuity is now worth $80,000. If the contract has a 4 percent surrender charge, you'll get a check for $76,800. The $23,400 loss is deductible. If you are in the 35 percent tax bracket, you'll save $8,190 in taxes. This will give you $84,990 ($76,800 + $4,990) to reinvest, a $4,990 gain!

Michael David Schulman, M.B.A., M.A., CPA/PFS
Principal, Schulman Co. CPA P.C.

POINT ▶

Did you know that most annuities have very high costs, which may be justified by the tax-deferral advantage of these investments? However, these advantages are not useful in an IRA and therefore it is not a good idea to put an annuity in your IRA. Save the tax benefits of your IRA for otherwise taxable investments like CDs, taxable bonds and dividend paying stocks.

Clark M. Blackman II, CPA/PFS, CFP®,
ChFC, CFA®, CIMA, AAMS®
Managing Director, Post Oak Capital

SUPPORTING POINT ▶

Do not invest your IRA assets in a variable annuity. The primary benefit of a variable annuity is that it provides tax-deferred growth, but this is only useful when investing taxable (nonqualified) monies. Because an IRA is already tax-deferred, this benefit is unnecessary and you are paying higher annual expenses (1.0–1.5 percent higher than the average mutual fund) for nothing. Any advisor looking to sell you this kind of investment is looking out for his or her best interest (these typically provide broker commissions in the 5 to 12 percent range).

Mark Wilson, CFP®, APA
Vice President, Tarbox Equity, Inc.

◀IIII COUNTERPOINT

While some advisors suggest that using a variable annuity is not suitable for IRA money, you may disagree with that group once you fully understand the unique benefits a variable annuity provides. If you die, it provides a guaranteed value payable to your beneficiary that could be higher than the account's market value. Stock investments, while tending to perform the best, also come with risk of being worth less than what you paid. With this in mind, a variable annuity could be a great way for you to invest in the stock market and still guarantee your principle to your heirs when you die. During times of significant losses in the stock market, a variable annuity can give you and your heirs peace of mind.

Angie Hollerich, CEP, CAC
Author of Grab the Brass Ring of Financial Security

LONG-TERM CARE

As the new kid on the block, long-term care insurance is a product that almost everyone needs a course in. It is one of the most valuable products you can find, if your situation demands it. It has very few provisions to choose from and allows you the peace of mind to use long-term care facilities without fear of running out of money. These tips can help you understand the decisions you will need to make as you shop for this product.

◆◆◆

Don't buy more long-term care insurance than you need. Nursing homes cost about $100 per day in most areas, but you only need to insure for about $80 per day. The reason? Your Social Security or other retirement income will continue whether you are in a nursing home or not and will cover part of your nursing home costs. Only insure what you can't handle. Your premiums will be lower as a result.

Steve Johnson, CPA/PFS, CFP®
Owner, Johnson Financial

With more than 100 companies offering long-term care insurance, are you confused about whether it's a product you need? Here are my "Do I or don't I buy?" rules of thumb. If you have sufficient money to pay care costs for you and your spouse, then you don't need it. If you don't have enough money or will likely run out, then Medicaid (not Medicare) will take care of you. If the costs of care for one of you might impoverish the other, seriously look into this product to supplement your retirement income and other assets to provide funds for your long-term care needs.

Mitchell Freedman, CPA/PFS
Advisor to the Stars

When putting together your financial plan, be sure to ask yourself "How will I pay for long-term care?" Don't think that because you are young long-term care expenses will not affect you. Forty percent of the people needing long-term care services each year are between the ages of 18 and 64. Long-term care insurance is very affordable for younger individuals. You'll find your annual premiums in the hundreds, compared to the thousands later in life.

Lloyd E. Painter, CPA/PFS, CFP®, CLU, ChFC, CFS
President, Painter Financial

Inflation protection on a long-term care policy is a very important rider to consider when purchasing long-term care insurance. This option increases your benefit amount each year so that coverage keeps pace with the rising cost of care. The national annual average of long-term care costs exceeds $50,000 and costs are expected to quadruple by 2030. Without the rider, a 5 percent annual increase for 10 years means your benefit would equal 62 percent of the projected cost. Factors such as age, family health history, and availability of other financial resources need to be included in determining the need for this rider.

Patrick T. Hanratty, M.B.A., CPA/PFS, CFP®
Managing Director, Capital Advisors, Ltd.

HEALTH AND DISABILITY INSURANCE

The phrase "I need the insurance" has come to mean "I need the health insurance." The cost and controversy surrounding health insurance has been in the news for several years, with no end in sight. Even though families are acutely aware of their health insurance coverage, they may not pay any attention to their disability benefits. The potential for a disability to impact a family's financial security is greater than almost any other risk they face. So pay close attention as our experts bring you up to speed on this critical piece of your financial planning.

♦ ♦ ♦

The rule of thumb is to have disability insurance equal to 60 to 70 percent of your gross income. If you pay the premiums with after-tax dollars, then the benefits you receive will be tax-free. Considering income taxes are normally 20 to 30 percent of your income, the rule of thumb coverage of 60 to 70 percent will enable you to meet your needs. However, if you are using pre-tax dollars or if your employer is paying the premium, your benefits will be taxed, changing your calculation of how much coverage you will need.

Paul D. Lyons, CPA/PFS, CFP®
Manager, KPMG Personal Financial Planning

Don't be lulled into thinking that your employer-provided disability coverage eliminates your need for personal disability insurance. You may be surprised to learn how many restrictions exist in the company program. When shopping for your own supplemental disability policy, look for noncancelable, guaranteed renewable insurance with an inflation rider and a provision for partial/residual benefits. To check on reports of the insurance company rating agencies, you can go online for sources such as: Moody's (www.moodys.com), Standard and Poor's (www.standardandpoors.com), or A.M. Best (www.ambest.com/index. html).

John E. Sestina, M.S.F.S., CFP®, ChFC
Author of Managing to Be Wealthy

Did you know that you are much more likely to become disabled for some portion of time than to die prematurely? For this reason, disability insurance should be a top priority in your financial plan. Many employers provide some level of benefits. However, if you have subpar benefits, lack of job security, or if you are self-employed, you need to evaluate the need for a personal disability policy.

Paul D. Lyons, CPA/PFS, CFP®
Manager, KPMG Personal Financial Planning

Sorting out the features of disability insurance contracts can be frustrating. You will need to educate yourself about waiting periods, definitions of complete and partial disability, tax consequences, and part-time work. At the least, you can start by using the websites of various insurers. Your insurance agent can provide answers to questions you have, but may have a vested interest in selling you a particular policy. After you have selected several possible policies, you may consider hiring a fee-based personal financial specialist to review the different policies and make a recommendation.

Jill Gianola, M.S., M.B.A., CFP®
Owner, Gianola Financial Planning

A key feature of disability policies is the elimination period. This is the number of days, after your disability begins, before you receive benefits. Base your choice of an elimination period (example: 90 days versus 30 days) on the adequacy of your emergency savings and the amount of accrued sick leave you have from your employer. The longer you make your elimination period, the lower your premium will be for a given amount of disability coverage.

Barbara O'Neill, Ph.D., CFP®, AFC, CHC
Author of Saving on a Shoestring

The most important item to look at when shopping for disability insurance is the definition of *disability*. The best definition is "unable to perform the duties of your *own occupation.*" An *any occupation* definition means that you will only receive benefits if you can't perform any occupation, no matter what type of job it is.

Paul D. Lyons, CPA/PFS, CFP®
Manager, KPMG Personal Financial Planning

IN MONEY WORDS

There's no such thing as a stupid question ... It's your money

---

Have life insurance that you don't need, but unable to get disability insurance you would like to have? Consider keeping—or even increasing—your life insurance, even if it's only term and even if it's only through your employer. If you become seriously ill, you will be able to use the policy to get money—either by taking an accelerated benefit or by selling ("viaticating") the policy for a lump sum.

Peg Downey, M.A., CFP®
Partner, Money Plans

Employers can now start a new free benefit, an HRA. Like an IRA, a Health Reimbursement Account allows employees to take advantage of much fatter pre-tax dollars—stretching purchasing power. HRAs are brand new, recently passed by Congress and approved by the IRS. HRAs allow reimbursements for out-of-pocket medical expenses. Employees may pay up to the deductible amount of their health insurance plan and are reimbursed periodically. For a list of qualified medical expenses, order IRS publication 502 at www.irs.gov/forms_pubs. HRAs allow employers to take a tax deduction for every dollar of benefit paid and employees to receive tax-free income—bypassing the 7.5 percent deductible adjusted gross income threshold.

Steve Wightman, CFP®
Life Advisor Specializing in Money, Lexington Financial Mgmt.

An estimated 90 percent of hospital bills contain at least one error, such as data coding errors that change a minor procedure into a major one, duplicate charges for the same service, and billing for the wrong number of days. Never pay a hospital bill without examining it carefully. Request an itemized bill that contains a description of services and prices. Then ask for explanations about questionable items.

Barbara O'Neill, Ph.D., CFP®, AFC, CHC
Author of Saving on a Shoestring

With costs of prescription drugs rising almost daily and insurance coverage diminishing, we all look for ways to lower costs. If you are over 65, you might consider HMO coverage instead of regular Medicare. Where it is available and for the drugs that it covers, it can be a big help. If you are a veteran, it is possible for you to get your prescription drugs through the VA at fairly nominal costs (in many cases, $7 for a month's supply). You must apply and normally wait for some period, and have a VA doctor prescribe it for you. Compared to hundreds of dollars for some prescriptions, it could be well worth it.

Henrietta Humphreys, M.B.A., CFP®
Financial Advisor, The Henrietta Humphreys Group

As you approach age 65, you may find you are not ready to retire. It probably does not make sense to apply for Social Security benefits if you continue working. However, it is still important to apply for Medicare benefits even if you will continue to be covered by your employer's health insurance plan. Contact your local Social Security office a few months prior to reaching age 65 for details.

Frank L. Washelesky, J.D., CPA/PFS, CVA
Director, Ostrow Resin Berk & Abrams, Ltd.

Are you taking full advantage of your employment benefits? Paying for medical expenses on a pre-tax basis saves you money. Take advantage of your employer's Medical Reimbursement Account. Money is taken from each paycheck and put into your personal fund. As you pay for medical expenses, you get reimbursed. The savings work like this: A $100 medical bill paid with pre-tax dollars from your Medical Reimbursement Account costs you $100 versus the $161 you would need to earn to have $100 after tax (assuming a 31 percent marginal federal tax rate and a 7 percent state income tax rate). So you are saving $61 in taxes!

Elaine E. Bedel, M.B.A., CFP®
President, Bedel Financial Consulting, Inc.

If your health insurance policy has multiple coinsurance rates, file the claims for expenses with the lowest company coinsurance rate (50% versus 80%) first and you'll save money! For instance, with a $500 annual deductible, a $600 bill to be reimbursed at 50%, and a $1,000 bill to be reimbursed at 80%, if you file them both together or the 80% coinsurance first, the reimbursement will be 80% × ($1,000 – $500) + 50% × $600 = $700. If, however, you file the 50% reimbursable first, it will look like this: 50% × ($600 – $500) + 80% × $1,000 = $850—a savings of $150 just because of the order in which you filed your claims!

Peg Downey, M.A., CFP®
Partner, Money Plans

Consider taking advantage of flexible spending accounts, if offered by your employer. These can create a tax-advantaged way to pay your family's medical expenses. Instead of paying your annual medical expenses with after-tax dollars, sign up for your employer's flexible spending account program and receive a tax deduction for the amount set aside to pay your medical expenses. Here's the catch: If your medical expenses are less than the amount you put into your medical spending account, you'll forfeit that difference unless it is spent on medical costs by year-end. So, estimate medical expenses conservatively. And, if you end up with an unused balance near year-end, go to the dentist, or buy an extra pair of contacts or something else so that you don't waste the money you set aside.

Barbara J. Raasch, CFA®, CPA/PFS, ChFC
Partner-in-charge of Wealth Management Solutions, Ernst & Young

Your affordable choices for health insurance aren't limited to HMOs and PPOs. If you are self-employed, or work for an employer with 50 or fewer employees, check into a Medical Savings Account. MSAs are high-deductible, major medical plans that often have much lower premiums, plus the ability to contribute tax-deductible contributions to a separate account. Deductibles are in the $1500 to $5000 range. How much you save depends on where you live and could be as much as 50 percent. A monthly MSA premium can actually end up costing about $18 a month (after you figure in your tax savings) if you contribute the maximum allowed to your MSA account.

Randall Kratz, CFP®
Owner, Kratz Investment Advisory Network

OTHER INSURANCE PRODUCTS

As if all that is not enough to think about and spend money on, there are other forms of insurance that you need to be familiar with. Here are several tips to help you make good decisions in those areas.

♦ ♦ ♦

An important risk management strategy is the large loss principle. This means spending the bulk of your insurance premium dollars to protect against risks that can wipe you out financially. Small expenses, such as a dented fender, can be covered through insurance deductibles or emergency fund savings. Examples of large financial risks are loss of income due to disability, loss of a household earner's income due to death, destruction of one's home, liability losses resulting from a court judgment, and high medical expenses.

Barbara O'Neill, Ph.D., CFP®, AFC, CHC
Author of Saving on a Shoestring

Make sure you discuss umbrella liability insurance with your property and casualty insurance agent. If you are sued for any reason, you may find that the limits of your home and auto liability insurance are far too low. A personal umbrella policy, which supplements the liability coverage provided by both policies, can be purchased in increments of $1 million. When purchased from the same company that insures your home and your auto, it can be relatively inexpensive, too. It is a small price to pay for more peace of mind!

Raj Pillai, Ph.D., CFP®
NAPFA-Registered Advisor, Financial Fitness Network of Solon

Think twice before buying an extended warranty on any new purchase. Most new durable goods like washing machines and vacuum cleaners are just not as susceptible to breakdown as they once were. Why waste your hard-earned money buying something that you don't need?

Michael L. Alberts, M.B.A., CFP®
President, Woodstock Financial Group, LLC

Make sure that your jewelry is covered under a jewelry floater. Under a homeowner's policy, if your diamond ring would lose one of its diamonds you would have coverage with a jewelry floater. The standard homeowner's policy does not cover property that is lost. But with a jewelry floater the lost diamond would be covered even when the setting has failed to keep the diamond in the ring.

Kent E. Anthony, CIC, CFP®, CMFC®
President, First Insurance Group

Save on health, auto, and homeowner's insurance premiums by increasing your deductible. According to the Insurance Information Institute, by requesting higher deductibles on auto collision and comprehensive insurance, you can lower your costs substantially. For example, increasing your deductible from $200 to $500 could reduce your collision cost by 15 to 30 percent. Use the premium savings to self-insure your smaller claims. Save even more by using the same company to insure both your auto and home. Inquire about any other possible discounts. (See www.pueblo.gsa.gov/cic_text/cars/autoinsu/autoinsu.htm for an auto insurance discount checklist.)

Deborah O. Levine, M.B.A, M.S.T., CPA/PFS, CFP®
Financial Planner, AFP Group

When insuring commercial property, be sure you write it under blanket coverage. The full blanket amount is then available to pay claims. Let's say you have $200,000 coverage on the building and $100,000 on the contents. If you have a loss on contents of $110,000, you would still be covered because you have a full $300,000 coverage for any one loss. This can help protect you from being underinsured on any one item.

Kent E. Anthony, CIC, CFP®, CMFC®
President, First Insurance Group

In order to protect yourself from the potentially huge liability associated with household employees such as a nanny, be sure to notify your property and casualty insurance agent to discuss the in-home services being provided by your employee. Your agent will help to make sure you comply with your state's requirements for worker's compensation insurance. You'll also want to consider adding the worker to your homeowner's policy and, if they drive on the job, you'll want to address auto insurance as well.

Brad R. Cougill, CFP®, CMFC®
Partner, Deerfield Financial Advisors, Inc.

If your business is dependent on another business, you should consider dependent properties coverage for business income. If your business buys parts from a supplier and that supplier has a fire loss, it could put you out of business if you don't have another supplier. By endorsing your policy to include dependent property business income coverage you can protect your income that you would lose when your supplier suffers a covered loss.

Kent E. Anthony, CIC, CFP®, CMFC®
President, First Insurance Group

Is your son or daughter joining an active-duty military unit? If so, one of the best investments they can make is joining United Services Automobile Association (USAA). With few exceptions, this member-owned organization is only available to active-duty military personnel and veterans. This insurance and financial services firm is continually rated one of the best firms in the country by consumer rating organizations and USAA members for their low costs and top-notch service.

Michael L. Alberts, M.B.A., CFP®
President, Woodstock Financial Group, LLC

Make sure that you insure commercial property at replacement cost. With replacement cost, the adjuster will not take any depreciation on the loss. To guarantee ahead of time that you are adequately insured to replacement cost, purchase an agreed amount endorsement on the policy. In this way, the company agrees in advance of the claim that you are adequately insured to replacement cost and will not take a coinsurance penalty for being underinsured.

Kent E. Anthony, CIC, CFP®, CMFC®
President, First Insurance Group

Still not your favorite topic, I bet! But you are so much closer to getting it under control. Most of these tips are easy to put into action with a couple of phone calls or mouse clicks. Your ability to procrastinate is the only thing standing between you and a better insurance portfolio. Put those skills aside for a few days and take some action toward better financial security for your family.

7

RETIREMENT PLANNING

He that riseth late, must trot all day.

Benjamin Franklin (Poor Richard's Almanack)

Terms from the Top

contingent beneficiary Person named in an insurance policy to receive the policy benefits if the primary beneficiary dies before the benefits become payable.

fiduciary Person, company, or association holding assets in trust for a beneficiary. The fiduciary is charged with the responsibility of investing the money wisely for the beneficiary's benefit.

lump-sum distribution Large payment of money received at one time instead of in periodic payments. People retiring from or leaving a company may receive a lump-sum distribution of the value of their pension, salary reduction, or profit-sharing plan.

Monte Carlo simulation A simulation technique used to calculate the probability of success or failure of a specific strategy. Thousands of scenarios are run and in each scenario factors like investment performance and inflation are randomly changed (within defined ranges) to simulate different results for the strategy being tested. The final result is a usually stated as: Your strategy works X percent of time and fails Y percent of time. It is a valuable tool to see how different market conditions can produce different results and how likely it is you will reach your goals (rather than just a single yes/no answer).

pre-tax contributions Amounts deposited into pension or retirement investment accounts prior to income tax being levied on them.

present value Value today of a future payment, or stream of payments, discounted at some appropriate compound interest—or discount—rate.

Source: reprinted by permission of Jordan Goodman, Dictionary of Finance and Investment Terms *(Barron's, 5th Edition)*

With all the pressures of everyday life, it seems difficult to plan for a time that may be 20, 30, or 40 years away. But with life expectancy growing and average years in the workforce shrinking, there is an increasing possibility that you will spend more years retired than you did working.

When Social Security was enacted, the life expectancy of males was just over 60. Retirement benefits under that system were intended to be for widows who lived too long. The weight that it must now carry as the foundation of our retirement security is causing it to crumble. However Congress decides to address the problem, the interim solution is clear: We must each be responsible for our own financial independence in retirement.

All tips in this chapter are intended for informational purposes only. Should you find one potentially helpful to your situation, you should consult with your legal, tax, or investment professional familiar with your individual situation to determine its suitability prior to taking any action or investing any money.

PLANNING TO PLAN

The hardest part of any planning process is getting started. The following tips give you some starting points and motivation to move on to more advanced strategies regarding your retirement planning. It's never too late to make a difference in your future security.

♦ ♦ ♦

Calculate what you need to save for retirement. Research consistently shows that people who do this save more than those who have not attempted a savings calculation. Use the amount from your annual Social Security benefit statement to help complete your savings calculation and request a pension benefit estimate from your employer, if applicable. Online resources to do a simple retirement savings calculation can be found at www.asec.org, www.money.com, www.smartmoney.com, and www.financenter.com. Links to additional retirement resources can be found at www.investing. rutgers.edu, and www.ces.purdue.edu/retirement.

Barbara O'Neill, Ph.D., CFP®, AFC, CHC
Author of Saving on a Shoestring

The Social Security Administration now sends you a copy of your total Social Security contributions and your projected benefits every year, and you don't even have to ask! But, you do want to check that they have correct information about you. Most importantly, check their accounting of the salary you earned each year that you worked. They give you 3 years, 3 months, and 15 days after the year in which the wages were paid (and sometimes longer) to fix your earnings record. So contact the Social Security Administration (www.ssa.gov) as soon as you spot a discrepancy.

Peg Downey, M.A., CFP®
Partner, Money Plans

Start planning for retirement early! Estimate how many years you will be retired and start planning that many years before you hope to retire. For example, if you plan to retire at 65 and live to 85 (20 years) you would need to start planning by at least 45.

Judy Ludwig, CPA/PFS, CFP®, ChFC, AEP
Advisor, Tandem Financial Services, Inc.

MIND OVER MONEY

Knowing when you have reached financial independence is very simple to figure out—when your money is growing faster than what you are making at work—you are there!

Craig Olson, CPA/PFS
Partner, Parrott Partnership

Saving for retirement is like dieting. You need to budget calories in a diet plan by saving some for later in the day or tomorrow, instead of consuming them all at once. By saving some of our earnings today, we will have more available for the future when other sources of income are not available. You will need to look for a balance between saving and spending that enables you to live within your budget.

Sid Blum, CPA/PFS, CFP®, ChFC, ATP
President, Successful Financial Solutions, Inc.

Those in fiduciary roles for endowments and pension plans establish their investment strategy in writing. This document, called an Investment Policy Statement, establishes a specific asset allocation plan, describes the allowable asset classes, and sets maximum levels for individual holdings. Consider yourself a fiduciary for your family's wealth and for your retirement. Once you have determined your goals and objectives, work with your financial advisor to create your own Investment Policy Statement. You will be more likely to achieve those goals by documenting and monitoring your investment strategy.

Timothy P. Thaney, CPA/PFS
Principal, DeJoy, Knauf & Blood, LLP

Think of retirement as financial freedom and then consider what you love to do with each day. You can plan on early retirement by pursuing full-time or part-time work in a field you enjoy to supplement your savings and retirement funds … and end up with a better life with time to do what you love.

Lesley J. Brey, M.B.A., CFA®, CFP®
President, L.J. Brey, Inc.

For the countdown to retirement, put household remodeling and major fix-up tasks on the priority list while you are still receiving regular paychecks. Those bills can put a big dent in the retirement cash flow if you wait until post-employment days.

John E. Sestina, M.S.F.S., CFP®, ChFC
Author of Managing to Be Wealthy

IN MONEY WORDS

He who laughs last, laughs best ... Sell high; buy low

Whether or not you should pay off your home mortgage when you retire depends on the estimated length of your retirement and, more importantly, on your investment risk tolerance. The more years you expect to live and the higher your risk tolerance, the more you should consider investing the money you would have used to pay off the mortgage. You would then be able to rely on the income or appreciation from these investments to cover your retirement living expenses, including your mortgage payment.

Pay off your mortgage in full if you expect to live fewer years and you have a lower risk tolerance.

Deborah O. Levine, M.B.A, M.S.T., CPA/PFS, CFP®
Financial Planner, AFP Group

Everyone wants to know how much they can afford to withdraw from their investment accounts during retirement, without worrying about running out of money during their lifetime. Financial planners can spend hours running the numbers, but there is a shortcut that works great. Just remember the number 4.5 percent. If your investments are invested at least 50 percent in equities (which historically have provided the necessary growth to sustain investments over a long retirement), you can plan on withdrawing between 4.0 and 4.5 percent during retirement. For example, if you have $500,000 of investment assets when you retire, you should not withdraw more than $22,500 each year.

Donna Skeels Cygan, M.B.A., CFP®
President, Essential Financial Planning, Inc.

If you are self-employed, you might wait until tax time to make your contribution to your retirement plan. You know that good cash flow management includes not paying a bill before it is due. But it's actually wiser to make your contributions equally throughout the tax year to dollar cost average into the stock market. This reduces your risk of volatility in today's markets. This strategy will also help you to even out cash flows so that a large contribution is not required all at once.

Timothy P. Thaney, CPA/PFS
Principal, DeJoy, Knauf & Blood, LLP

Let's say you have a choice to put $100,000 in your IRA, either as a variable annuity or a mutual fund, for your retirement in 25 years. The investments in the variable annuity are comparable to those in the mutual fund. You're aware that variable annuities cost more than mutual funds, which is reflected by a 1.25 percent annual expense charge on the value of your assets in this particular variable annuity. If you earn an average of 8 percent per year before expenses, how much will that 1.25 percent per year charge cost you over 25 years? Approximately $180,000.

John J. Feyche, M.S., M.B.T., CPA/PFS
Manager, Z&W Wealth Management

T. Rowe Price (www.Troweprice.com). The retirement calculator uses a Monte Carlo simulation to calculate probability of outliving one's money.

If your plan is to have your retirement assets last an extended period of time in retirement, consider taking advantage of the historical performance of the market by keeping a portion of your portfolio in equities. Make sure you have three to five years' worth of distributions in a stable, conservatively invested account for the purpose of drawing payments from. Periodically, at a point where you're comfortable with their value, sell off equities to make sure you always have money in your conservative fund to draw money from. This way, you aren't forced into selling equities in a "down" market to fund your retirement. You control when your equities are sold!

Cathie E. Cobe, CPA/PFS, CFP®, CLU, ChFC
Retirement Management Spec., Nationwide Retirement Solutions

Are you getting close to retirement and wondering how much you can withdraw from your retirement funds? You might be surprised to find out that over a 30-year time period, history has shown that you can only withdraw around 4 percent of your portfolio and have a high probability of not running out of money. For example, if at age 60 you have $500,000 saved for retirement, you would only be able to withdraw approximately $20,000 per year, increasing with inflation each year, from your retirement funds to have a good chance of not running out of money by age 90.

Chad P. Tramp, PFS, CFP®
Wealth Management Advisor, RSM McGladrey

Adding structure to your cash flow will help you sleep at night during retirement. Ask your brokerage firm to set up a monthly paycheck for you with automatic distributions from your investment account into your local checking account. Select the amount based upon your estimate of cash flow needs, after subtracting any other source of income. That amount will be transferred electronically every month on the day you select. It helps even out your cash flow so you won't be worrying about how to pay the bills. Every six months, review the amount and adjust it as necessary.

Donna Skeels Cygan, M.B.A., CFP®
President, Essential Financial Planning, Inc.

If you're one of those retired folks who doesn't receive Social Security, check your earnings record to see what it takes to start receiving monthly payments. All it might take is a little yard work or babysitting for neighbors and you could be receiving hundreds of dollars a month for life! You receive credit for a quarter of coverage for each $870 of earnings. All you need is 40 quarters of coverage to receive benefits. You may already have as much as 38 or 39 quarters, and a bit of part-time earnings could get you to 40!

Peg Downey, M.A., CFP®
Partner, Money Plans

You may not be paying enough attention to the contingent beneficiaries you name on your retirement accounts. You should never name minor children as outright or contingent beneficiaries. The contingent beneficiary of retirement plans should rarely be your estate. When the children are minors, trusts that exist should generally be the contingent beneficiaries.

Stuart Kessler, J.D., M.B.A., CPA/PFS
Past Chairman of AICPA—Personal Financial Planning Division

GETTING THE MOST OUT OF YOUR 401(K) PLAN

When most pension plans were managed by pension administrators, employees were happily ignorant. As more employers installed 401(k) plans, more employees became aware of their need to understand investment choices and tax laws. The stability of 401(k) plans has become a great source of concern in recent years. It is imperative that you learn as much as possible and establish solid guidelines for your own 401(k) account.

♦ ♦ ♦

When planning for your retirement income needs, consider the effects that a down year in the market would have on your portfolio. In your projections, you may assume an average rate of return and use that return each and every year. However, in reality, you are going to have up years and down years. Even if the average return is the same, the result will be much different. Investor B outperformed Investor A by over 2 percent, even though they had the same average rate of return. The impact of such a difference when doing savings projections into the future can become very large, and throw you off plan by not making realistic assumptions. This makes it important to consider investments that have lower volatility to help provide for more consistent returns. Consult your financial advisor to have them run a Monte Carlo simulation, which will simulate the effects of up and down years on investment returns.

For example, take two investors: Investor A and Investor B. Each invests $1,000 in a mutual fund. Investor A's fund earns 20 percent the first year but loses 10 percent the following year, giving him an average return of 5 percent. Investor B's fund earned only 5 percent the first year but earned 5 percent again in the second year, giving him an average return of 5 percent. Which investor earned the most at the end of the two-year period? Take a look below:

	Investor A	Investor B
Initial Investment	$1,000.00	$1,000.00
Year 1 earning	200.00 (20% gain)	50.00 (5% gain)
Balance at end of year 1	$1,200.00	$1,050.00
Year 2 earnings (loss)	(120.00) (10% loss)	52.50 (5% gain)
Balance at end of year 2	$1,080.00	$1,102.50

William K. Kaiser, CPA/PFS
Financial Advisor, Howard Financial Services, Inc.

If you own your employer's stock inside of your retirement plan and it has substantial gains (current value over cost when contributed), be sure you consider the little-known rule which allows you to defer the tax on any net unrealized appreciation of the employer's stock. This rule requires that you take a lump-sum distribution from your retirement plan. For example, you are considering retiring (or leaving your employer) and you have 500,000 in your retirement plan of which $250,000 consists of employer securities that have a cost basis of $50,000. It may be more beneficial to take a lump-sum distribution whereby you put the nonemployer funds into an IRA and take a total distribution of the $250,000 employer securities. You would currently only be taxed on the $50,000 cost basis. The $200,000 of net unrealized appreciation would be taxed at long-term capital gain rates when you sold the stock. You will want to consult a qualified advisor to help you make this decision.

Chad P. Tramp, PFS, CFP®
Wealth Management Advisor, RSM McGladrey

When your employer provides a matching contribution for your 401(k) deferrals, take it! This will be one of the best investments you will ever make. For example, when your employer matches 10 cents for each dollar you contribute, you are receiving an immediate 10 percent return on your investment. When the match is made in employer stock, the deal can still be quite good. Even in the worst of cases, as when the employer stock goes down by 90 percent, you still receive some free money.

Mark Wilson, CFP®, APA
Vice President, Tarbox Equity, Inc.

When you're signing up for your 401(k) plan at work, make sure you get all the matching money coming to you from your employer. Often the employer matches a part of every contribution made. If you make the maximum number of contributions possible by spreading your contributions throughout the entire year instead of getting the maximum amount in as fast as you can, you'll get matching money every time! If you get to the maximum dollar amount before the year is up, you'll be missing out on some employer matches!

Peg Downey, M.A., CFP®
Partner, Money Plans

MIND OVER MONEY

Fear will keep you from your dreams. Commit yourself to learning. Knowledge conquers fear.

Joseph E. Sedita, CPA/PFS, CFP®
Owner, Joseph E. Sedita and Co. Certified Public Accountants

You may well be one of the growing number of employees whose employer is sponsoring a SIMPLE retirement plan. These plans are popular with small employers because of low administrative costs. They should also be popular with you because they require an employer match. Make sure you take advantage of the match by contributing at least 3 percent of your compensation to the SIMPLE. In most years, your boss has to match you dollar for dollar up to 3 percent of your compensation. That's a 100 percent return on your savings in the year of contribution.

Frank B. Arnold, CPA/PFS
Vice President, Panfeld, Edelman & Arnold

With all the new rules on pensions and retirement benefits, you and your spouse can now contribute to your combined profit sharing and 401(k) plans, up to $40,000 each. If you are 50 years old or older, then add another $1,000 each to the contribution. These contributions are fully tax-deductible. The available deductions have never been higher. Further planning can be done to allocate the pension contributions between the husband and wife by adjusting compensation levels between them.

Stephen A. Drake, Ph.D., CPA/PFS, CFP®
President, Optima Financial Resources

Do you know that the IRS will give you money if you contribute to a retirement plan? Based on your income level, the new tax law offers individuals a nonrefundable credit of up to $1,000 on their tax returns for contributing to a retirement plan. You have to be 18 or over, not a full time student and not claimed as a dependent on any other tax return. Also note that the credit will be reduced if you are taking retirement plan distributions. The table is as follows:

Married Filing Jointly	Head of Household	Other Filing Status	Credit Rate
$0–$30,000	$0–$22,500	$0–$15,000	50% of up to $2,000
$30,000–$32,500	$22,500–$24,375	$15,000–$16,250	20% of up to $2,000
$32,500–$50,000	$24,375–$37,500	$16,250–$25,000	10% of up to $2,000
Over $50,000	Over $37,500	Over $25,000	0%

Paul D. Lyons, CPA/PFS, CFP®
Manager, KPMG Personal Financial Planning

Remember to periodically review the beneficiary designations on all of your retirement plans. These plans include IRAs (regular and Roth), 401(k) and 403(b) plans, as well as employer-sponsored profit-sharing and pension plans. This is particularly important after a change of marital status (or spouse). For example, if you have your ex-spouse listed by name as your IRA beneficiary (as opposed to naming "my spouse"), upon your death the wrong person will receive your pension.

Michael David Schulman, M.B.A., M.A., CPA/PFS
Principal, Schulman Co. CPA P.C.

Consult an attorney who is experienced in the creditor/debtor provisions of your state law before you roll over funds from qualified plans (such as pensions or 401[k] plans) into IRAs. Qualified plans enjoy creditor protection under federal Employee Retirement Income Security Act (ERISA) provisions, while IRAs aren't covered under ERISA. If you are concerned about keeping your retirement funds out of the reach of creditors, make sure your state's laws offer you good protection before you transfer funds into IRAs.

Raj Pillai, Ph.D., CFP®
NAPFA-Registered Advisor, Financial Fitness Network of Solon

Retirement Living (www.retirementliving.com/RLtaxes.html). Important tax information, state by state.

If you are a small business owner with fewer than 10 employees and are a little behind in saving for your retirement, consider implementing a defined benefit (DB) plan. With this type of plan, you can put away a significant amount of retirement dollars on a tax-deferred basis. For example, due to recent law changes an individual 50 years old who makes $160,000 per year may be able to put away about $100,000 per year into a DB plan for their own retirement. To determine the appropriate retirement plan design for your specific situation, see a qualified retirement plan specialist.

Chad P. Tramp, PFS, CFP®
Wealth Management Advisor, RSM McGladrey

Defined benefit pensions, or the old "gold watch" pensions, are often worth the most but given the least value in divorce. This is because the pension statement balance shows contributions and interest. This most often is not the true value of the pension. A "present value" is a calculation that considers all the future monthly payments paid after retirement until death and then reduces them to a lump-sum amount.

Depending on a person's age and when they expect to receive the pension, the present value could be several hundred thousand dollars. Don't guess—get the facts before you negotiate your settlement.

Joan Coullahan, M.B.A., CDP
Co-author of Financial Custody: You, Your Money, and Divorce

If you are a high earner, consider an employee leasing arrangement with a U.S. corporation combined with an Irish corporation, for preferable tax treaty purposes. First, an Irish corporation retains you for your worldwide services. A U.S. domestic, employee-leasing corporation enters into a leasing agreement with the U.S. corporation, your current employer. Your employer pays the leasing company and the leasing company pays the Irish corporation for your services. The Irish corporation sets aside a substantial deferred compensation amount for you. This is not taxed until you take the compensation. Bottom line: The U.S. domestic employer gets a large tax deduction and you are currently taxed on only a fraction of the compensation.

Stephen A. Drake, Ph.D., CPA/PFS, CFP®
President, Optima Financial Resources

Individual Retirement Account Strategies

Congress continues to emphasize and increase the benefits from Individual Retirement Accounts. Even with new rules, these are fairly simple instruments that may fit into your overall retirement plan. Our experts help you sort out some of the new changes and best options for your situation.

♦♦♦

Good news if you are saving for your children's education and you are within certain income guidelines. The Economic Growth and Tax Relief Act has increased the contribution limits for Coverdell Education Savings Accounts (formerly called Education IRAs). The annual contribution limit is now $2,000 per designated beneficiary. Withdrawals are free from federal income tax when used for qualified higher education expenses. For example, a $2,000 deposit at age 0 with 10 percent annual growth could result in tax savings of $1,824 at age 18. Cover-dell accounts can be opened at most financial institutions and are usually funded with mutual funds.

Patrick T. Hanratty, M.B.A., CPA/PFS, CFP®
Managing Director, Capital Advisors, Ltd.

Where do your store the copies of your IRA and retirement plan beneficiary forms? Yes, the beneficiary forms. The ones you probably completed years ago when you rolled that IRA over or became eligible for your employer's 401(k). You may find it interesting that those forms will determine who receives those assets in the event of your death regardless of what your will states. Request copies today from each of your accounts. Review them, update them, and store them with your other important documents in a safe location. And make sure that location is communicated to those responsible for settling your estate!

Paul D. Knott, CPA/PFS, CFP®
Financial Consultant, Smith Barney

By starting your annual Roth IRA contributions of $2000.00 at age 25 rather than at age 30, you will spend an additional $10,000 (5 years × $2,000). At an annual return of 9.4162 percent, you will increase your total Roth account by over $308,000 at age 65. Sound good? Then consider this trick that doesn't cost you any more: Make your contribution at the beginning of the eligible year rather than the end of the eligible year. This technique will increase your account by over $73,000.

Parke Stratford Teal, CPA/PFS
Principal, Dreggors, Rigsby, and Teal, P.A.

IN MONEY WORDS

It's not over 'til the fat lady sings ... Retirement distributions

---

If you are over 50 and are contributing to a retirement plan, you can contribute more than the regular limits. So-called "catch-up" provisions will now allow you to make additional contributions to these plans. The catch-up amounts are:

Year	Defined Contribution Plans (including 401[k] plans)	IRAs	SIMPLE IRAs (Reg. and Roth)
2002	$1,000	$500	$500
2003	$2,000	$500	$1,000
2004	$3,000	$500	$1,500
2005	$4,000	$500	$2,000
2006	$5,000	$1,000	$2,500

Paul D. Lyons, CPA/PFS, CFP®
Manager, KPMG Personal Financial Planning

Did you know that some people who don't earn any money can build an IRA nest egg? If you make less than $150,000 and file a joint tax return, your nonworking spouse can contribute up to $3,000 ($3,500 if 50 or older) to a Roth IRA or a deductible IRA in 2002. There's no income limitation if your spouse funds a nondeductible IRA instead. Just call a no-load mutual fund family such as Vanguard or Fidelity and ask for an IRA application and list of funds.

Jill Gianola, M.S., M.B.A., CFP®
Owner, Gianola Financial Planning

Before you take your IRA distribution under the "substantially equal periodic payments" exception to avoid the 10 percent penalty on early distributions, include a cost-of-living adjustment (COLA) in the calculation of the periodic payment. If you don't include any COLA, you will be stuck with the same amount for the longer of five years or until you reach age 59½. The IRS has "blessed" this change in your IRA distributions through a Letter Ruling that permitted an annual COLA increase only because it was built into the original IRA distribution calculation.

Loyd J. Stegent, CPA/PFS, CFP
Director of Financial Planning, Cornelius, Stegent & Price

If you have after-tax money in a retirement plan, you can roll over those amounts into an IRA and continue to defer income taxes on their earnings. You can also roll over these amounts from one qualified plan to another, if certain provisions apply. Under previous tax law, only the pre-tax contributions and earnings could be rolled over to an IRA. After-tax balances had to be distributed to you and the earnings portion counted as income.

Paul D. Lyons, CPA/PFS, CFP®
Manager, KPMG Personal Financial Planning

Social Security Administration (www.ssa.gov). To check your Social Security and Medicare benefits online.

If you take 100 shares of stock from your IRA to roll over to another IRA account and you put cash instead of the 100 shares in the new account, you will have to pay income tax at your current marginal rate and perhaps an early withdrawal penalty of 10 percent on the stock you kept if you are under age $59^1/_2$ at the time you take the distribution.

Jim Wagenmann, CPA/PFS
Advisor, Watkins, Meegan, Drury & Co., LLC

Once you invest money in an IRA, there are rules for when the money (age $59^1/_2$) can be withdrawn. Exceptions available for distributions prior to age $59^1/_2$ include "substantially equal" payments. These payments must be made at least annually over the owner's life expectancy, or the owner's and the beneficiary's joint life expectancy, and must continue for the greater of five years or until age $59^1/_2$. Follow a few simple rules and you will avoid a 10 percent penalty and maximize the benefits of your IRA assets.

Patrick T. Hanratty, M.B.A., CPA/PFS, CFP®
Managing Director, Capital Advisors, Ltd.

If you need or want to make a pension contribution but have not been able to do so because your main source of income is from rental property or other passive income, here is an answer. First, set up a limited liability company (LLC) or family limited partnership. Contribute your rental property, stocks, and bonds into the LLC. Then pay yourself a guaranteed payment from the LLC for your management time and expertise, qualifying you to make a pension contribution. This guaranteed payment will be subject to FICA tax, but this should be more than offset by the income tax savings from the pension contribution.

Stephen A. Drake, Ph.D., CPA/PFS, CFP®
President, Optima Financial Resources

The issue here is time. A very small amount of time spent thinking about and planning for your retirement will be the highest earning period of your life. You could realize tens or hundreds of thousands of dollars available for your retirement security from the results of only a few hours of planning. Every day that you wait to complete this task is a day that is no longer on your side in your planning horizon.

8

ESTATE PLANNING

*The favour of the Great is no
inheritance.*

Ben Franklin (Poor Richard's Almanack)

TERMS FROM THE TOP

gift tax   Graduated tax, levied on the donor of a gift by the federal government and most state governments when assets are transferred from one person to another. The more money given as a gift, the higher the tax rate. A $10,000 exemption per recipient is allowed per year.

kiddie tax   Tax filed by parents on Form 8615 for the investment income of children under age 14 exceeding $1400. Tax is at parent's top tax rate. In some cases, however, parents may elect to report such children's income on their own returns.

living trust (*inter vivos* trust)   Trust established between living persons—for instance, between father and child. In contrast, a testamentary trust goes into effect when the person who establishes the trust dies.

per stripes   Formula for distributing the assets of a person who dies. Under such a distribution the estate is allocated according to the number of children the deceased had, and distributed accordingly to those surviving the decedent. If any children predeceased the decedent, the share allocated to them would be equally divided among their children and so on.

probate   Judicial process whereby the will of the deceased person is presented to a court and an executor or administrator is appointed to carry out the will's instructions.

stepped-up basis   Increase in the basis up to the fair market value of assets when they are passed to an heir at the owner's death.

testamentary trust   Trust created by a will, as distinguished from an *inter vivos* trust created during the lifetime of the grantor.

unlimited marital deduction   Provision in the federal estate and gift tax law allowing spouses to transfer unlimited amounts of property to each other free of tax. Such transfers may be made during the life or at the death of the transferor, and are intended to treat a couple as an economic unit for transfer tax purposes.

Source: reprinted by permission of Jordan Goodman, Dictionary of Finance and Investment Terms *(Barron's, 5th Edition)*

As you make good decisions throughout your life to build your wealth, you then have more responsibility to plan your estate well. You may have some idea about how your estate will pass to your heirs and may have developed some legal documents to put your wishes into place. Our experts were full of warnings that what you expect to happen may not happen. Constant monitoring of your choices is necessary to ensure your plan is carried out.

Even if you haven't amassed your fortune yet, you have many decisions to make to protect your family and your assets. Maybe you have life insurance in place to provide cash for your family in the event of an early death. This simple decision has many aspects that can help or hinder an overall estate plan. Wills are a necessary document for most people but may not hold as much power as you think. The tips in this chapter will give you some interesting insight into whether your estate plan is what you think it is.

All tips in this chapter are intended for informational purposes only. Should you find one potentially helpful to your situation, you should consult with your legal, tax, or investment professional familiar with your individual situation to determine its suitability prior to taking any action or investing any money.

ESTATE AND GIFT TAX ISSUES

Congress continues to debate the usefulness of estate and gift tax revenues, making it important that you work with a professional who is current on how their revisions may affect your planning. The exemptions for these taxes are rather high, leaving many with estates that will never be taxed. But those who are taxed have several very effective planning strategies to consider that can minimize the tax impact.

◆ ◆ ◆

The numerous changes in estate law make it important that you have a professional review of your current estate plan. Do you have the proper documents and will they provide for the plan that you envisioned? In addition, you may have had a change in your life, such as divorce, death, the birth of a child, or a move to a different state that requires a change in your will or trust documents.

Jill Gianola, M.B.A., CFP®
Owner, Gianola Financial Planning

Think the estate and gift taxes have been repealed? Think again. The federal estate tax will only be repealed if you happen to die in 2010. It doesn't take affect until that year, and by 2011, it is gone! Congress calls this a "sunset" provision, and it was the only way they could get the bill passed. Estates of less than a million dollars need not worry, but the estates of those millionaires who pass on in any other year will still have to deal with the IRS. Also know that the federal gift tax has not been repealed for any year. Careful estate planning is and will continue to be necessary.

Paul D. Lyons, CPA/PFS, CFP®
Manager, KPMG Personal Financial Planning

If the estate tax is repealed, don't underestimate the tax your beneficiaries will pay in income taxes that would have been avoided if they had inherited them under the current estate tax system. This would be caused by the loss of "stepped-up basis" at your death. Your heirs would have to pay income taxes on the capital gains of the assets they inherit from you if the Estate Tax is repealed. Action item: Keep good cost basis records for all valuable assets, especially your home, with your estate planning documents.

Susan J. Bruno, CPA/PFS, CFP®
Principal, Winged Keel Financial Advisors, LLC

Do you know who owns your assets? If you don't, you have lots of company! For estate planning purposes, it's a good idea to know how all your assets are titled. Joint assets can be held in any one of four methods, depending on with whom you hold them and in what state you reside. They can be held as:

- Community property: Belonging to a married couple jointly, in a community property state. Each spouse owns half of property. Passes through probate. Surviving spouse receives a complete step-up in basis. Included in probate estate.
- Tenancy in common: Belonging to more than one person, each of whom has the right to dispose of their share in the estate. Included in probate estate.
- Tenancy by the entirety: Belonging to a married couple with each share passing to the surviving spouse at death, outside of the probate process. Neither tenant can dispose of their share without consent of spouse.
- Joint property with rights of survivorship belonging to more than one person, but divided equally among tenants. On the death of one tenant, ownership passes to the remaining tenants, equally, outside of the probate process.

Each one has a different effect on who gets your property, how they get it, and what taxes will be paid. Be sure to check this out before you have any will or trust document drafted.

Paul D. Lyons, CPA/PFS, CFP®
Manager, KPMG Personal Financial Planning

Did you know that how you title a certificate of deposit or other investment account could mess up even the best estate plan? Say you have numerous investment accounts and three children. For convenience you have the child living locally named on the investment accounts. Upon your death, this one child will probably inherit all of these investments. Avoid this problem by requesting that your CPA, attorney, or financial planner review titling based on the data you gather for tax return preparation. This simple step will go a long way in making sure your assets go where you want and that you can maximize estate tax savings.

Frank B. Arnold, CPA/PFS
Vice President, Panfeld, Edelman & Arnold

Did you know that your will may not direct your assets? If you have money in retirement plans, annuities, or jointly held assets (joint tenants with right of survivorship or tenancy by the entirety), your will has no bearing on where these assets go. They pass outside of the probate process and will go directly to the named beneficiary, regardless of what your will says. It is possible to name your estate as the beneficiary, but that creates other problems. This would subject those assets to the lengthy and costly probate process, which can delay when your beneficiaries receive the assets.

Paul D. Lyons, CPA/PFS, CFP®
Manager, KPMG Personal Financial Planning

If you're a typical married couple, you probably have his assets, her assets, our (joint) assets, contract assets, children's assets and possibly assets that have already been transferred to trusts. A well-designed estate plan could have disastrous unintended consequences unless the title of each and every asset is confirmed. For example, if all of the family assets were titled in only your name and your spouse passed away first, there would be no assets available to fund a credit shelter trust pursuant to the terms of the will.

Susan J. Bruno, CPA/PFS, CFP®
Principal, Winged Keel Financial Advisors, LLC

IN MONEY WORDS

Life's only certainties are death and taxes ... Live rich, die broke

---

Are you the beneficiary of an estate but would prefer to have your heirs receive the money instead? Did you know that you do not have to accept the inheritance? By filing a disclaimer, you may be able to have the inheritance pass on to your heirs without a gift or estate tax issue. The disclaimer must be filed within nine months of the date of inheritance and you cannot receive any benefits during that period. You will need the help of a knowledgeable attorney to draft and file the disclaimer. The benefits of avoiding estate taxes at your death and benefiting the next generation now could be great.

Frank L. Washelesky, J.D., CPA/PFS, CVA
Director, Ostrow Resin Berk & Abrams, Ltd.

You might find that life insurance is an attractive way to pay estate settlement and transfer costs. Generally the one type of policy to have is a *second-to-die* or *joint survivor* policy with your spouse. Why? Because the majority of estate costs are due at the death of the second spouse and that is when the insurance pays the benefit. This type of policy also has a lower premium than a single life policy for the same face amount. Remember, to avoid the death proceeds from being included in the insured's taxable estate the policy should be owned and payable to a third party, such as a child or an irrevocable trust.

J. Victor Conrad, CPA/PFS, CFP®, ChFC
Financial Advisor, The MONY Group

Do you have a large estate? Do you want the government to get up to 55 percent of your estate? If you own a personal residence, farm, or yacht, consider donating it to charity while retaining the right to enjoy the full use of it. You have your choice of a term of years or the lifetime of one or more individuals. This is called a Life Estate Agreement. You could ask your planner, attorney, charity, or combination of all three. The cost is a few thousand dollars depending upon the property's value. You'll need an appraisal, a deed transfer, and an environmental survey. It is an excellent tool to create a legacy and lower your estate at the same time.

Cary Carbonaro, M.B.A., CFP®
President, Family Financial

As you and your children get older, you may have excess cash while they are fighting to make ends meet. However, the tax law only allows for annual gifts of $11,000 each year without a gift tax issue. You can increase the amount of support you provide your children each year by taking advantage of a few overlooked provisions in the tax law. You may pay medical and health providers and certain education expenses directly to qualified providers on behalf of your children without gift tax consequences. For example, pay your children's medical insurance premiums or your grandchildren's private school tuition each year.

Frank L. Washelesky, J.D., CPA/PFS, CVA
Director, Ostrow Resin Berk & Abrams, Ltd.

One of the most ingenious techniques that you can employ to help your adult children, grandchildren, or other heirs prepare for their retirement while you reduce your estate is to fund their contributions to employer-provided savings programs like 401(k) and 403(b) plans. Here's an example: You agree to provide up to $11,000 per year to your daughter, who increases her 401(k) contribution to take advantage of your generosity. Your estate has just been reduced without any tax implications to you, your daughter's retirement assets have received a much-needed boost, and the hidden benefit is that her federal taxable income will be reduced by the amount that her contributions are increased!

Michael L. Alberts, M.B.A., CFP®
President, Woodstock Financial Group, LLC

Want to help your grandchildren while helping yourself? Look at 529 plans. These plans allow you to fund a grandchild's college education and remove these funds from your estate without incurring the gift tax or generation-skipping tax. You can do this by contributing up to $55,000 per grandparent to each grandchild. The funds contributed will grow tax-free, and for a child born this year, a $55,000 contribution earning an 8 percent average annual return will grow to almost $220,000 at the age of 18. (Note: The $55,000 is indexed for inflation, and may increase.)

John J. Feyche, M.S., M.B.T., CPA/PFS
Manager, Z&W Wealth Management

Making annual gifts to your children can be an excellent estate planning strategy. At the same time, you can also attempt to minimize the impact of income taxes. If your child is not yet 14, you can use investments that generate growth of principal rather than current income. Since the growth in these investments will not be taxed until they are sold, with proper timing you can avoid the kiddie tax by generating income of $1,500 or less each year. If your child's income exceeds $1,500, you will pay your highest tax rate on their income.

Alexis M. Jensen, CPA, CFP®
President, Z&W Wealth Management

One reason to convert to a Roth IRA is to stretch your IRA for generations. You never have to take Required Minimum Distributions. You can stretch it over your children's and grandchildren's lifetimes. If you don't need it, let the nest egg grow and leave your grandchildren a legacy! If you convert to a Roth IRA, you will have taxes due the year you convert. One way to avoid the tax bite in the same year is to donate appreciated stock to charity. In some cases you can wipe out the tax bill for the year.

Cary Carbonaro, M.B.A., CFP®
President, Family Financial

BENEFICIARIES

This section of the book got the award for the most tips submitted on the same subject. It seems all our experts agree that this seemingly simple piece of financial planning is so often overlooked that they wanted the world to know! Beneficiaries show up on life insurance, pensions, IRAs, and other documents. You fill in the blank and then forget about them. Who you pick and how they are listed makes a great deal of difference. Don't assume you have this issue figured out until you read these tips.

♦ ♦ ♦

You may not realize how important it is to pay attention to the contingent beneficiaries you name on your life insurance policies. If you're like many people who have a will, you have probably decided that after you and your spouse both die your assets will go to your children through a trust. Your children would then receive the principal at designated ages. If you name your minor children as contingent beneficiaries of a life insurance policy, they would receive the proceeds outright.

In turn, this could result in guardians *ad litem* being appointed by surrogate courts with accompanying fees. To avoid this undesirable outcome, the contingent beneficiaries of your life insurance policies should be your estate.

Stuart Kessler, J.D., M.B.A., CPA/PFS
Past Chairman of AICPA—Personal Financial Planning Division

Do you have a son or daughter named as a beneficiary of your IRA or retirement plan? Are you aware of how the proceeds from that plan would be paid out if they predeceased you? Their family would receive their portion ... correct? No, not necessarily. If you intend your child's family to participate in your plan's eventual distribution, then make sure your beneficiary form states so. This is commonly handled by inserting the words "per stripes" after the names of those beneficiaries. Make sure the plan or IRA custodian allows this language.

Jill Gianola, M.B.A., CFP®
Owner, Gianola Financial Planning

IN MONEY WORDS

The acorn never falls far from the tree ... Make sure to plan your estate and charitable giving

---

Be sure to review the beneficiary designations listed on your tax-deferred retirement accounts to ensure they work in concert with your established plan to distribute assets at your death. Estate planning is an important component of the comprehensive financial planning process, but beneficiary designations are often overlooked. In some cases these accounts may be a substantial part of your total estate, and because the funds within these accounts pass by beneficiary designation, they will not follow your well-thought-out, carefully coordinated path contained in the trust you recently completed.

Kristofor R. Behn, CFP®, CTC
Director of Strategic Planning & Coordination, Fieldstone Financial

Did you know that you could name a special qualified trust as beneficiary of your IRA and still preserve all the income tax benefits associated with an IRA for your heirs? You will need to have a testamentary trust created (effective at your death), and you will need to change your IRA beneficiary designation to ensure that the IRA is transferred to this trust at your death. A knowledgeable attorney will be able to create the appropriate trust language to ensure that IRA tax benefits are preserved. This is a fairly straightforward trust and should not be too costly to have the document created if the attorney has done this before.

Clark M. Blackman II, CPA/PFS, CFP®, ChFC, CFA®, CIMA, AAMS®
Managing Director and Chief Investment Officer, Post Oak Capital

WILLS, TRUSTS, AND OTHER LEGAL DOCUMENTS

One of the hardest parts of estate planning is coming face-to-face with your own mortality. In order to decide what should happen after you die, you have to admit freely that you will be dead someday. As obvious as it sounds, this simple notion is what keeps many from ever taking any steps to plan their estate. Once over that hump, the documents that get the process started are relatively routine and resolve many issues that will save your family money and time when you die.

♦♦♦

You may be neglecting your estate plan because the thought of seeing an estate attorney and discussing legal issues you don't understand seems overwhelming. Promise yourself a reward when you are finished, and then schedule the appointment. Interview several estate attorneys until you find one you like. Have your will or trust documents prepared, along with a Power of Attorney for health care issues and a Power of Attorney for financial issues. Review the beneficiary designations for your IRAs, 401(k), life insurance policies, and annuities with the attorney. After you have signed your legal documents and you know everything is in good order, reward yourself with something very special.

Donna Skeels Cygan, M.B.A., CFP®
President, Essential Financial Planning, Inc.

Most inheritance problems can be avoided if addressed early. Don't leave everything to your spouse. A "sweetheart will," which essentially was the husband saying, "I give everything to my wife when I die," gives his heirs a large tax bill after she dies, depending on the size of the estate and the extent of any pre-planning. You can remove $1 million from your estate today and shelter it from estate taxes forever by putting it into a ByPass or Credit Shelter Trust. When you die, the $1 million plus any appreciation passes directly through to your spouse and on to your heirs and is never subject to estate taxes.

Phyllis Bernstein, CPA/PFS
President, Phyllis Bernstein Consulting

Remember not to put your will inside your safe deposit box. Once you die, the box will be sealed and access to the box will be restricted. Leave the original will with your attorney or in a secure location inside your house.

Michael David Schulman, M.B.A., M.A., CPA/PFS
Principal, Schulman Co. CPA P.C.

Did you know that in many states going through probate is less expensive than setting up a living trust? Recently a client of mine paid $2,000 for a probate filing. The will had been prepared previously for $750. Many times the creation of a living trust runs between $4,000 and $5,000, and often probate is not entirely avoided. Before you decide on utilizing a living trust get a second opinion to verify that it is a good idea for you and really accomplishes what you want. Ask for referrals to qualified estate tax attorneys or check the yellow pages for Board Certified Estate Tax attorneys.

Frank B. Arnold, CPA/PFS
Vice President, Panfeld, Edelman & Arnold

If your assets and life insurance coverage will leave a substantial inheritance, consider having your will create a testamentary trust that will be funded by the proceeds of your life insurance policies. Trusts can allow you flexibility in dealing with issues such as postponing distributions of substantial assets to children after they turn 21 years old. Many

21-year-olds would blow a lot of that money on expensive cars and vacations rather than put it to a use you may believe more appropriate.

Barbara J. Raasch, CFA®, CPA/PFS, ChFC
Partner-in-charge of Wealth Management Solutions, Ernst & Young

Take advantage of the new Principal and Income Acts being adopted in several states. These statutes allow your trustee to distribute more than trust income to traditionally income-only beneficiaries. The trustee may elect to distribute capital gain proceeds or capital appreciation to your income beneficiaries if certain requirements are met. This will allow your trustee to invest trust assets for total return rather than having to choose between investing for dividend and interest income or investing for capital appreciation. You should check with your legal counsel, CPA, or other financial advisors to determine the availability of this planning opportunity for your trust.

Jack B. Capron, Esq., CPA/PFS
Director-TLS, PriceWaterhouseCoopers, LLC

Consider hiring a third-party administrator (TPA) to help you comply with the Crummey provisions in your life insurance trusts in order to prevent unintended (and potentially disastrous) results. The services of the TPA would include:

- Sending Crummey notices to all necessary parties
- Applying for the tax identification number for the trust
- Setting up a separate checking account for the trust
- Seasoning the money when needed

Naming your brother-in-law as your trustee may sound like a good idea, but he could find himself in serious trouble when the IRS challenges your life insurance trust after you die!

Susan J. Bruno, CPA/PFS, CFP®
Principal, Winged Keel Financial Advisors, LLC

Consider selling appreciated assets to an intentionally defective grantor trust. For income tax purposes, this trust treats all income as being taxed back to the grantor. But, for estate and gift tax purposes, the trust is not in the grantor's estate. This saves substantial estate/gift taxes at rates as high as 50 percent. In effect, an asset can potentially be transferred to children without an income tax and the asset still is not in the grantor's estate.

Stephen A. Drake, Ph.D., CPA/PFS, CFP®
President, Optima Financial Resources

No matter how you receive that next dollar—get your paycheck, win the lottery, receive an inheritance or find it on the street—it has the same utility in the real world. You can put it to work for you, use it to further your dreams, or use it buy more stuff. Compare where you are at that moment relative to where you want to be, then decide how to "dispose" of your next dollar—toward long-term or short-term goals or immediate gratification.

Lesley J. Brey, M.B.A., CFA®, CFP®
President, L.J. Brey, Inc.

Just because you aren't a millionaire doesn't mean that you don't need a will. If you have minor children you need a will to name their guardians. And make sure that the guardians that you select agree to the responsibility! Also, the will can instruct the guardian in how you want your assets managed for the benefit of the kids. For example, do you want the guardian to move into your house, saving your children the anxiety of moving into a new neighborhood and school district? Or should the house be sold and the proceeds left to the guardian to provide for the kids?

Michael David Schulman, M.B.A., M.A., CPA/PFS
Principal, Schulman Co. CPA P.C.

Structure your assets to be creditor-claim proof by using a limited liability company (LLC) or partnership to accumulate family assets. Once this is done, you transfer a variety of assets into the LLC. This can be rental property, stocks and bonds, etc. This technique has tremendous estate planning consequences, because the assets in the LLC can be structured in such a way to pass them to younger generations at a large discount. For example, $1,000,000 in assets transferred to the

LLC may be, for IRS purposes, only worth $600,000 with modern valuation techniques. The benefit is that many more of your assets can be passed along to your heirs before gift or estate taxes are due.

Stephen A. Drake, Ph.D., CPA/PFS, CFP®
President, Optima Financial Resources

Want to make sure your brokerage account passes directly to your heir without probate, but don't want to make a gift to that person now by making them a joint owner of your account? Ask your broker to make the account "payable on death" to your heir. All it takes is filling out an easy form.

Peg Downey, M.A., CFP®
Partner, Money Plans

You may have drafted a will to distribute all of your assets exactly as you want. Now you need to make sure that your will actually controls these assets at death. Anything that is titled as joint tenants with rights of survivorship (JTWROS) will not flow through your will. Neither will accounts with a beneficiary designation such as your IRA, 401(k) plan, or life insurance. Bonds or CDs with a transfer on death (TOD) designation will not either. Don't let a well-drafted document go to waste. Review the ownership status and beneficiary designation on all your assets as part of your estate planning.

Helen L. Modly, CFP®, ChFC, CLU
Vice President, Focus Financial Consultants, Ltd.

A letter of last instructions may be the most important love note you'll ever write, but don't wait until Valentine's Day to get it done. Remember that your will is not always read immediately after you die. Your letter of last instructions covers those details your family will need to know right away. This personally prepared letter is an explicit way of saying in your own words how you want to assist those you love in your passing. Let family members know where important papers are located. Be specific. You'll find this file in the bottom-left drawer in my desk.

John E. Sestina, M.S.F.S., CFP®, ChFC
Author of Managing to Be Wealthy

CHARITABLE GIVING

Giving is a wonderful thing to do, for numerous reasons. Giving with a plan that saves taxes and maximizes the amount available to the charities is an even better thing to do. There are several creative vehicles that you can use to accomplish a variety of goals for yourself and your charitable interests.

♦ ♦ ♦

Do you have close ties to your alma mater, church, or synagogue? Consider leaving your favorite charity a portion of your qualified retirement plan at your death. The charity can realize the benefits and your heirs will not be saddled with the income tax and estate tax costs they would incur if this asset were left to them. Leaving qualified retirement accounts to your children can cost as much as 70 cents on the dollar in estate and income taxes. A charitable beneficiary can receive the entire amount without any tax cost. You simply need to change the beneficiary of the account to the charity you prefer by completing a new beneficiary designation form available from the plan's trustee.

Frank L. Washelesky, J.D., CPA/PFS, CVA
Director, Ostrow Resin Berk & Abrams, Ltd.

MIND OVER MONEY

Money causes an enormous amount of stress, and some people allow money to hold a very powerful position in their life. If you look at money objectively, you can change your attitude and put money on a much lower pedestal so you will control it instead of it controlling you. Money is a tool. It is to be used wisely. It buys nice things, but it does not bring happiness. Take the time to determine what brings you happiness, and what you value in life. Focus on those things, and you will inadvertently be forcing money to a lower position on the pedestal.

Donna Skeels Cygan, M.B.A., CFP®
President, Essential Financial Planning, Inc.

It is better to give and also receive. Charitable Gift Annuities can lower your estate, lower your taxes, and pay above-market interest rates. If you are retired and have highly appreciated stock in your portfolio, you can take an immediate deduction on your taxes. You will get an above-market interest rate based on your age. For example, at age 70 you would receive 7.2 percent with an income stream for life. Since it is an annuity, up to 50 percent of the income is tax-free! To buy these products, contact a fee-only advisor or your favorite charity directly!

Cary Carbonaro, M.B.A., CFP®
President, Family Financial

Consider setting up a charitable remainder trust to sell your highly appreciated asset(s) without paying any capital gains taxes. This can be combined with an insurance trust that will give your children an income- and estate-tax-free inheritance. Income is paid to you from the charitable trust for your joint lives and you receive an immediate income tax deduction for making a deferred charitable donation (no money goes to charity until both of you have passed on). This is a great tax planning idea for those with charitable intent who would like to avoid capital gains taxes.

Stephen A. Drake, Ph.D., CPA/PFS, CFP®
President, Optima Financial Resources

Consider including a nonbinding request in your will for your surviving spouse to make a charitable deduction, as opposed to including it as a charitable bequest in your will. If you were the first to die, your estate would typically not pay estate tax due to the unlimited marital deduction. The nonbinding request will prevent your estate from wasting a charitable contribution deduction and allow your surviving spouse to generate an income tax benefit for the charitable deduction. For example, a $50,000 charitable bequest could result in zero estate tax savings, while the same contribution from the surviving spouse could result in up to a $25,000 income tax savings!

Susan J. Bruno, CPA/PFS, CFP®
Principal, Winged Keel Financial Advisors, LLC

Don't forget your favorite charity when constructing your estate plan … Surprisingly, naming a charity as one of your beneficiaries may work to your benefit in the long run. A carefully crafted estate plan should include an option for your immediate beneficiaries to disclaim a portion of their interest in your assets to others further down on the list of beneficiaries. By listing a charity as a contingent beneficiary, you provide an estate planning opportunity to your beneficiaries, which may enable them to reduce or eliminate the tax paid on the inherited assets.

Kristofor R. Behn, CFP®, CTC
Director of Strategic Planning & Coordination, Fieldstone Financial

At this point you must have figured out that this is a complicated area of your financial life. Several professionals are required to make sense out of it for most people. Yearly reviews of the plans are necessary to keep up with financial, tax, and legal changes. Find people you enjoy working with because you'll be seeing them often, and your heirs will need to work with them while they are grieving for your passing. This is a wonderful gift you can give them: a well thought out plan for handling the distribution of your estate with competent professionals to translate it for them.

9

FAMILY MONEY MANAGEMENT

*So what signifies wishing and hoping
for better times. We may make these
times better if we bestir ourselves.*

Benjamin Franklin (Poor Richard's Almanack)

Terms from the Top

529 Plan   Tax-free savings plans sponsored by states for the purpose of accumulating money for education expenses.

credit-reporting bureaus   Agency that gathers information about the credit history of consumers and relays it to credit grantors for a fee. Credit grantors look at this information, which is constantly being updated, in making their decision as to whether or not to grant credit to a particular consumer, and if so, how much credit is appropriate.

executor/executrix   Administrator of the estate who gathers the estate assets; files the estate tax returns and final personal income tax returns, and administers the estate; pays the debts of and charges against the estate; and distributes the balance in accordance with the terms of the will.

expected family contribution   Actual tuition payment required of a student attending an institution of higher learning, calculated based on government formulas that take into account income, assets, and family size.

Family and Medical Leave Act   Federal law enacted to give employees more flexibility and job security, while attending to personal crises that require time off work.

identity theft   Crime involving the acquisition and use of personal identifying information, such as Social Security number, bank account numbers, and credit card information, for the purpose of financial gain.

pre-nuptial agreement   Agreement between a future husband and wife that details how the couple's financial affairs are to be handled both during the marriage and in the event of divorce. The agreement may cover insurance protection, ownership of housing and securities, and inheritance rights.

Source: reprinted by permission of Jordan Goodman, Dictionary of Finance and Investment Terms *(Barron's, 5th Edition)*

When you're single, no one asks where your paycheck goes. When you have kids, you don't have to ask where it goes. You know. Family money management is really a big puzzle: How to take care of everyone's needs with multiple sources of income. At the same time, the issues of planning for everyone's ongoing security become more complex.

Getting married, having kids, getting the kids out of the house, or getting divorced all present different financial questions and stressors. All the joys and benefits of families are often overshadowed by financial worries. Let our experts help show you some ideas for creating a financially stable family life.

All tips in this chapter are intended for informational purposes only. Should you find one potentially helpful to your situation, you should consult with your legal, tax, or investment professional familiar with your individual situation to determine its suitability prior to taking any action or investing any money.

FAMILY ISSUES

Let's start this chapter with an overview of some of the issues that come up in families that may need some additional attention in your family. If you have them all under control, great! If not, pick one or two and call a family meeting to discuss the next steps to getting a handle on them.

◆ ◆ ◆

To measure your true wealth, focus on your total personal net worth—not just the value of your stocks. First, your financial net worth includes more than just your equities. Add in your money market cash, CDs, bonds, real estate, fixed-income annuities, life insurance cash value, and your possessions. For the bigger picture of your total personal net worth, add important nonfinancial assets including family, friends, health, spiritual well-being, freedom, work, hobbies, achievements, wisdom, happy memories, pets, and all that brings you joy. In other words, the real value of everything you have is worth much more than only your stocks.

Kathleen M. Rehl, Ph.D., CFP®
Owner, Rehl Financial Advisors

MIND OVER MONEY

Would you like to know more about how money impacts your behavior? Find out by writing a money autobiography. Use question starters such as these:

- My father's (mother's) message about money was ...
- I first began to realize we were rich or poor when ...
- With money, it always seems as though ...

Once you have these new insights, it will be easier to form new habits.

Judi Martindale, M.Ed., CFP®, EA
Author of No More Baglady Fears

IN MONEY WORDS

Don't try this at home ... Buying on margin, speculative investing, day trading

---

Get a free financial check-up. Take Rutgers Cooperative Extension's interactive Financial Fitness Quiz online at www.rce.rutgers.edu/money2000 (click on Money and Investing resources to access the quiz). The Financial Fitness Quiz will help you identify the strengths and weaknesses of your financial situation. Questions about financial behaviors where you indicate a seldom or never response are areas of financial planning where you need improvement. Just like an annual physical with your doctor, a financial check-up can identify problems before they get worse.

Barbara O'Neill, Ph.D., CFP®, AFC, CHC
Author of Saving on a Shoestring

Are you and your spouse both involved in your family's financial matters? If you have all the information and you die first, it will be difficult for your spouse to pick up where you left off. A helpful tool is to create a list of your assets and where they are located, including account numbers. Discuss the list with your spouse and provide him or her with a copy of it. This will relieve a substantial area of worry if you die first.

Harvey D. Aaron, J.D., CPA/PFS, CFP®
VP and Director of Tax Services, Tandem Financial Services

Family and Medical Leave Act (FMLA) time can be used during a medical crisis to care for a family member or for your own serious medical condition. If you are eligible, you can receive up to 12 weeks of leave over a 12-month period. Your employer is required to maintain your health coverage and return you to your same job or one with equivalent pay, seniority, and benefits. FMLA leave can be taken in small increments, such as a week off after chemotherapy treatments, and spread out over time. You do not need to use the 12 weeks all at once.

Barbara O'Neill, Ph.D., CFP®, AFC, CHC
Author of Saving on a Shoestring

It is time to rethink the traditional view of loaning money to family members. If you have a child who cannot afford the growing costs of housing but you want and have the financial means to help, just do it! In your zeal to do so, just don't forget to complete the proper steps to be IRS-compliant. Some of these include following a basic loan structure and leaving a paper trail. An intra-family loan is often a win-win situation for all parties. You can transfer wealth, avoid costly gift taxes, and give your child a lower mortgage rate all at once.

Howard Safer, M.B.A., CPA/PFS
EVP, Regions Morgan Keegan Trust Co.

If you are ever asked to serve as an executor to a family member, beware of the real fiduciary responsibilities and potential conflicts of interest, especially if you are also a named beneficiary. Many of us consider being named an executor/executrix an honor of faith and trust bestowed on the oldest or most successful son or daughter by parents, aunts, and uncles. Real problems faced by the family executor: legal responsibility to act in the best interest of the estate and heirs. In many cases, this can take 6 to 12 months or even years for little or no pay. Most professional trustees and investment fiduciaries charge a percentage of the assets. But family members serving in the similar positions are asked to serve without compensation.

Ray Julian, CFP®
Executive Vice President, Compass Capital Corporation

RECORD-KEEPING

Now we've hit the most exciting part of money management. If you're like most Americans, you spend at least three hours a day on your books! *Not!* Probably the only thing we are worse at than saving is record-keeping. If we didn't have an income tax system that required us to keep some records, we'd have little more than a couple of bank statements to refer to. And now, with ATM and computer access to our accounts, we rarely keep our own records.

♦ ♦ ♦

All families—including those renting an apartment—need to purchase a fireproof box for critical household papers. Found in the aisles of virtually every hardware or office supply store, a well-built storage container is an ideal place for insurance policies, a letter of last instructions, loan agreements, automobile registration, credit card numbers, etc. Let your children or parents know where the box is located.

John E. Sestina, M.S.F.S., CFP®, ChFC
Author of Managing to Be Wealthy

To avoid becoming a victim of identity theft, don't routinely carry around identification cards or papers with your Social Security number on them, such as college transcripts, college IDs, and health insurance or prescription drug cards. Carry them when needed, of course, such as when you are visiting a doctor or hospital or needing identification to board a plane. Otherwise, carry a copy of your identification with the Social Security number crossed out.

Barbara O'Neill, Ph.D., CFP®, AFC, CHC
Author of Saving on a Shoestring

Many class action suits cover things that we, individually, have suffered, and which could prove financially beneficial to us. An announcement from the Court is published in the newspaper asking if you wish to be excluded from the class. Unless you ask to be excluded you will, with no further action on your part, be included in any settlement of that case, at which time another announcement will appear in the newspaper informing of the settlement and proposed distribution. If you have a monetary claim, follow the instructions for filing a claim and eventually you will share in the settlement of that case. It can pay to be vigilant.

Henrietta Humphreys, M.B.A., CFP®
Financial Advisor, The Henrietta Humphreys Group

IN MONEY WORDS

The pot of gold at the end of the rainbow ... Financial independence

---

Get rid of those stick-on notes and scraps of paper that have your user names and passwords scrawled on them. Put special numbers in a computerized spreadsheet that contains frequent traveler accounts, toll-free reservation numbers, organizational membership records, subscriber codes, etc. Do not store the spreadsheet in an unprotected hard drive file. Instead, put the data on a floppy disk and mark it with some obscure name such as "trips." This way you can get to your information when you need it but the scoundrels can't.

John E. Sestina, M.S.F.S., CFP®, ChFC
Author of Managing to Be Wealthy

Help protect yourself from credit card fraud by photocopying the front and back of each item kept in your wallet, such as your ATM and credit cards, driver's license, checks, and passport. Keep the list in a safe place at home and also with a trusted friend so that if you are traveling you can place one call and initiate the cancellation of each card. You'll also want to keep the names and contact information of the three major credit-reporting bureaus on your list—TransUnion (www.transunion.com), Equifax (www.equifax.com), and Experion (www.experion.com). If your wallet is lost or stolen, contact one of the bureaus immediately for specific steps to take.

Brad R. Cougill, CFP®, CMFC®
Partner, Deerfield Financial Advisors, Inc.

Get a Hotmail e-mail account or one of many other free e-mail addresses. You can use it for those times when you don't want to give out your primary personal or business e-mail address, such as online purchases or where you are required to provide an address but don't want to expose your personal e-mail address to a lot of junk mail.

Henrietta Humphreys, M.B.A., CFP®
Financial Advisor, The Henrietta Humphreys Group

When making a purchase of any product or service, especially major purchases such as home improvements, major appliances, and electronic equipment, follow the Rule of Three and compare at least three competing product or service providers. Do this for financial products also, such as insurance policies, mutual funds, and credit cards.

Barbara O'Neill, Ph.D., CFP®, AFC, CHC
Author of Saving on a Shoestring

College Costs

Before you totally freak out about how much college costs these days, read through this insight from our experts. Children who want to go to college will go. Parents who become educated about the costs and options for financing will go to the head of the class.

♦ ♦ ♦

When a newborn arrives, set aside money for college from your next paycheck—even if it is only a few dollars.

John E. Sestina, M.S.F.S., CFP®, ChFC
Author of Managing to Be Wealthy

Make sure you understand the concept of expected family contribution (EFC) as you start saving for your child's college education. (Go to www.collegeboard.com for a preview). Chances are, you won't have to pay sticker price—which means you won't have to tear your hair out worrying about it!

Raj Pillai, Ph.D., CFP®
NAPFA-Registered Advisor, Financial Fitness Network of Solon

Need to save for college and retirement? Consider using a 529 Plan for college saving. If there is money left after college is paid for, you can get the money back for your own retirement. You pay tax on the earnings left in the 529 Plan and a 10 percent penalty. Not a bad way to cover both needs! The 529 Plans are provided by the States and not the federal government. However, you are eligible to participate in any State's plan, not just your state of residence. The provisions and investment selections can be different with each plan. Check out all your options at www.savingforcollege.com.

Elaine E. Bedel, M.B.A., CFP®
President, Bedel Financial Consulting, Inc.

Federal Student Aid (www.ed.gov/studentaid). This is the federal government's comprehensive site for educational matters; it contains links to many related issues.

If you have two children in college at the same time, your cost need not be double what it costs to enroll one. In fact, your expected family contribution (EFC) may remain the same. Make sure you understand how EFC is calculated. Even if you don't qualify for financial aid when only one child is in college, you may qualify when the second one follows suit.

Raj Pillai, Ph.D., CFP®
NAPFA-Registered Advisor, Financial Fitness Network of Solon

Having a difficult time trying to figure out how to fund your children's college educations? How about letting your state assist you? Some states will provide free college tuition for students attending state schools who agree to serve in state Army or Air National Guard units. Call your local National Guard recruiter to find out if this option is available in your state.

Michael L. Alberts, M.B.A., CFP®
President, Woodstock Financial Group, LLC

FinAid (www.finaid.org). This site has comprehensive information regarding financial aid, as well as links for everything else related to college.

Set up a 529 Plan college fund for your child, and then sign up with a program like Upromise.com or BabyMint.com so that rebates you earn in the course of your normal shopping can be credited to that account. You'll earn rebates when you patronize participating vendors—grocery stores, car manufacturers, long-distance carriers, restaurants, and so on. What's more, anyone—even your friends or colleagues—can credit their rebates to your account. If you have family members whose children are past their college years, encourage them to help you at no cost!

Raj Pillai, Ph.D., CFP®
NAPFA-Registered Advisor, Financial Fitness Network of Solon

MARRIAGE AND DIVORCE

Money issues seem to be the number-one cause of divorce, and divorce is one of the biggest causes of bankruptcy. However we look at it, money and love are terribly intertwined. Managing money in a marriage through open, honest communication is easier said than done. Time is tight, issues are deep, and money is limited. Don't ignore the advice in this section. It could save you your marriage, a lot of money, or both.

◆ ◆ ◆

Has financial communication in your marriage become SHADY (Sneak, Hide, Avoid, Deceive, or Yell)? If you have discovered conflicting styles and expectations about money, start to think like a shrink! Conflict will reign unless ways of dealing with your differences are found. First, try bringing light to the shade by diplomatically sharing your goals and expectations in specific and positive terms. Take turns and limit each turn to three to five minutes. Listen for understanding, not planning a response. As listener, restate your partner's comments and ask if you understood accurately. Then brainstorm solutions and decide which ones to try.

Susan Zimmerman, M.A., LMFT, ChFC, CLU
Author of The Power in Your Money Personality

Don't forget to enter into a pre-nuptial agreement if you have assets over one million dollars and expectations of an inheritance or are entering into a second marriage. A pre-nuptial agreement can protect your separate assets from being divided with a future spouse. Although not an easy subject to approach your fiancé with, protecting your children from a prior marriage or pressures from your own family members takes some of the heat off of you. Make sure you find an attorney who specializes in the preparation of marital agreements. These are very technical documents, and an improperly drafted agreement could create more problems than it solves.

John R. Connell, M.B.A., CPA/PFS
Personal Financial Specialist, Causey, Demgen, & Moore

MIND OVER MONEY

Divorce is one area where you don't want to let emotions overcome your common sense. Too often one or both spouses will let anger, guilt, or fear be the driving factor in how they negotiate their divorce settlement. Unfortunately, this has made many divorce attorneys wealthy and frustrated. No one really wins when emotions dictate actions, especially children. Talk with a therapist, counselor, clergyperson, or friend. Emotions must be dealt with, but not at the negotiating table.

Joan Coullahan, M.B.A., CDP
Co-author of Financial Custody: You, Your Money, and Divorce

If you are a widow or widower and were married for at least nine months, don't forget that you can begin drawing your Social Security benefits at age 60 based upon your late spouse's earnings, instead of waiting until age 62. This widow(er)'s benefit will continue even if you remarry after age 60 and will be unaffected by your new spouse's work. If you don't remarry, you can switch to full benefits based upon your own earnings, when you do reach age 65 (or age 62 if you retire early), if the monthly amount would be greater. Your local Social Security office will help you to determine the highest benefit available.

Helen L. Modly, CFP®, ChFC, CLU
Vice President, Focus Financial Consultants, Ltd.

You've probably noticed that he says "potayto" and she says "potahto." It's a natural dynamic of couples—they tend to dichotomize. So he'll become the spender and she'll become the saver, or the other way around, even though, objectively, their spending values are very similar. With this in mind—and a sense of humor—when you are developing a spending plan, you and your spouse or partner may find it much easier to see each other's viewpoint and come to agreement.

Peg Downey, M.A., CFP®
Partner, Money Plans

IN MONEY WORDS

No one said it would be easy ... Sticking to a financial plan

---

You can have a successful divorce. What? You didn't think that such a thing existed? Well it does, but only if you approach the divorce process in the right way. This means getting all the details about your situation. The right starting point is to list all your assets, debts, and living expenses. Too often negotiations start before the whole picture is known. You wouldn't start a vacation without knowing how you were going to get there—divorce is the same way. Get organized!

Joan Coullahan, M.B.A., CDP
Co-author of Financial Custody: You, Your Money, and Divorce

I hope you grabbed your spouse, the kids, your parents, and anyone else who impacts or is impacted by your financial decisions—and read them a tip! Sharing information, strategies, and overall goals with each other is essential to a happy family life and successful financial life. You may have always known something you just read in a tip, but your family didn't believe you. Now you can point to an expert to back you up and begin to move closer to financial security.

10

SAVINGS STRATEGIES

For age and want, save while
you may;
No morning sun lasts a whole day.

Benjamin Franklin (Poor Richard's Almanack)

TERMS FROM THE TOP

emergency savings   Cash reserve that is available to meet financial emergencies. Most financial planners advocate maintaining an emergency reserve of two to three months' salary in a liquid interest-bearing account.

IRA (Individual Retirement Account)   Personal, tax-deferred, retirement account that an employed person can set up with a deposit historically limited to $2000, but recently increased by Congress to $3000 with additional increases through 2008, ending with a limit of $5000. IRA contributions are deductible regardless of income if neither the taxpayer nor the taxpayer's spouse is covered by a qualified plan or trust.

principal   Basic amount invested, exclusive of earnings.

Roth IRA   Individual Retirement Account permitting account holders to allow their capital to accumulate tax free under certain conditions. Individuals can invest up to the yearly limit and they can withdraw the principal and earnings totally tax free after age 59½, as long as the assets have remained in the IRA for at least five years after making the first contribution.

SEP (Simplified Employee Pension)   Pension plan in which both the employee and the employer contribute to an Individual Retirement Account (IRA). Employees may elect to have employer contributions made to the SEP or paid to the employee in cash as with cash or deferred arrangements (401[k] plans).

solo-k   A one-person 401(k) plan designed for self-employed small business owners.

Source: reprinted by permission of Jordan Goodman, Dictionary of Finance and Investment Terms *(Barron's, 5th Edition)*

In the United States we have one of the most dismal savings rates in the world. We just don't value the practice of holding on to our earnings. We have become too dependent upon consumer credit to take care of instant needs that measure more than our weekly paycheck. What savings we do accumulate is often locked into tax-deferred accounts that are inappropriate for short-term needs.

Whether it is motivation, strategies, or systems for increasing your savings rate, you'll find some great advice in this chapter. All our experts are united in the need to help you find new and easy ways to build your ability to save more. Pick a couple of tips and try them out!

All tips in this chapter are intended for informational purposes only. Should you find one potentially helpful to your situation, you should consult with your legal, tax, or investment professional familiar with your individual situation to determine its suitability prior to taking any action or investing any money.

A Savings Mentality

To many, *savings* is the same as *not spending*. Since we enjoy spending, savings sounds like no fun. Instead, what if we thought about *savings* as *spending later?* Setting savings goals and reaching them is a wonderful feeling. Look for some help from our experts to bring you closer to that feeling.

♦ ♦ ♦

It is more important to get your money invested somewhere than to postpone your investment while you chase higher returns. $100 invested monthly at 6 percent will grow to $6,977 in five years. Of that amount $6,000 is your principal! At 8 percent, you will accumulate $7,348. But, if you increase your investment to $105 monthly, your 6 percent investment will grow to $7,326. Moral: Instead of chasing a 33 percent higher interest rate, simply increase your monthly contribution by 5 percent.

Michael David Schulman, M.B.A., M.A., CPA/PFS
Principal, Schulman Co. CPA P.C.

One great way to save more money is to automatically save 50 to 100 percent of any salary increases (and all of your bonus).

As soon as your raise is effective, have that amount automatically deducted from every paycheck to be added to your investment portfolio. You are used to living on your old salary. Investing steadily is the best way to accumulate wealth.

Constanza Low, M.I.M., and John Henry Low, M.B.A.
Vice President and President, Knickerbocker Advisors Inc.

Do whatever you can to contribute to your 401(k), SEP, or IRA. You are reducing your taxes as well as providing for your retirement. If you are salaried and regularly receive a refund on your taxes, try the following. At the beginning of the year, increase your withholding exemptions (less money will be deducted from your paycheck for taxes) and increase deductions to your retirement accounts. If before year's end not enough has been withheld for taxes, you can compensate by de-creasing your withholding exemptions. The federal government does not penalize salaried taxpayers for uneven withholding tax payments throughout the year.

Deborah O. Levine, M.B.A, M.S.T., CPA/PFS, CFP®
Financial Planner, AFP Group

MIND OVER MONEY

Don't let the task of making money divert you from life's bigger goals of spending time with family and friends, and enjoying life! After all, no one has ever been overheard on his or her deathbed regretting not investing in a particular stock, or not spending more time at the office!

Raj Pillai, Ph.D., CFP®
NAPFA-Registered Advisor, Financial Fitness Network of Solon

Establish a disciplined approach to enable yourself to save for your home purchase. Determine a set amount to save each month and, if available through your savings vehicle, have an automatic deposit of this amount credited on a monthly basis.

Alternatively, have the first check you write each month be the check you write to your savings vehicle. The easiest way to calculate how much to save each month is to determine how much you'll need in X number of months in the future and save the amount each month that when multiplied by X will reach your goal. For example, if you'll need another $1,200 in 12 months, save $100 per month. You'll pick up a little interest along the way, which will give you a little cushion on that special day when you reach your goal.

Barbara J. Raasch, CFA®, CPA/PFS, ChFC
Partner-in-charge of Wealth Management Solutions, E&Y, LLC

Learning how to use the SMarT Plan makes it easy to save more in your 401(k) plan, a wonderful savings tool. SMarT = Save More Tomorrow. Pledging a percentage of future pay raises (say 50 percent) to increase your 401(k) savings raise still allows for a raise to appear in your paycheck. Say you are saving 6 percent of salary now and want to increase that to 8 percent. Every future raise you get, contribute half of it to the 401(k) plan, keeping the other half as a pay raise. A 4 percent raise in salary increases your 401(k) savings by 2 percent and you have already reached your goal!

Bill Pomeroy, M.S., CFP®, CRC
Executive Vice President, The Shobe Financial Group

Ready to make the last payment on your car? Don't! Continue paying it! After you make your final payment to the bank, begin a new bank account and pay yourself the amount of your monthly car payment. When your current car is ready to be replaced, you'll have a nice down payment ready, and won't even need to adjust your current budget. For example, if you have a car payment of $350, saving for just 18 months before you buy your next car could save you interest of $1,500 and shorten the life of your next loan by over a year!

Patrick T. Hanratty, M.B.A., CPA/PFS, CFP®
Managing Director, Capital Advisors, Ltd.

IN MONEY WORDS

The early bird catches the worm ... It's never too soon to begin saving

---

If you know you'll need a new car in several years, save for it now rather than financing it then. Not only will you save the interest on the loan, but you'll lower the total amount needed by the amount you earn on your savings. For example, if you're buying a car that costs $20,000, and you're financing at 6 percent over five years, your interest expense would add another $3,200 to the total cost. By saving for five years instead at a 4.75 percent return on your savings, you'll only need to put aside $17,760, for a combined total savings of $5,440.

Timothy M. Hayes, M.B.A., RFC, CMFC®
President, Landmark Financial Advisory Services, LLC

On a daily basis for a couple of months, detail each dollar spent on a spreadsheet with spending categories for columns (utilities, coffee shop, gifts ...) and each day as a row. Include all purchases, whether made by cash, credit card, check, or electronically. Review this record and challenge yourself as to the best use of your money. This exercise takes some discipline, but can be very rewarding when you find the potential savings. You might decide that you have an additional $80 per month to invest in a mutual fund when you notice that you spent $80 on coffee last month!

Nate Wenner, CPA/PFS, CFP®, CIMA
Personal Financial Counselor, Ernst & Young

Congratulations, you just got a raise! Now don't forget to give your emergency fund a raise, too. For example: Prior to the raise you made $50,000 a year, and you have decided that three months' pre-tax salary is a sufficient emergency fund for your current lifestyle. This would give you an emergency fund of $12,500. However, your 5 percent raise dictates that you contribute an additional $625 for a total of $13,125. Going through this process at every raise will ensure that your lifestyle doesn't outgrow your rainy day fund and leave you all wet.

Patrick T. Hanratty, M.B.A., CPA/PFS, CFP®
Managing Director, Capital Advisors, Ltd.

SAVINGS TOOLS

If you're now in the mood to save, this section will help you make some good choices with your dollars. The financial institutions have come up with options for just about every need. Your only job is to evaluate your needs well and then find the tools that match your situation. We are so fortunate to have so many convenient and efficient products to choose from. Happy shopping!

◆◆◆

Automate, automate, automate. Get money automatically deposited into savings before you get a chance to spend it. Specific places that make automated savings easy and affordable include tax-deferred employer retirement savings plans, mutual fund automatic investment programs, credit unions, direct stock purchase plans, and the U.S. Treasury Department's EasySaver program for U.S. savings bond purchases (see www.easysaver.gov). Contact your employer and/or investment advisor for information about available automated saving and investment opportunities. You won't miss the money if you "pay yourself first."

Barbara O'Neill, Ph.D., CFP®, AFC, CHC
Author of Saving on a Shoestring

To help guard your emergency fund, deposit the money in a money market account at a bank on the other side of town, and at a bank that is different than the one you use for your normal banking activities. Keeping the bank separate and inconvenient will make you less likely to make a run on your emergency savings.

Patrick T. Hanratty, M.B.A., CPA/PFS, CFP®
Managing Director, Capital Advisors, Ltd.

A great way to invest and also accrue airline miles is to buy your Series I savings bonds online at www.savingsbonds.gov. If you are single, you can purchase up to $30,000 in any one calendar year. If you are married, the two of you can purchase up to $60,000. By using your credit card, you earn miles. That's at least one round trip a year!

Judy A. Stewart, M.B.A., CFP®, EA
Owner, Stewart Financial Services

IN MONEY WORDS

A penny saved is a penny earned ... The power of compounding

Passbook savings accounts may have been our grandparents' choice of investments, but they're not generating much income these days. If you still have a few of your own bank savings accounts around the house, track down the current interest rate. You may be surprised! As of the summer of 2002, one of the regional banks in our area was paying only 0.6 percent on passbook accounts. Note where the decimal is! Even though money market mutual funds are also at rock bottom yield levels, those accounts are better places to park your cash. Plus, they offer check-writing privileges.

John E. Sestina, M.S.F.S., CFP®, ChFC
Author of Managing to Be Wealthy

Having a difficult time getting started with your 401(k)? Just can't seem to give up any take-home pay? Check into the employer-provided pre-tax benefit plans, such as the Medical Reimbursement Account and the Dependent Care Reimbursement Account. Taking advantage of these plans will reduce the amount of income tax withheld from your paycheck. Use this tax savings to get your 401(k) started.

Elaine E. Bedel, M.B.A., CFP®
President, Bedel Financial Consulting, Inc.

When you have payments to the same creditor in the same amount each month such as a student or other installment loan, it becomes routine to write the check every month. After you have made the last payment, continue to write the check each month, only write it to yourself and deposit it into a savings account or mutual fund. If you are paying electronically, arrange with your bank or mutual fund company to take the same amount from your account each month. This is a painless way to save for that next vacation or to just accumulate a rainy day fund.

Harvey D. Aaron, J.D., CPA/PFS, CFP®
VP and Director of Tax Services, Tandem Financial Services

If you own your own business and have no employees, the best way to save for your retirement is through a plan you create for yourself. If you are younger and need flexibility in the amount you contribute, look into a Simplified Employee Pension (SEP) or a solo-k (one-person 401[k]). Generally, if you are satisfied with contributions of 25 percent of your compensation (maximizing your contribution of $40,000), go with the SEP. If you have a lower compensation level and would like to save more than 25 percent, look toward the solo-k. If you are older and wish to save more aggressively, a Defined Benefit plan can be quite attractive.

Mark Wilson, CFP®, APA
Vice President, Tarbox Equity, Inc.

Invest $720—end with $2,000 federally guaranteed! You may be eligible for a 50 percent tax credit for dollars you contribute to your retirement plan from 2003 through year 2006. Are you 1) over age 17, 2) not a full-time student, 3) not a dependent on another person's return? Is your Adjusted Gross Income (line 33 on your 1040) less than $50,000 Married Filing Jointly, $37,500 Head of Household or $25,000 Single? The IRS will refund the lesser of up to half the contribution of up to $2000 or 100 percent of the tax liability for the year contributed—plus a tax deduction.

Steve Wightman, CFP®
Life Advisor Specializing in Money, Lexington Financial Mgmt.

Instead of making music in your pocket with that spare change, start a pot of gold with it. Every time you break a bill and receive change back, throw that change in a jar and forget about it. Once a month, you should count it, wrap it, and make a deposit into savings. That's a different spin on a coin collection. In a year's time, this could add up to several hundred dollars.

Samuel O. Sanders, Jr., CCCC
Director of Education, CCCS of Baton Rouge

When saving for a home down-payment, maximize your rate of return on the savings vehicle by using a Roth IRA if your situation allows you to wait five years before buying the house and your adjusted gross income does not exceed the eligibility limit (currently $110,000 for single taxpayers and $160,000 for married couples filing a joint return). This could add another $2,700 to your home purchase pot if you're in the 27 percent tax bracket (or another $3,000 if you're in the 30 percent bracket!)

Barbara J. Raasch, CFA®, CPA/PFS, ChFC
Partner-in-charge of Wealth Management Solutions, E&Y, LLC

COLLEGE SAVINGS

Of course your kids are going to college. And you don't even want to hear how much it is going to cost! It's depressing, frustrating, and scary to think that they might get into a great school and then you have to mortgage the house to be able to afford it. Obviously, the earlier you start, the better chance you have of keeping up with the rising costs. It's an area that can cause tremendous anxiety but these tips should relieve a great deal of it.

♦ ♦ ♦

When evaluating the many options available for college savings plans (Section 529), look to contribute first to your own state's plan—up to the amount of the state tax deduction, if available. Then, choose a plan with low expenses (less than 1 percent annually) and a diversified portfolio mix. Remember, in those final years before college, a large portion of the account will likely be in fixed income. Plans with low expenses will allow your savings to compound faster, easing the burden of that first tuition bill.

Timothy P. Thaney, CPA/PFS
Principal, DeJoy, Knauf & Blood, LLP

You have so many things to save for, but especially college for your children and retirement for you. What if you cannot afford to save for both? Maximize the dollars you put into a tax-deferred retirement plan for you first. Come college time, you can take money from your retirement plan for qualified higher-education expenses—tuition, books, fees, and supplies—without penalty. In addition, since the assets are not in the child's name, they will not lessen the opportunity for financial aid.

Peg Downey, M.A., CFP®
Partner, Money Plans

In an effort to protect your child's college savings, you may have considered gifts to a trust. Then you discovered that trusts are heavily taxed. Look into having a trust invest in a Section 529 College Savings Plan. The assets are protected from creditors by the trust and they grow tax-deferred or tax-free. Have competent legal counsel to ensure that this action would not conflict with any provisions of your trust.

Frank B. Arnold, CPA/PFS
Vice President, Panfeld, Edelman & Arnold

Opt for automatic deductions out of your paycheck for retirement or 529 Plan accounts to combat your common emotional tendencies, potential adversaries to your achieving long-term goals. Our natural tendency is to be optimistic and only buy when the stock market is doing well. We are fearful and avoid the stock market when it is down. We sometimes overreact and buy or sell impulsively. Or we waffle and avoid any decision about investing. We spend today rather than plan for tomorrow. Automatic deductions are our best investment friend.

Deborah O. Levine, M.B.A, M.S.T., CPA/PFS, CFP®
Financial Planner, AFP Group

IN MONEY WORDS

Save for a rainy day … Minimum three months of after-tax contingency savings

---

Did you know money in Section 529 Plans can now be taken out tax-free? Under previous tax law, and depending on the state involved, you could take distributions from Section 529 Plans and not pay state income tax on the accumulated earnings, but you still had to pay federal income tax. Now, distributions made for qualified education expenses are free from federal tax, too!

Paul D. Lyons, CPA/PFS, CFP®
Manager, KPMG Personal Financial Planning

As you look for ways to save for your child's college education, consider establishing a 529 Plan for your youngster. They come in two flavors: Pre-Paid Tuition or Savings Plan. The most flexible is the Savings Plan, and it affords its investors a variety of professionally managed investment strategies, potential state income tax benefits, funding limits in excess of $150,000, and accelerated estate and gift tax advantages. They are great for accelerating gifts from grandparents. For more information and links to each state plan, visit www.collegesavings.org.

Jonathan S. Dinkins, CPA/PFS, CIMA, CMFC®
Senior Consultant, Glass Jacobson Investment Advisors, LLC

FastWeb (www.fastweb.com). This is a scholarship search site.

Pay children over age 6 for household chores or through your family business up to the annual limit of IRA contributions, $3,000 till 2004, $4000 in 2005–2007, and $5,000 thereafter. With new kid IRA accounts, contribute the lesser of the limit or 100 percent of earned income to the Kiddie-tax limit ($1500 in 2002) in a Roth and the rest in a deductible IRA until they reach age 14, then 100 percent in a Roth thereafter. After 16 years, income tax deductions may hit $80,000; your net college savings cost may be as low as $40,000. With an average 7.9 percent untaxed interest rate, your child may end up with $160,000—an ivy legacy for your kids and theirs.

Steve Wightman, CFP®
Life Advisor Specializing in Money, Lexington Financial Mgmt.

College Savings Plans Network (www.collegesavings.org). Learn about 529 plans and how to save for college expenses.

When your child receives an acceptance letter from the college of their choice, don't accept it! Look in the top right corner. It says *initial*, not *final* offer! This means that the college is open to negotiate financial terms with you. They understand that they cannot know your entire situation from financial aid documents. Also, colleges know all too well what kind of endowments they have and how much they are willing to contribute. Parents who refuse to accept the initial letter and instead meet with college staff often see their child's education expenses cut by

50 percent. The more expensive colleges offer the steepest reductions because they often have the largest endowments.

Steve Wightman, CFP®
Life Advisor Specializing in Money, Lexington Financial Mgmt.

Don't fall into the trap of saving college education funds in your child's name to save on taxes. The meager tax savings would be more than wiped out by the loss of college financial aid, if your child qualifies for it. Remember, even children from families with incomes of $100,000 can qualify for financial aid at the expensive colleges. For every $10,000 you put in your child's name in a non-IRA account, you could be foregoing up to $7500 of financial aid, depending on your income and assets.

Raj Pillai, Ph.D., CFP®
NAPFA-Registered Advisor, Financial Fitness Network of Solon

So what are you waiting for? So many simple strategies and great reasons to save—the only decision is when. How about now? Make it fun. Attach great expectations to the security and freedom you will achieve by establishing a solid savings strategy. If you aren't yet convinced to increase your savings rate, reread these tips until you find one that gets you going.

11

KIDS AND MONEY

*What maintains one vice, would bring
up two children.*

Benjamin Franklin (Poor Richard's Almanack)

Terms from the Top

beneficiary   Person to whom an inheritance passes as the result of being named in a will; or a recipient of the proceeds of a life insurance policy; or one to whom the amount of an annuity is payable; or a party for whose benefit a trust exists.

Coverdell Education Savings account   A tax-advantaged investment tool created for the purpose of paying for the future cost of a child's qualified education expenses. This includes elementary, secondary, and post-secondary education. The maximum annual contribution is $2,000 (AGI limits apply) per child, and earnings on contributions grow tax-free as long as distributions are used for eligible expenses. Any unused funds can be rolled over to another family member provided they are under age 30.

financial literacy   A level of competency regarding information and decision-making surrounding personal finance issues that leads to reasonable expectations of financial stability.

financial planning   Process of preparing a program to meet financial needs and objectives.

intra-family loan   Debt instrument issued between members of a family for business, real estate, or other purposes, backed with an agreement documenting the terms of the loan.

savings bond   U.S. government bond issued in face value denominations ranging from $50 to $10,000. From 1941 to 1979, the government issued Series E Bonds. Starting in 1980, Series EE and HH bonds were issued. Series EE bonds, issued at a discount of half their face value, range from $50 to $10,000. Series HH bonds, interest-bearing, range from $500 to $10,000. The interest from savings bonds is exempt from state and local taxes, and no federal tax is due on EE bonds until redemption.

Source: reprinted by permission of Jordan Goodman, Dictionary of Finance and Investment Terms *(Barron's, 5th Edition)*

Think back, way back. What is your earliest memory of money? What messages did you receive about how to manage it? Was it a big secret or a big problem in your family? Kids are always learning about money, sometimes by listening, sometimes by watching, and sometimes by earning and spending their own.

Supporting kids, educating kids, saving for kids, and getting kids out of the house on their own are all major undertakings. This area of personal finance, like many others, has become complicated in recent years. The rising cost of college and the changing tax laws are only two of the big reasons to learn more about your options.

All tips in this chapter are intended for informational purposes only. Should you find one potentially helpful to your situation, you should consult with your legal, tax, or investment professional familiar with your individual situation to determine its suitability prior to taking any action or investing any money.

TEACHING CHILDREN ABOUT MONEY

Without knowing it, you may be repeating with your children the same lessons that were shown to you as a child. It is important for you to become very deliberate about how you send messages to your children about money. It isn't hard and shouldn't take any more of your time than they already do—which is all of it! Have some fun with it and watch them grow up into financially functional adults.

♦ ♦ ♦

The best way to teach children about financial decision-making is by sharing with them how both good and bad decisions are made. Vocalize your thought process so that your child can hear. For example, "I like this very much, but I do not need it and so I won't buy it." Or "I will call three companies to compare quotes on auto insurance." Or "I invested in this company without looking at its balance sheet and without understanding how the company made money. I made a mistake and I learned from it."

Deborah O. Levine, M.B.A, M.S.T., CPA/PFS, CFP®
Financial Planner, AFP Group

A recent study in California showed that only 12 percent of high school graduates learned about personal financial literacy in school. That means it's up to the parents of all those other children to provide these essential lessons. To do your part, involve your children in the family budgeting and bill-paying process every month. Explain where the money comes from and what each bill is for as you pay it. It takes no additional time, and helps prepare the children for adult financial responsibilities. They may not appear interested now, but the lessons will sink in for years to come. And what a bonus if your kids demand less of you now that they understand how the family finances work!

Jeff Michael, Director of Education
Springboard Non-Profit Consumer Credit Counseling

Jump$tart Coalition (www.jumpstart.org). Find great ideas and educational resources for financial literacy.

Is your child financially literate? If so, she is in the minority. Help your child attain fiscal fitness by taking them to the Jump$tart Coalition for Personal Financial Literacy website (www.jumpstartcoalition.org). Introduce her to the recently released "12 financial principles that every young person should know." The average high school senior in the United States can't pass a simple quiz dealing with personal financial concepts. In fact, over the past six years quiz scores have been consistently declining. Give your child the gift of becoming an informed consumer, investor, taxpayer, and borrower.

Mitchell Freedman, CPA/PFS
Advisor to the Stars

As soon as your youngster can identify and understand numbers, take them to the local toy store with that $5 bill from Grandma. Explain how the price tags work and turn them loose to pick anything they want that they can afford with $5. (You may have to pony up the tax.) This building block of fiscal responsibility works best if there is a sense of scarcity!

> *Lesley J. Brey, M.B.A., CFA®, CFP®*
> *President, L.J. Brey, Inc.*

Kids think stock trades happen in Kmart and Wal-Mart. Tell them about Wall Street and show them the *Wall Street Journal*. Better yet, take them on a trip to New York City they will never forget!

> *Cary Carbonaro, M.B.A., CFP®*
> *President, Family Financial*

MIND OVER MONEY

Make sure you teach your kids about money by example. What they learn by observing you will stick with them a lot longer than what you preach!

> *Raj Pillai, Ph.D., CFP®*
> *NAPFA-Registered Advisor, Financial Fitness Network of Solon*

Ten Commandments of Personal Finance … To Teach Young People

1. Manage your expenses so they don't exceed your income.
2. Spend money thinking of your future as well as your present.
3. Begin saving early to take advantage of compound interest.
4. Avoid collecting credit cards and using them for borrowing.
5. Always honor your debts and other financial obligations.
6. Project your income and expenses for the next 12 months and track variances.
7. Focus on the relationship between the risk and projected return of investments.

8. Maintain organized records for tax and general financial planning purposes.
9. Have a plan and a purpose for your investing.
10. Obtain a financial education to be in a position to make good decisions.

Paul S. Richard, RFC
Executive Director, Institute of Consumer Financial Education

---

In Money Words

If I had only known ... The value of financial planning

To raise fiscally fit kids, think in terms of A-B-C, for Allowance, Balance, and Charity. Provide an *allowance* with no strings attached, even if it's small. This gives your children valuable practice in financial decision-making. *Balance* their experience by suggesting ways they can earn more money and always save a portion of their income. Show them how it is being saved and discuss it. Finally, model *charity*. Decide together ways their time and money can be contributed to a good cause. Guide, share, and discuss financial and societal responsibilities throughout your kids' childhood for happy fiscal fitness results!

Susan Zimmerman, M.A., LMFT, ChFC, CLU
Author of The Power in Your Money Personality

ALLOWANCES AND OTHER STRATEGIES

Most parents have tried an allowance system. Some work well and some don't. Usually, it's the parents who have trouble keeping up with complicated systems. So, our experts are ready with advice on how to keep it simple and still effective to teach the basic notions that will live on to help your child grow up financially literate.

◆ ◆ ◆

Teach your children about money when they're young. When you give them an allowance, tell them they can spend 25 percent; give you 25 percent for overhead (clothes, food, etc.) or use that portion for their clothes; 25 percent to savings; and 25 percent to church or charity. They'll learn from the beginning that income and outgo must be balanced.

Judi Martindale, CFP®, EA
Author of No More Baglady Fears

MIND OVER MONEY

If you have ever wondered where your financial management style came from, you can learn a great deal by asking yourself some questions about your childhood. You may discover some unconscious beliefs have guided some of your choices. How did your parents handle money and conflict? Do any memories stand out? Your most vivid memories may cause distorted conclusions that misguide you. Next time you feel a strong emotion about a financial matter, look to see if you have an all-or-nothing belief about it that is limiting your options. Then instead of making that black-or-white choice, choose something gray!

Susan Zimmerman, M.A., LMFT, ChFC, CLU
Author of The Power in Your Money Personality

If you are a sole proprietor or small business owner, don't forget to take advantage of a great tax-saving opportunity by hiring your kids. You can put them on your payroll to clean your office, help with computer work, or even model for the company website. The wages they earn are tax-deductible against your business income and can be invested into a Roth IRA or a Section 529 college savings plan on behalf of your children. Why not have the government pay for 20 to 35 percent of your child's education or retirement?

Gregory C. Fenton, CFP®
Principal, Cambridge Cape Cod Advisors

Encourage your child to apply for a paying job with a local employer by age 16. Help them accumulate their earnings by opening a no-cost checking account at a local credit union or bank to help with college costs. Teach them to prepare their own tax return to claim a refund for taxes withheld. If they can afford to put their money away indefinitely, explore opening an IRA with them. Saving $2,000 per year earning 10 percent from ages 19 to 26 will give them back more than $1 million by age 65.

Bonnie A. Hughes, CFP®
President, A&H Financial Planning and Education, Inc.

Since it is hard to teach an old dog new tricks, involving your children in a savings strategy when they are young is vital. As soon as they start working, sit down with them and show that with just a part-time job at $6.00 an hour, four hours a day, three days a week, they could make $3,456.00. If they save half, $1,728.00, they could open a savings account or a mutual fund. Help them develop a budget with the remaining 50 percent. With $72.00 a week to spend, they can purchase their CDs, games, clothes, etc. Developing good money habits while your children are young will positively influence their financial well-being.

Angie Hollerich CEP, CCA
Author of Grab the Brass Ring of Financial Security

Start an allowance plan for your kids in five easy steps:

1. Pay your child according to your paydays.
2. Encourage saving.
3. Play devil's advocate and point out when they attempt to over-spend.
4. Don't give in by making loans or advances—this teaches money discipline.
5. Encourage them to save a portion and allow them to spend the rest on things they ask you to buy like video games and movie rentals, candy, or ridiculously expensive shoes.

This will help you avoid having to say no, reduces guilt, and eliminates misspending when you spend just to make the kids happy. It also helps to control the gimmes.

Samuel O. Sanders, Jr., CCCC
Director of Education, CCCS of Baton Rouge

Teach your kids the value of compound interest. Pay them a small allowance for weekly chores and make them set aside a portion of it for investment in a 529 Plan or Coverdell Education Savings account. Keep track of what they've invested over the years and periodically teach them how to compare what they've invested to the current value. They'll learn to love saving and have a nice nest egg for education or a home purchase. At the end of 13 years, just $5 a week at a 9 percent rate of return would grow to $6,410, a $3,030 gain.

Patrick T. Hanratty, M.B.A., CPA/PFS, CFP®
Managing Director, Capital Advisors, Ltd.

IN MONEY WORDS

What's in it for me? … Understanding investment risk and reward

---

Studies show that taking your kids to the grocery store can cause you to spend more. Here's a spin on that concept: Have your children plan the meals for the week in advance. Let them prepare the shopping list before you head out to the store. Allow them to shop while you supervise and you can teach them about money management, sales shopping, and wants versus needs. What a great life lesson!

Samuel O. Sanders, Jr., CCCC
Director of Education, CCCS of Baton Rouge

Consumer Jungle (www.consumerjungle.org). This is a kid-friendly site that promotes consumer literacy.

If your children will someday be required to be good stewards of wealth, you can continue their education (and assess their responsibility) by turning over some portion of their college savings accounts to them. Communicate expectations, such as, "This should last for two years and cover all college expenses, recreation, and incidentals" and watch how they behave. It's better that they risk mishandling $10,000 to $50,000 now than ruin a strong family legacy years later.

Lesley J. Brey, M.B.A., CFA®, CFP®
President, L.J. Brey, Inc.

When giving children an allowance or income, give the money in denominations that encourage saving. For example, if the amount is $5, give out five $1 bills and encourage at least one be set aside in savings. Just saving $5 a week at 6 percent interest compounded quarterly will total about $266 in a year, $1,503 in 5 years, and $3,527 in 10 years.

Paul S. Richard, RFC
Executive Director, Institute of Consumer Financial Education

As you attempt to instill an appropriate work ethic in your children, consider providing them with an "employment bonus" for outside employment. You may consider a higher bonus for less desirable but more relevant work. For instance, bookkeeping or acting as a teacher's aide may be less desirable to a child looking for part-time employment than higher-paying, blue-collar positions. You can steer them toward more desirable areas with a financial incentive that covers the short-term pay differential.

Frank L. Washelesky, J.D., CPA/PFS, CVA
Director, Ostrow Resin Berk & Abrams, Ltd.

Help your kids grow financial wings that will make them financially independent adults. At least by the teenage years, sit down with each of your children and create a budget. It should include his or her clothes, shoes, toiletries/makeup, haircuts, movies, video rentals, snacks, sports equipment, etc. Calculate the average amount he or she needs per month and transfer it into his or her bank account. Everybody wins! The kids learn how bank accounts work, how to balance an account, how to plan for large expenditures, and how to shop for value. No additional money is required from the family budget over the planned deposits to their accounts. Watch the squabbles over their impulsive needs disappear.

Marsha G. LePhew, CPA/PFS, CFP®, ChFC
President, LePhew Financial Services, Inc.

Your children do not need a new car just because they have a driver's license. Let them work up to one. If they start with a new BMW, where do they go from there? And what has that taught them?

H. Lindsey Torbett, CPA/PFS, CFP®
President, Wealth Development Group

For your business or household, you should consider employing high school students part-time, particularly in areas of technology. Many schools in cities and towns across the country have a referral agency, which can put your message out to any number of students, many of whom are more qualified and industrious than one can ever imagine. In San Francisco, there is Enterprise for High School Students, which we have used on several occasions and have never been disappointed. In addition to getting quality work done at minimum price, you'll have the opportunity to meet some quality young people, many of whom will be friends for life.

Henrietta Humphreys, M.B.A., CFP®
Financial Advisor, The Henrietta Humphreys Group

As a business owner, there is a great way to teach your kids the value of work, saving, and the compounding of interest. As soon as they are physically able, have them clean the office. About seven hours a week at minimum wage would earn your children $2,000 dollars a year to deposit in an IRA. If they contributed this amount from age 14 through age 17 (4 years only) and the investment averages a 10 percent rate of return, the account would have approximately $900,496.00 when they reached age 65. Oh, let's not forget that if the wages are in fact earned, their contribution could be gifted from you.

Parke Stratford Teal, CPA/PFS
Principal, Dreggors, Rigsby, and Teal, P.A.

I have a "tween" who became a little "mouthy," so we developed a jar that was called Mouth Money. Every time our son used his mouth inappropriately, he had to put a quarter of his allowance in the glass jar. After he began seeing how quickly the jar was filling and how much of his money was in the jar, he began correcting his own behavior! He did not like seeing me buy something for myself with his money. Every once in a while I set the jar back out, when he forgets! It reinforces the old saying: Your mouth will get you into trouble!

Kathy Adams-Smith, M.P.A.
Director, Credit Counseling Services

FINANCIAL TOOLS

This is the fun part of financial management. Helping your kids to build a financial foundation for their future is so rewarding. The more you can bring them into the decision-making process, the better. They love learning about the stock market, taxes, and insurance. It is surprisingly exciting to them. Pick a tip and read it to your kids!

♦ ♦ ♦

One simple way to get your kids or grandkids started on a path of saving for a lifetime is to help them set up an IRA as soon as they start working. Then give them a gift of enough to begin funding the account right away with the lesser of their earned income or $3,000. Just $2,000 each year beginning at age 16 would grow to $1,000,000 when they turn 65 if they earn a 7.6 percent rate of return. Involve your child in the investment decision-making as part of the learning process.

Clark M. Blackman II, CPA/PFS, CFP®, ChFC, CFA®, CIMA, AAMS®
Managing Director, Post Oak Capital

Regardless of the type of work they choose, your children will likely have a difficult time saving money in the early years. As your children are getting established or working part-time while attending school, consider funding a Roth IRA contribution for them. For instance, contributions of $2,000 per year for five years during high school and college could easily grow to well over $300,000 when your child reaches age 65. The ability to grow the account tax-free over many decades will provide a wonderful nest egg for their future. Also, your children will learn the value of saving by watching the fund grow.

Frank L. Washelesky, J.D., CPA/PFS, CVA
Director, Ostrow Resin Berk & Abrams, Ltd.

If you own a closely held business, pay your child a salary equal to the Roth IRA limit (currently $2,000), which you then contribute to a Roth IRA in the child's name. Starting this strategy by the age of 14 (or earlier, depending upon your circumstances) will accomplish two things:

- You are moving income from your tax bracket to a zero percent tax bracket for your child.
- You are setting up a Roth IRA for your child at a very young age, which will allow the power of compounding over time.

If contributions are made for nine years (until age 22) totaling $18,000 at 8 percent, there will be over $316,000 when the child is 65 or over $632,000 at age 74.

Robert S. Seltzer, CPA/PFS
Financial Advisor

Tips for Kids (www.tipsforkids.com). An educational sight that puts kids right in the middle of real life money situations.

Would you give your kids money if you knew they couldn't spend it? If you want to give money to your child or grandchild for education or that rainy day, consider using the UGMA. This stands for Uniform Gifts to Minors Act. Money or stock that is put under the UGMA is taxed at the child's rate but the investment is controlled by the custodian and cannot be spent by the child until the child reaches the age of majority.

Kent E. Anthony, CIC, CFP®, CMFC®
President, First Group Insurance

The summer before seventh grade, get your child a checking account. Seed it with a small amount and have them write a few test checks over the summer. Reconcile it with them each month until school starts. Give them a lump sum to cover all clothing, gifts, and recreation spending for the next 12 months. Work with them to estimate a reasonable amount but don't make it large enough to eliminate tough choices! If they run out of money they need to make due or work—don't bail them out now or you risk doing it for life. Repeat this process annually until they are off to college or on their own.

Lesley J. Brey, M.B.A., CFA®, CFP®
President, L.J. Brey, Inc.

Give your child or grandchild the gift of stock instead of stuff. Put it in their name with you as the custodian. Buy kid-friendly companies that they will know. For example, Pixar sends a movie poster or toy with their annual report. The toy will be out of date in a few weeks but your gift of stock could last forever along with the lessons they will learn!

Cary Carbonaro, M.B.A., CFP®
President, Family Financial

Escape From Knab (www.escapefromknab.com). Kids take an adventure to the planet Knab while learning life skills.

As soon as your child is born, make sure you execute a valid will that designates a guardian to be responsible for your child's day-to-day well-being following your death. This is important even if you are married to the child's parent because both you and your spouse could die in a common disaster. Failure to designate a guardian for your child in a validly executed will results in a judge deciding who will take care of your child. The judge may select someone you would not. It will probably cost $1,000 to $2000 to have an experienced attorney prepare your wills, but it is worth it to make sure your child is raised by the person you believe is most appropriate.

Barbara J. Raasch, CFA®, CPA/PFS, ChFC
Partner-in-charge of Wealth Management Solutions, Ernst & Young

Money is certainly one area where we hope our children become more skilled than we are. We want the best for them, and we know that it is only possible with good financial habits and attitudes. Learn with your children and grow together. It is a delight to watch them come up with new ideas and strategies on their own—that might never have occurred to you before! Just for fun, have them pick a chapter in this book and see how many of the concepts they have heard of—you may be surprised!

12

HOUSING AND MORTGAGES

When you have bought one fine thing,
you must buy ten more. 'Tis easier to
suppress the first desire, than to satisfy
all that follow it.

Benjamin Franklin (Poor Richard's Almanack)

Terms from the Top

equity Difference between the amount a property could be sold for and the claims held against it.

mortgage Debt instrument by which the borrower (mortgagor) gives the lender (mortgagee) a lien on property as security for the repayment of a loan. The borrower has use of the property, and the lien is removed when the obligation is fully paid.

permits Permission issued by local governments to build, develop, or change real property.

Private Mortgage Insurance (PMI) Type of insurance available from lenders that insures against loss resulting from a default on a mortgage loan and can substitute for down payment money. Normally required of those borrowers with less than 20 percent equity.

reverse mortgage Arrangement whereby a homeowner borrows against home equity and receives regular payments (tax-free) from the lender until the accumulated principal and interest reach the credit limit of equity; at that time, the lender either gets repayment in a lump sum or takes the house. Reverse mortgages are available privately and through the Federal Housing Administration (FHA).

title insurance Insurance policies, written by title insurance companies, protecting lenders against challenges to the title claim to a property. Title insurance protects a policyholder against loss from some occurrence that already has happened, such as a forged deed somewhere in the chain of title. Title insurance premiums are usually paid in one lump sum at the time the policy is issued, and the policy remains in force until the property is sold.

Source: reprinted by permission of Jordan Goodman, Dictionary of Finance and Investment Terms *(Barron's, 5th Edition)*

For most, the purchase of a home is a time-consuming, anxiety-producing, complicated, and yet ultimately rewarding experience. Some dwell on every detail and every decision to the point where it feels like a second full-time job. Others delegate the details to spouses or professionals and just look for the special features that they value in a home.

Homeownership changes your status in our economy. Financial strategies, access to secured debt, tax deductions, and the responsibility of maintenance and property taxes all add complexity to a family's financial life. Picking out the house is only the first step in a lifelong set of decisions that frame your financial security.

All tips in this chapter are intended for informational purposes only. Should you find one potentially helpful to your situation, you should consult with your legal, tax, or investment professional familiar with your individual situation to determine its suitability prior to taking any action or investing any money.

PURCHASING A HOME

Some of the best advice ever offered on purchasing a home is to buy the third home you fall in love with. We often let our emotions take over in this decision. But so much of the decision is based in financial reality that it is fun to see what our experts have offered you from their perspective. Homeownership is a key component to a solid financial plan. When to own, what to own, and when to sell are not easy decisions.

◆ ◆ ◆

Have the right size house. If you're like most Americans, your home is the most significant investment you will ever make. Buy a home valued at 2 or $2^1/_2$ times your annual income, with a mortgage of at least 50 percent or more of its value. If the value of the home reaches 100 to 125 percent of your income, sell it and trade up to a new home using the same formulas. Someday, when you sell, your gain on your investment in your home will be tax-free up to $250,000 for a single individual and $500,000 for a married couple.

Robert B. Walsh, CPA/PFS CFP®
President, Lighthouse Financial Advisors, Inc.

After you have a family and can afford to replace the starter home with your family home, search for a home in a good school district that you can reasonably expect to live in until your children graduate from high school. It is very expensive to move, so take your time and do a lot of research before selecting your family home. Don't just look at average SAT scores and colleges that last year's graduation class got accepted into; also look for trends that can dictate the best school districts in the future (i.e., new principal, school board, initiatives, etc.).

Barbara J. Raasch, CFA®, CPA/PFS, ChFC
Partner-in-charge of Wealth Management Solutions, E&Y, LLC

MIND OVER MONEY

I'm especially tempted to buy things I shouldn't when that little voice pops into my head and whispers, "You work hard and you deserve to have everything you want. Why should you have to do without?" In these moments of weakness, I just remind myself that things like peace of mind, being debt-free, and having money in the bank are really the good things in life. Too many of us live beyond our means in an attempt to impress other people. We need to realize that the things we possess don't make us better people or more successful in life.

Jennifer Delcamp, CCCC
Director of Operations, CCCS of Oklahoma

If you purchase a home jointly with someone who is not legally your spouse, it is important for both tax and financial reasons to have your ownership and obligation desires properly reflected in the asset title and mortgage loan documents. The percentage ownership should reflect your agreement concerning costs. For example, if each of you owns 50 percent of the property, both of you should be included on the mortgage. In order to maximize your tax deductions, each of you should pay 50 percent of the loan interest payments and real estate taxes.

Barbara J. Raasch, CFA®, CPA/PFS, ChFC
Partner-in-charge of Wealth Management Solutions, E&Y, LLC

When deciding to purchase a home, make sure you verify that all permits for past work had been acquired by the previous owners. You might be surprised at what can happen if there is a complaint after you have purchased the home. If all the necessary permits were not obtained, it is possible that the town officials may require you to remove the improvements. This would depend on the laws of your municipality. Before making a purchase, go to Town Hall to verify that all improvements have permits. If permits are missing, investigate the necessary steps to rectify the situation.

Ann D. Jevne, CPA/PFS, CFP®
Partner, Schwartz & Hofflich LLP, CPA

IN MONEY WORDS

Dreams really do come true ... Plan ahead for home ownership, college education, vacation

---

MORTGAGES

When you buy a home, you make a second purchase that is actually more expensive than the real estate. You buy the money in the form of a mortgage. Since it is a rare real estate transaction that is conducted in cash, mortgage decisions have been very intertwined with real estate decisions. It is important to see them as independent areas that require special attention. Here are a few tips on how to get the most from the mortgage options available to you.

◆ ◆ ◆

Ignore outdated "rules" about refinancing and consider getting a low-cost home equity loan instead of a new mortgage. Interest on home equity loans of under $100,000 is tax-deductible. When fees and points are low, interest rate reductions of 1 percent or less can pay. Simply compare the monthly after-tax savings from a refinanced loan (old payment minus new payment) with the time you expect to live in your house to determine if refinancing is cost-effective. I've refinanced twice with home equity loans in the last five years, once for a fee of $35 and the second time for $50. Both loans paid for themselves in about a week.

Barbara O'Neill, Ph.D., CFP®, AFC, CHC
Author of Saving on a Shoestring

Refinancing? You already paid for title insurance once, so don't pay for all new title insurance. Save yourself a hefty fee by requesting a reissue of the original title insurance instead. Your settlement officer can handle this for you.

Peg Downey, M.A., CFP®
Partner, Money Plans

Don't pay more for title insurance than you need to! Title insurance premiums are likely the most expensive component of your closing costs and pay as much as 80 percent commission back to the selling agent. Ask for good faith estimates from several approved title companies. Then compare their cost estimates for closing your loan. For example, on a $300,000 mortgage loan, the title search will range from $400 to $500 and the title premium will approximate $1,500. Try negotiating your fees beforehand and save those hard earned bucks!

Jonathan S. Dinkins, CPA/PFS, CIMA, CMFC®
Senior Consultant, Glass Jacobson Investment Advisors, LLC

It is almost always a good deal to pay points up front in exchange for a lower interest rate, if you plan to keep the property for more than five years. To estimate the trade-off, ask your lender to calculate your monthly payments for each loan option. If you can "pay off" the additional points with four to five years of lower payments (the difference in mortgage payments), and your mortgage is 15 years or more, you are probably better off paying the extra points.

Lesley J. Brey, M.B.A., CFA®, CFP®
President, L.J. Brey, Inc.

Those letters from your mortgage company about all the interest you can save by making extra payments tell only half the story. First, the interest you will save is partially offset by increased income taxes on the federal and many state returns. Second, the interest savings may be less than what you could earn if you invested the extra payments elsewhere. Finally, extra principal payments increase your investment in your home, which reduces return on equity. Your house appreciates at the same rate no matter how much you have invested in it. If you have a $100,000 home, 3 percent appreciation on 20 percent equity is 15 percent return on equity. The same 3 percent appreciation on a home with 60 percent equity is 5 percent return on equity.

Bob Schumann, M.A., M.Div., M.B.A., CFP®, ChFC, EA
President, Cambridge Financial Advisors, LLC

When refinancing a home, be aware that not all points are created equal. There are a few rules to follow when considering the deductibility of your mortgage points. To be deductible, your principal or secondary residence must secure the new mortgage. Additionally, points are deductible in the tax year paid only if they are for improvements to your primary residence. Points paid to refinance a mortgage or not used for home improvements are amortized over the life of the loan. Knowing these rules before you meet with your lender will help you maximize your deductions.

Patrick T. Hanratty, M.B.A., CPA/PFS, CFP®
Managing Director, Capital Advisors, Ltd.

If you don't have 20 percent for a home down payment, talk with lenders about using a piggyback loan to avoid paying Private Mortgage Insurance (PMI). If you only have 10 percent down you can get two mortgages, one at 80 percent and one at 10 percent, instead of getting a single mortgage for the remaining 90 percent. By doing this, you avoid paying PMI. Though the 10 percent mortgage is often at a higher interest rate, the interest paid is tax-deductible, making your after-tax payments typically cheaper than the PMI premium.

Don A. Gomez, CFP®
President, Momentum Financial Advisors

You may be considering utilizing one of the mortgage programs where bi-weekly payments are drafted from your checking account. Make sure the program is actually applying these payments to your loan every two weeks by reading the contract and asking for an annual transaction statement. Many of these plans accumulate your money over a year and then make one extra payment. Why not, instead, put $1/12$ of your monthly payment into an interest-bearing account each month? Then you can make one extra mortgage payment a year, earn interest income, and pay no fees.

Frank B. Arnold, CPA/PFS
Vice President, Panfeld, Edelman & Arnold

If you put less than 20 percent down on your home when you purchased it, make sure you recognize when you have 80 percent equity. This can happen two ways:

- The value of your home has appreciated through improvements or market conditions.
- You have paid down the principal of the loan through your payments.

Then, talk to your lender about being able to stop paying for Private Mortgage Insurance (PMI). If they don't let you at that time, you can consider refinancing with another lender to avoid this unnecessary expense. You should save money by doing this depending on the amount you borrowed.

Don A. Gomez, CFP®
President, Momentum Financial Advisors

Your home is your castle, and most likely you want to stay in it as long as possible no matter your health or wealth. A little-known resource is a reverse mortgage. It works like this: Instead of paying a bank every month to live in your house, you can actually have a bank send you a check every month for as long as you live in your house. These once questionable deals are now a home saver for many seniors! For example, a 75-year-old living in Montgomery County, MD, in a $150,000 home could receive either an $87,000 lump sum or $595 a month for life. You are required to participate in a free counseling session (which can even be done by phone) before you apply. Call the Department of Housing and Urban Development (HUD) for a counseling agency near you.

Peg Downey, M.A., CFP®
Partner, Money Plans

FINANCIAL STRATEGIES

Being a homeowner allows you some unique opportunities to build your wealth and financial security. These opportunities can be confusing, however. Let our experts help you think about some of the decisions you may be facing.

♦ ♦ ♦

Owning a home is the American dream, but is it right for you? It usually takes two to three years to break even on the purchase of a house, so if you move around a lot or your job isn't secure, you're probably better off renting. If the purchase of a home would leave you without extra cash, you're smart to rent while you build up an emergency stash equivalent to about three months of living expenses. While you're renting, you can enjoy some of the benefits of owning real estate by investing a small portion (10 percent or so) of your retirement funds in a real estate mutual fund (REIT).

Jill Gianola, M.S., M.B.A., CFP®
Owner, Gianola Financial Planning

If you are like many successful retirees, you might like to purchase a second home to enjoy during retirement. If you accumulate substantial wealth in your retirement plan and do not need the income to meet your lifestyle expenses, consider this. One effective planning strategy is to use a mortgage to purchase the second home and use your income from the retirement funds to make the payments. A significant portion of the taxable income from your tax-deferred savings may be offset by the deductible mortgage interest.

Gregory M. Railsback, CPA/PFS, CFP®
Senior Plan Design Consultant, Allmerica Financial

Pay off the mortgage or refinance—the ongoing dilemma. Assuming some level of ongoing inflation, if your money is out of the house and invested in anything that has the ability to match inflation, you can have your cake and eat it, too. The house should increase in value, your loan proceeds should at least break even with inflation, and your net after 10 to 20 years may be as much as double the non-loan choice. The other emotional yet strong solution is to pay off the house and take the mortgage payment money and save it. This is the right choice for those who might be tempted to spend loan proceeds, those who can't resist high-risk investments, or those who simply want no debt so they can sleep better.

Joe Harper, CFP®
President, Harper Associates, Inc.

IN MONEY WORDS

Don't put all your eggs in one basket ... Diversify

One practical method of reducing mortgage debt is to increase your payments by the same percentage your salary increases each year. The small payment increase each year will not be significant in any one year and will keep the ratio of mortgage payment to income constant over time. Assuming an annual 5 percent increase, you would be able to pay off a $100,000, 30-year mortgage with a 7 percent interest rate in less than 15 years!

Gregory M. Railsback, CPA/PFS, CFP®
Senior Plan Design Consultant, Allmerica Financial

If you're behind on your mortgage payments, there may be many options to help you avoid foreclosure. In some situations, missed payments can be added back into the loan balance or even deferred. Contact the Department of Housing and Urban Development (HUD) at 1-888-466-3487 to find a HUD-approved counseling agency near you or visit www.hud.gov for help weighing your options and saving your home.

Jennifer Delcamp, CCCC
Director of Operations, CCCS of Oklahoma

If you're behind on your mortgage payments, beware of companies that promise to help you save your home ... for a hefty fee. They can't do anything for you that you can't negotiate yourself. If you do need guidance, contact a HUD-approved housing counselor by calling 1-888-466-3487 or visit www.hud.gov to locate free or low-cost assistance.

Jennifer Delcamp, CCCC
Director of Operations, CCCS of Oklahoma

One of the common mistakes in divorce settlements is keeping the house and trading away retirement assets. This usually happens because the wife wants the security of living in the house and the husband wants his retirement or pension. If the wife has adequate income from her own salary, pension, or Social Security, keeping the house could be a good option. But too often the wife keeps the house and ends up with no retirement assets and little or no savings. This sets up a bad scenario of getting into debt trying to pay monthly expenses or for those unexpected home repairs. Before deciding on a settlement, make a sensible monthly budget to make sure keeping the house is affordable without the retirement assets from the marriage.

Joan Coullahan, M.B.A., CDP
Co-author of Financial Custody: You, Your Money, and Divorce

Tightening your budget and curbing your impulse spending can help you find the money to repay debts rather than taking out a loan against your home's equity. After all, you don't want to risk losing your home by hocking it for everyday goods that you previously financed. A good budgeting session might help you identify "nips" and "tucks" to stretch that budget further.

Samuel O. Sanders, Jr., CCCC
Director of Education, CCCS of Baton Rouge

Mind Over Money

Remember that you make your money when you buy.

H. Lindsey Torbett, CPA/PFS CFP®
President, Wealth Development Group

Make sure to create a file called "Cost Basis—home address" when you purchase your home and put the closing statement in the file for future reference. Any time you make capital additions to your home (e.g., major renovations or landscaping, as well as capital assessments such as sewer), put receipts from those projects in the file to enable you to determine your home's cost basis in the future when you sell it.

Barbara J. Raasch, CFA®, CPA/PFS, ChFC
Partner-in-charge of Wealth Management Solutions, E&Y, LLC

INSURANCE HINTS

Insuring your most valuable asset is a given. But keeping yourself protected is not always simple. There are some smart ways to use your insurance dollars.

♦♦♦

Don't overinsure for small losses with low ($250) deductibles on your homeowner's insurance policy. Select deductibles of $500 or $1,000 instead. A higher deductible could lower your premium by as much as $100 annually. If you invest this savings, you should be able to afford several small, self-insured claims during your lifetime.

Barbara O'Neill, Ph.D., CFP®, AFC, CHC
Author of Saving on a Shoestring

If you have a home-based business, beware! Homeowner's policies exclude liability coverage for business activities. The good news is that many homeowner's policies can be endorsed to provide coverage for certain types of home-based businesses. If you cannot add your home-based business to your homeowner's policy by endorsement, make sure you buy a commercial policy to protect yourself from potential financial loss.

Kent E. Anthony, CIC, CFP®, CMFC®
President, First Group Insurance

Do you keep contents used in a business around your home? Be careful! Most homeowner's policies only give you $2,500 of coverage for business equipment and inventory kept at your home. For more coverage, buy a business inland marine policy to provide coverage for your contents at any location.

Kent E. Anthony, CIC, CFP®, CMFC®
President, First Group Insurance

So many times homeowners have bit off more house than they could chew, only to become "house poor." In this rich country where we enjoy some of the safest housing, best neighborhoods, and most functional real estate system in the world, that is a shame. If you make homeownership part of your financial landscape, look for ways to make it work for you so that you can enjoy all the benefits it has to offer.

13

CONSUMER CREDIT MANAGEMENT

For industry pays debts, while despair
encreaseth them.

Benjamin Franklin (Poor Richard's Almanack)

Terms from the Top

balance transfers   The movement of funds from one debt account to another, commonly used with credit card balances to achieve better terms.

consolidation loan   Loan that combines and refinances other loans or debt. It is normally an installment loan designed to reduce the dollar amount of an individual's monthly payments.

Fair Debt Collection Practices Act   A federal law passed in 1977 that outlawed unfair collection practices by third party collectors including debtor harassment.

FICO score   Objective methodology used by credit grantors to determine how much, if any, credit to grant to an applicant. Some factors in scoring are income, assets, length of employment, length of living in one place and past record of using credit.

rule of 78's   Method of computing rebates of interest on installment loans. It used the sum-of-the-year's-digits basis in determining the interest earned by the finance company for each month of a year, assuming equal monthly payments, and gets its name from the fact that the sum of the digits 1 through 12 is 78. Thus, interest is equal to $^{12}/_{78}$ of the total annual interest in the first month, $^{11}/_{78}$ in the second month, and so on.

zero percent financing   A financing strategy used by vendors of consumer products, such as automobiles, where the finance company is paid by the vendor from proceeds of the sale and the consumer perceives no calculated interest on a purchase over time, but has in fact effectively paid interest in the form of a higher purchase price for the goods.

Source: reprinted by permission of Jordan Goodman, Dictionary of Finance and Investment Terms *(Barron's, 5th Edition)*

The consumer credit industry has exploded in the last 10 years, leaving many households carrying excess high-interest debt. Other households have been able to use the availability of low-interest credit to their advantage, while keeping their liquid assets working for them in well-placed investments. Which strategies you use regarding credit may have more impact on your overall financial security than all the investment choices you will make in your lifetime.

The availability of credit has changed the nature of our consumer choices. In essence, we can have things before we can afford them. Merchants know that we will spend more in their stores if we have a credit card in our wallet. We are different consumers with and without credit. The consequences of this excess consumption may not be felt for months or years later. It is as important to have a solid credit management plan as a good investment strategy.

All tips in this chapter are intended for informational purposes only. Should you find one potentially helpful to your situation, you should consult with your legal, tax, or investment professional familiar with your individual situation to determine its suitability prior to taking any action or investing any money.

CREDIT MANAGEMENT STRATEGIES

Certain credit strategies work well for some but are devastating to others. It is very important to look at your own attitudes and behaviors regarding credit to understand what will work for you. Financial advisors talk about risk tolerance with regard to investment choices, but it is also relevant with regard to credit choices. How much are you willing to risk by being in debt and pledging future earnings toward repayment of that debt?

◆ ◆ ◆

Be very careful if you find yourself using credit as a substitute for income. If you can't afford to pay your bills, you should work as hard as you can to find other ways to come up with what you need rather than resorting to cash advances or running up high credit card debt. Get a second job, rent a room in your house, or tap into retirement funds in extreme cases. Human beings are survivors—we'll find a way to get by in a crisis. Abusing credit is not the way; it's a recipe for financial disaster.

Jeff Michael, Director of Education
Springboard Non-Profit Consumer Credit Counseling

Point ▶

Do you pay cash for all your major purchases? Do you believe all borrowing is bad? Don't forget that there are positive uses of credit. If you find a zero percent financing deal on a car, take it! Keep your money where it is and growing. Don't liquidate your portfolio to get access to cash. You most likely will be selling at an inopportune time. You will also have a taxable event! Keep a line of credit on your house. You can get it near prime and with a low annual fee. Use www.bankratemonitor.com to find the best deal. The interest is tax-deductible and your money gets to keep growing!

Cary Carbonaro, M.B.A., CFP®
President, Family Financial

◀ Counterpoint

Zero percent deals aren't always what they seem to be. Some of these deals cost you money with hidden costs or very restrictive conditions. These rates are usually for special vehicle types, so the car of your choice might not become yours. The car salesman will do his part and get you in a car anyway if you let him. The point of these promotions is to get you on the lot.

Samuel O. Sanders, Jr., CCCC
Director of Education, CCCS of Baton Rouge

So, you have credit card debt and just want to pay it back as quickly and cheaply as possible. If you have a good payment history, you may have more power than you think. Try simply calling your creditor to request a lower interest rate. The key is to ask for a low fixed rate instead of one of those introductory rates that will expire in a few months. I know of one instance where a consumer got his interest rate reduced from 12 percent to 6 percent just by asking, saving him up to $600.00 per year on a $10,000.00 balance.

Angie Hollerich, CEP, CCA
Author of Grab the Brass Ring of Financial Security

Have you ever wondered what a debt-to-income ratio is? It is a widely used measure of financial stability that is calculated by dividing your monthly minimum debt payments (excluding mortgage or rent payments) by your monthly gross income. For example, if you have a gross monthly income of $2,000 with minimum payments of $400 on loans and credit cards, you have a debt-to-income ratio of 20 percent ($400 / $2000 = .20). Some lenders may use slightly different formulas but the overall concept is still the same: a debt-to-income ratio compares your monthly debt obligations to your income. A ratio of 36 percent or less indicates that gross income is adequate and should decrease as you grow older.

Preston Cochrane, AFC
Executive Director, AAA Fair Credit Foundation

MIND OVER MONEY

You need to understand what is important to you about your money. What are you trying to accomplish, how will you feel if you accomplish it, how much are you willing to sacrifice now to accomplish it? Related to this, you also need to understand your tolerance for risk, and how it will impact your ability to handle your money in an appropriate way. You also need to take your focus off short-term market trends and put it on your long-term goals. Design an investment plan specific to your goals and appropriate for your individual tolerance for risk, and your odds for financial success will increase.

Bill Cratty, M.S., CPA/PFS
Senior Financial Planner, MetLife Securities

Learn the difference between good debt and bad debt. Use good debt only for the production of income and avoid bad debt. Examples of good debt are buying a house and funding a college education. Examples of bad debt are financing the purchase of a luxury car and any type of consumer debt. Good debt will allow your net worth to grow, while bad debt will consistently decrease your net worth.

Robert B. Walsh, CPA/PFS CFP®
President, Lighthouse Financial Advisors, Inc.

Here are five novel ideas to limit your credit card spending:

1. Shop only on specific days of the week. This limits the amount of time you see things to buy.

2. Take elevators in department stores. Escalators let you scan the floor to think of more to purchase.

3. Go shopping with a Money Buddy who will support you to stick to your lists.

4. Put your credit cards in a safety deposit box and shop only on the weekends when you can't get to your cards.

5. Freeze your credit cards! You'll be forced to go home and thaw them before you can spend.

Judi Martindale, M.Ed. CFP®, EA
Author of No More Baglady Fears

Many credit card companies offer to let you transfer a balance to their card with a guaranteed low fixed interest rate. Sounds great, right? Well, there may be a slight catch. While the rate for balance transfers may be low, the rate for purchases may be much higher. The credit card company will apply all of your payments to the lower interest rate balance transfer until it's paid off. Your best bet is to find a card with a low fixed interest rate for balance transfers as well as purchases. Better yet, don't use the card for new purchases at all.

Jennifer Delcamp, CCCC
Director of Operations, CCCS of Oklahoma

Be safe using your credit cards with these 10 steps:

1. Reduce the number of cards you carry and use just one or two.
2. Use them only for essential purchases.
3. Cut up and return all unwanted credit cards.
4. Keep unused cards in a safe place.
5. Carry credit cards separately from your wallet or purse.
6. Keep your card in view whenever you hand it to a merchant.
7. Never lend your cards to anyone.
8. Promptly report questionable charges.
9. Avoid signing blank charge vouchers.
10. Don't give card numbers out over the phone, especially on a call you didn't originate.

Paul S. Richard, RFC
Executive Director, Institute of Consumer Financial Education

MAINTAINING GOOD CREDIT

Your credit report may not be as important to protect as your children, but it runs a close second. It is rather easy to maintain a good credit report once you have established one. Our experts have some tips that make it even easier.

♦ ♦ ♦

To ensure that your credit record is as accurate as possible, it's very important to review your credit report once per year. Check to make sure all of the accounts are really yours and that the balances are accurate. Sometimes creditors can be lax about updating account balances, so it may look like you still owe money that was paid years ago. To access your credit report online, go to one of the websites of the three main credit bureaus (www.transunion.com, www.equifax.com, or www.experian.com). If you've been denied credit, are unemployed, are a victim of fraud, or live in certain states, you can get a free copy of your report.

Jennifer Delcamp, CCCC

Director of Operations, CCCS of Oklahoma

One credit card is all you need. If you find a second card with a better interest rate and lower fees, by all means apply—but destroy your other card as soon as you get the new one.

Jeff Michael, Director of Education
Springboard Non-Profit Consumer Credit Counseling

If you revolve a credit card balance, pay your monthly bills no more than a day or two after they arrive to lower the average daily balance upon which interest is charged. Even if you don't carry a balance, pay bills promptly to avoid late charges, which can also lead to penalty annual percentage rates (APRs) of 20 percent or more. Many creditors today allow only two weeks to mail a statement and get a payment posted to your account. Another option is to pay credit card bills electronically via phone or online. Be careful to time the payment correctly, however, so that it is credited to the proper billing cycle.

Barbara O'Neill, Ph.D., CFP®, AFC, CHC
Author of Saving on a Shoestring

ID Theft (www.consumer.gov/idtheft). This is the essential online government resource for victims of identity theft.

It has become increasingly important to check your credit reports regularly in order to spot identity theft. It's the fastest-growing crime in America, and sometimes checking your credit report is the only way to detect it. The average victim of identity theft will spend 175 hours and $800 recovering from the crime. Those who don't check their credit reports regularly won't discover that they've been a victim for an average of 15 months. Check your report for unfamiliar accounts and inquiries. You'll be able to see if an identity thief has used your information with lenders, landlords, or employers.

Jeff Michael, Director of Education
Springboard Non-Profit Consumer Credit Counseling

Beware of free credit report offers. Often, you'll be signed up for a costly credit report monitoring service. Read the fine print. You can usually save a lot of money by just checking your report occasionally yourself instead of paying these hefty fees. You can easily dispute any incorrect information for free so it's unnecessary to pay someone to do it for you. Remember: No one can legally do anything for you that you can't do for yourself regarding your credit.

Jennifer Delcamp, CCCC
Director of Operations, CCCS of Oklahoma

Acting as a cosigner for any type of credit or becoming an authorized user on someone else's credit accounts can help you build credit, but can be extremely dangerous. If anything happens, even if the person is financially stable at the moment, your credit can and will be ruined if they default on the loan. Be extremely careful of who you choose to share credit with.

Carolyn Baker, CCCC
CEO, Minnesota Credit Association

Whether you're looking to get a mortgage, car loan, or home-equity loan, you're going to get scored. Named after Fair, Isaac & Co., your FICO score is calculated using a computer model that compares the information in your credit report to what's on the credit reports of thousands of other customers. FICO scores range from about 300 to 900. Generally, the higher the score, the lower the credit risk. A credit score that one lender considers satisfactory may be regarded as unsatisfactory by other lenders for comparable credit instruments. The higher your FICO score, the easier it should be to obtain credit and low interest loans.

Preston Cochrane, AFC
Executive Director, AAA Fair Credit Foundation

If you ever suspect you are the victim of credit card fraud or identify theft, immediately contact one of the following credit bureaus to initiate the steps necessary to resolve the problem. You should also consider visiting the websites of the credit bureaus to review valuable information that might help you reduce the risk of this happening to you. Print this list of credit bureau fraud departments to use and keep for reference:

- TransUnion (www.transunion.com), 1-800-680-7289
- Equifax (www.equifax.com), 1-800-525-6285
- Experian (www.experian.com), 1-888-397-3742

Brad R. Cougill, CFP®, CMFC®
Partner, Deerfield Financial Advisors, Inc.

As you look for ways to improve your credit report, consider this payment strategy. On accounts that are delinquent, pay the amount that would bring the account current, continue paying the required amount for a few months, and then pay off the balance. As an example, on a credit card with a $500 balance and a delinquent amount of $125, pay the $125 to bring the account current, pay two minimum payments, and then pay off the balance. By bringing the account current and maintaining a current status for a few months, the account will be reported as a "1," the best rating you can have!

Sandra E. Dunaway, CCCC
Director, CCCS of Mobile

Don't carry your Social Security card in your purse or wallet. Doing so makes it too easy for the scam artist looking for a new victim.

Samuel O. Sanders, Jr., CCCC
Director of Education, CCCS of Baton Rouge

Keep monthly debt payments, such as credit cards and a car loan, below 15 percent of net (after-tax) pay. When more than 20 percent of your income goes to repay debt, this is a sign of financial distress. A 20 percent debt-to-income ratio means that you are working for five days and it feels like you are only getting paid for four because a full day's pay is already spoken for. For some families with high expenses, such as child care, a 10 percent debt-to-income ratio is advisable.

Barbara O'Neill, Ph.D., CFP®, AFC, CHC
Author of Saving on a Shoestring

RESOLVING CREDIT PROBLEMS

As much as we try to manage our credit and debt responsibly, we might find a time when it gets tough to keep up with the payments. These time periods are reminders to us of the risk we take when we use consumer credit and might help us to rethink our strategy for credit usage in the future. In the meantime, our experts are ready with some great strategies to minimize the pressure during these times.

♦ ♦ ♦

During a financial crisis, make a creditor priority list and pay as many as possible. Start by ranking your creditors according to the consequences associated with not paying them. Think about basic needs: shelter, food, utilities, and transportation to get to work. Don't be bullied into paying lower priority creditors ahead of more important ones. Often, the ones who hassle you the most are probably somewhere near the bottom of your list.

Jennifer Delcamp, CCCC
Director of Operations, CCCS of Oklahoma

If you or a loved one suffers a temporary disability and you anticipate short-term difficulty in making monthly payments, talk to your creditors early. Many banks, credit card companies and mortgage holders have hardship programs that will work to preserve your credit and give you relief during your period of disability. When you call, ask for their "Hardship Department" or a supervisor. Explain your situation, including the accommodation you are seeking. Many times payments can be postponed for periods of 30 to 90 days or more, at your request, giving you a better chance to get back on your feet, both physically and financially.

Richard A. Vera II, M.B.A., CPA/PFS, CDP, CSA
CEO, CPA & Financial Services, LLC

One of the biggest mistakes you can make during financial hardship is avoiding your creditors. They will be much more willing to work with you if you contact them before you fall behind on your payments. Call the customer service number on the statement. Ask to speak to a supervisor. Explain that you want to pay them but may be unable to do so for a while. In certain situations, they may allow you to defer payments or make reduced payments. If the situation goes on for several months, keep them updated in writing. If creditors see you as someone who wants to pay them, they'll treat you with much more respect than if they think you're trying to avoid them.

Jennifer Delcamp, CCCC
Director of Operations, CCCS of Oklahoma

Federal Trade Commission (www.ftc.gov/os/statutes/fdcpajump.htm). This is the Federal Trade Commission's site on the Fair Debt Collection Practices Act.

If you're ever in a situation where collection agencies are calling you, it's important to know your rights under the Fair Debt Collection Practices Act (FDCPA). Visit http://www.ftc.gov/os/statutes/fdcpajump.htm to find all the information you need. The bottom line is: If you feel that a collector is harassing you, he probably is. Tell the collector that you know your rights under the FDCPA, and they'll almost certainly back off. If they don't, visit the Federal Trade Commission online at www.ftc.gov and report the violation. Remember, the law is on your side.

Jeff Michael, Director of Education
Springboard Non-Profit Consumer Credit Counseling

IN MONEY WORDS

Look out for number one ... Pay yourself first

If you're dealing with collectors, it is very important not to be bullied into making a promise to pay that you can't keep. Stay calm and tell them that you will pay them as soon as you can. Don't tell them you'll make a payment just to make them go away. If you break a promise to pay, it can hurt your credibility later when you're trying to negotiate payment arrangements that you can keep.

Jennifer Delcamp, CCCC
Director of Operations, CCCS of Oklahoma

Many folks get into financial difficulty at some time in their lives. If you have reached the point when you need to look for a credit counseling agency, keep these tips in mind.

1. Choose a not-for-profit organization.
2. Make sure they will help in getting your accounts re-aged and showing current on your credit report.
3. Make sure you are not being promised something that can't be delivered.
4. Remember the old saying: If it sounds too good to be true, it probably is.
5. Ask a lot of questions! A reputable agency will be happy to answer all of them.

Randall L. Leshin, Esq.
Executive Director, Express Consolidation, Inc.

MIND OVER MONEY

If you are one of millions of learning-disabled consumers, you may be looking for different strategies to cope with your phobias about saving, record-keeping, and money in general. An aversion to money awareness needs some type of incentive. The computer may be your salvation. Quicken is magic for many. It's visual, requires no math skills, and reminds you about things you used to forget. Think of it as a game and have fun with your money for the first time ever!

Suzi Marsh, LCSW
Host of Choosing Life

If you have a student loan, it's important to notify the lender in the event of a financial crisis. Lenders are usually very cooperative and will work with you to either temporarily delay or reduce payments. If you default on student loans (no special arrangements made and no payment for 210 days), you will be charged with a collection fee that equals 20 percent of your balance. Therefore, it is essential that you keep your loan in good standing even during the rough times.

Jennifer Delcamp, CCCC
Director of Operations, CCCS of Oklahoma

In an effort to become debt-free, you might consider offering a settlement to a creditor, which means you would usually pay only 50 to 75 cents for each dollar owed. A great deal, right? Not necessarily, as any amount forgiven over $600 can be considered as income by the IRS. The result will be that you have eliminated that debt, but possibly increased the amount of income taxes owed this year. Be wise and consult your CPA before using this strategy.

Sandra E. Dunaway, CCCC
Director, CCCS of Mobile

GETTING OUT OF DEBT

As you think through your true tolerance for carrying debt, you may decide to lighten your load. Check out this section for some great tips on how to get out of debt faster than you thought.

◆ ◆ ◆

Don't simply make the minimum payment on your credit cards. Always strive to pay the minimum plus the interest charged for the previous month's balance. This way you pay down your principal faster and you never finance the interest since you always pay it in full. Example: If you owe $20.00 on a credit card with a $25 annual fee and 18 percent interest, simply paying the minimum payment plus last month's interest. This cuts payment time from 138 months to 76 months and saves you $1,000!

Samuel O. Sanders, Jr., CCCC
Director of Education, CCCS of Baton Rouge

If you are considering divorce, don't be caught by the common misconception that the divorce decree is the deciding factor of who is responsible for joint credit accounts. This goes for any joint credit. A divorce decree does not supersede the original financial agreement you make with a creditor. If possible, close any and all joint accounts with your ex-spouse and reopen your own. Most creditors will not allow this, but it is worth a try to have your name removed from an account if you are not responsible to repay it. You can also ask the credit reporting agencies to split the reporting of the accounts according to the divorce decree.

Carolyn Baker, CCCC
CEO, Minnesota Credit Association

When you receive an income tax refund, it's important not to think of it as found money, but rather *your* money. You worked for it, you earned it, and you should include it in your budget. Too many Americans put their tax refunds toward big-ticket items. Instead, consider using the refund to repay outstanding debt. The average consumer will save over $350 in interest if he or she applies one tax refund to a credit card balance, paying off the card five months faster. This strategy can help relieve your financial burdens in the long run and enable you to save up for that big-ticket item.

Jeff Michael, Director of Education
Springboard Non-Profit Consumer Credit Counseling

A consolidation loan may be workable *only* if the loan interest is less than the interest on the debts to be paid-off *and* the original accounts are closed. Make sure the extra cash flow is put toward paying off the consolidation loan even faster. Otherwise, in a year or two you may find yourself paying off a consolidation loan and also new credit purchases.

Paul S. Richard, RFC
Executive Director, Institute of Consumer Financial Education

Time Value Software (www.tcalc.com/calculators.htm). Find lots of financial calculators you will need.

Paying off debts as part of a divorce settlement is one of the smartest decisions someone could make. Monthly payments on credit cards and loans can actually prevent someone from accumulating wealth. Every dollar made on debt payments is a dollar lost to savings and investing. The secret to getting richer is simply to spend less than you make.

Joan Coullahan, M.B.A., CDP
Co-author of Financial Custody: You, Your Money, and Divorce

Pay a little more each time. Try to add an extra $10 or $20 to each payment on your credit card, auto loan, or other loans. Make your first goal to pay down debts with the highest interest rates.

Steve Johnson, CPA/PFS, CFP®
Owner, Johnson Financial

IN MONEY WORDS

Living on borrowed time ... Paying off one credit card with another

---

You may need to practice do-it-yourself plastic surgery if you find yourself making only the minimum payments on your credit cards. Cut up all your credit cards and start paying off the balances with the most dollars you can spare. Instead of spending your next raise, or your tax refund, pay down your debt. Take a less expensive vacation next time or scrimp a little when you eat out. Don't stop until the balances are paid off—you will find that your money goes farther without the baggage of 18 to 20 percent interest!

Raj Pillai, Ph.D., CFP®
NAPFA-Registered Advisor, Financial Fitness Network of Solon

Did you know that some car financing arrangements front load the finance charges in the first half of the loan? This is known as the rule of 78's. Three fourths of the interest on the loan is paid in the first half of the loan. So if you signed such a loan agreement and are thinking about paying off that car loan early, look toward other debt, such as interest-bearing credit cards, to put your hard-earned dollars toward. If you have no other debt, consider hiking your 401(k) or other qualified plans. You will come out ahead in the long run. You can tell what kind of loan you are signing by reading the finance charges and payments section of your loan agreement. If the contract does not specifically stipulate, ask for the method of computation in writing.

Leonard C. Wright, CPA/PFS, CFP®, CLU, ChFC
Principal, Strategic Financial Group

You may have found that, in an effort to be fiscally sound, you paid off all your credit card debt—and now it has magically appeared again. Before you try to get rid of this debt again with a lump-sum payment (from your home equity line, or your retirement money, or your investments ... wherever), make sure you have a spending plan (a.k.a. "a budget") in place that you are living on. Otherwise, the card balances increased once because of your lifestyle and they will again. A reduction in spending is the only way to permanently eliminate debt.

Peg Downey, M.A., CFP®
Partner, Money Plans

Did you know that if you just pay the minimum payment each month on your credit card it could take you over 22 years to pay off? The interest alone would be almost 400 percent of the principal! That's more interest than you would pay on a 30-year mortgage. No single tip in this book will save you more in the long run than this: *Pay off your credit cards every month!* If you don't have it, don't spend it. Save your credit for those times you really need it, like the purchase of big-ticket items.

Randall L. Leshin, Esq.
Executive Director, Express Consolidation, Inc.

This is probably the most powerful determinant of your long-term financial security: your attitudes toward and use of credit. All the wonderful investment strategies you choose can be undermined in a moment by excessive accumulated debt. The issuers of debt know that you can often be persuaded to incur more debt than you intended. It's very human to fall victim to their effective marketing strategies. Tips in this chapter give you the foundation to begin to make decisions based on what is best for you, not the creditors.

14

BUDGETING AND
CASH FLOW

*If you know how to spend less than you
get, you have the Philosophers-Stone.*

Benjamin Franklin (Poor Richard's Almanack)

TERMS FROM THE TOP

auto-debit discounts   A reduction in the interest rate charged to a debtor if permission is granted to the lender to automatically make the monthly payments by debiting a checking, credit card, or other account each month.

depreciating asset   A piece of equipment or other capital or consumer good that wears out over time, such as cars, computers, and furniture.

discretionary income   Amount of a consumer's income spent after essentials like food, housing, and utilities and prior commitments have been covered.

fixed expenses   Items in a family's budget that do not change from month to month due to a contractual arrangement with the provider, vendor, or debtor.

net worth   Amount by which assets exceed liabilities. For an individual, net worth is the total value of all possessions, such as a house, stocks, bonds, and other securities, minus all outstanding debts, such as mortgages and revolving-credit loans.

Quicken Cash Flow   Report function that is available in the popular personal finance software tool, Quicken, that allows a household to project the future differences in income and expenses.

spending categories   Organization system for a family's budget.

Source: reprinted by permission of Jordan Goodman, Dictionary of Finance and Investment Terms *(Barron's, 5th Edition)*

These two terms, Budgeting and Cash Flow, might make the all-time top ten list of the most hated words in the English language. In an attempt to not scare you, I put them at the end of the book! Financial professionals have taken to using terms that candy coat their meanings. Spending Plan is one that has been used extensively. They don't fool me! They really mean Not-Spending Plan, right? Budgets are freeing, we are told. They allow us to freely reach our goals, sometimes finding money for things we really value. Budgets are freeing, I guess, in the same way that control-top pantyhose allow us to wear a size smaller than we should. It's all about fitting more desires into a smaller income. Money is limited for most of us and it doesn't matter how much we have available to spend, we have the capacity to want more.

All tips in this chapter are intended for informational purposes only. Should you find one potentially helpful to your situation, you should consult with your legal, tax, or investment professional familiar with your individual situation to determine its suitability prior to taking any action or investing any money.

WHERE DOES IT ALL GO?

We've all asked this question. And no one is standing there with the answer. It's up to us to figure it out. Sometimes we just know that where we spend our money is within our budget. It works to allow us to reach our goals. But many times it isn't working or our goals change and our spending must adjust for new circumstances. Different tips advise very different approaches. I'm sure you can find one that might work for you!

◆ ◆ ◆

Have you been arguing with your spouse or partner about money? Have a monthly money meeting! Once a month, sit down with your Quicken Cash Flow report and review your previous expenses against the budget. Then discuss your future purchases. This way each person knows what the other is doing in advance, according to previously agreed upon goals. No surprises = less upset.

Judi Martindale, M.Ed. CFP®, EA
Author of No More Baglady Fears

POINT ⫸

Do it now! Take out a piece of paper and draw lines to form columns. The first column is your spending categories. Don't leave anything out: groceries, eating out, clothing, utilities, mortgage, etc. The second column is what you are spending now. The third column is the amount you could get by with in that category. Put the difference between the two in the fourth column. This is your potential savings. Add it up!

Connie Brezik, CPA/PFS
Investment Advisor, Asset Strategies, Inc.

⫷ COUNTERPOINT

You have tried to stick to a detailed budget, but it is time-consuming and difficult. Rather than tracking every expenditure, try paying yourself first. Each paycheck, set aside a fixed amount into savings and then pay your monthly expenses from the remainder. You can have the amount automatically withdrawn so you do not have to think about it. Better yet, have the payment sent directly to the mutual fund of your choice. Investing in a mutual fund in this manner will allow you to take advantage of dollar cost averaging. It also makes it more difficult to use the money for short-term needs.

Frank L. Washelesky, J.D., CPA/PFS, CVA
Director, Ostrow Resin Berk & Abrams, Ltd.

Quicken (www.Quicken.com). This site has lots of basic information, and useful calculators, in addition to providing valuable information for using Quicken.

Don't have a clue how much money you spend? Here is a quick and dirty way to find out using your tax return:

1. Identify your Gross Income.
2. Then subtract the total amount of federal taxes paid.
3. Subtract the total tax from your state tax return and FICA and Medicare taxes from your W-2 (or tax return if self-employed).

Your result will be your after-tax income. If you had any automatically reinvested income or dividends, subtract those, too. What's left is your approximate spendable income.

Brad R. Cougill, CFP®, CMFC®
Partner, Deerfield Financial Advisors, Inc.

Why does money management seem to work so well for some, while others have found it to be an impossible dream? It seems that some sabotage their own successes. Before you blame your lack of financial success on how much you make, take a look at what other factors affect how you earn, spend, save, and invest your money. Check out your environment, motivation, attitude, habits, family, budget, education, goals, time, age, needs versus wants, and risk. Once you identify what's been in your way, you may see a change in your financial successes.

Angie Hollerich, CEP, CCA
Author of Grab the Brass Ring of Financial Security

One of the hardest things people try to do is spend less than they make. In divorce, this is especially true as one household becomes two. One of the first actions someone should take when preparing for divorce is to find out how much they really spend each month. Some people use a software program like Quicken or MS Money and assign categories to each check and credit card purchase. Another way to make a budget is to look at a check register and assign categories to each check written. Doing this for three or four months shows a very accurate picture of where the money goes.

Joan Coullahan, M.B.A., CDP
Co-Author of Financial Custody: You, Your Money, and Divorce

Developing a spending plan can be tricky. If, when you are doing your monthly planning, you take a week's expense and multiply it by four, you will shortchange yourself—by four weeks out of the year! (That's as much as you are allowing for a month's expenses.) Watch for the fact that since there are 52 weeks in a year, there are 4.33 weeks in a month so you don't find yourself needing an entire month's additional income.

Peg Downey, M.A., CFP®
Partner, Money Plans

Where did all the money go? Does this sound familiar after you have paid all the bills, paid for extra activities for the kids, and purchased other small, unplanned items? The next time you hear that old familiar question, give your partner a money-tracking form and review it the next month along with your form. I'm sure the tone of the question will be different the next time!

Kathy Adams-Smith, CCCC
Director of Credit Counseling Services, LifeSpan, Inc.

Analyze Net Worth Change to Check Surplus Estimate. In order to check estimates of your spending and surplus, analyze your net worth at the beginning and end of the year. Your net worth will change because of your surplus (or deficit), principal payments on loans, and unrealized changes in assets. If you cannot explain why your net worth changed by a particular amount, it is likely that your estimate of spending is too high or too low.

Sherman D. Hanna, Ph.D.
Professor, The Ohio State University

GETTING CONTROL

It's one thing to know where your money went. It is another thing entirely to have control over where it is going to go in the future. Relationships, kids, impulses, emergencies, and assorted other human experiences just get in the way. Like dieting, sometimes we can follow a plan, but it may not last for long. And then the guilt sinks in. Will you ever be able to reach your goals? Read through the following tips and look for ones that speak to your situation. I know you'll find one that looks fun to try!

♦ ♦ ♦

If you're an impulsive spender, try putting things in perspective before you buy an unplanned item. How much does it cost and how many hours did you have to work to earn that much money? Is the item really worth all of that hard work? If your boss offered to give you a pair of shoes for an entire day's work, would it be a good deal? If not, why would you ever spend that kind of money on them?

Jennifer Delcamp, CCCC
Director of Operations, CCCS of Oklahoma

To keep a check on unnecessary spending, try this: Deposit your income or salary into two checking accounts. One pays for fixed expenses such as your mortgage and insurance premiums. The other pays for discretionary items such as entertainment and vacations. At the beginning of each year, fix the percentage of your income to be deposited between the two accounts. Determine the split by categorizing your previous year's expenditures (fixed versus discretionary). Go through a year's worth of credit card statements and checkbook entries. Adjust for possible changes in the new year's circumstances.

Deborah O. Levine, M.B.A, M.S.T., CPA/PFS, CFP®
Financial Planner, AFP Group

Kiplinger's (www.Kiplinger.com). This is a consumer-oriented forum for investors.

If you are paid weekly or biweekly, here's a painless way to achieve some of your financial goals. At the beginning of each year, mark your paydays on a calendar and identify those months with "extra" paychecks. If you are paid weekly, there will be four months with five paydays. If you are paid biweekly, there are two months with three paydays. Monthly expenses usually don't increase much during these months, so use this "extra" income to increase savings or reduce debt.

Barbara O'Neill, Ph.D., CFP®, AFC, CHC
Author of Saving on a Shoestring

When your urge to splurge is proving itself to have more muscle than your craving for saving, it is time to think RICH (Resist Impulse Commit Healthy Habits). Most spending and credit card debt is the result of impulse purchases on items that are rarely genuinely needed. Often these purchases have become a habit stemming from boredom, anger, or frustration. To have healthy financial habits, you need to have awareness of what you can truly afford without incurring debt. Try other boredom busters than shopping, but when you must be in the store, think RICH to be rich.

Susan Zimmerman, M.A., LMFT, ChFC, CLU
Author of The Power in Your Money Personality

If your money just seems to vanish, try giving yourself an allowance to use for unnecessary items. Decide how much you can comfortably afford to spend and withdraw that amount in cash each month. This will allow you to stick to a budget while still splurging on some of the things that you want. No one says that you have to suffer just because you live on a budget!

Jennifer Delcamp, CCCC
Director of Operations, CCCS of Oklahoma

MIND OVER MONEY

Spend money thinking of your future as well as your present. You have an obligation to be as good to the person you are going to be in 20, 30, or 40 years from now as you are to yourself today.

Paul S. Richard, RFC
Executive Director, Institute of Consumer Financial Education

---

If you are married with children, it pays to carefully calculate all the costs of both you and your spouse working. You will learn how much you will need to tighten your purse strings to enable one spouse to stay home. In addition to the obvious costs such as child care and transportation to and from work, you may also have increased costs for work-related clothing, charitable contributions and gifts at work, eating out, and housekeeping services. You may find that, after all these costs plus the taxes are paid, trimming your budget is a better alternative for your family. One family found that the additional $40,000 earned by one spouse was really only $10,000 additional spendable income after doing this analysis.

Barbara J. Raasch, CFA®, CPA/PFS, ChFC
Partner-in-charge of Wealth Management Solutions, E&Y, LLC

IN MONEY WORDS

Live within your means … Reduce debt; manage on a budget

If you're an impulse shopper, make a list before you go to the store. Don't allow yourself to buy anything that's not on the list. Estimate the amount of money it's going to take to buy what you need and only take that amount of cash with you. When you survive the shopping trip by actually sticking to your list, you may even come home with extra cash. If so, try saving the money for a big, fun purchase or treating yourself to a monthly night out on the town to celebrate your incredible willpower.

Jennifer Delcamp, CCCC
Director of Operations, CCCS of Oklahoma

Save for them and pay cash. That's why they call them *major* purchases.

Bonnie A. Hughes, CFP®
President, A&H Financial Planning and Education, Inc.

Every Little Bit Helps

Wow! What a collection of great ideas. The only problem is that many of them cost money. Save for a rainy day. Make sure your retirement is secure. Have enough disability insurance. Where do you get the money? Either make more or spend less. Right? Here are some "spend less" tips that will help you find a little bit here and there. It all adds up to help you reach your goals!

◆ ◆ ◆

Cars are a depreciating asset—who wants to own that?! Well, okay we all want at least one, but why pay a high price for an asset you *know* will depreciate and quickly? This is where it pays to buy used. Do your research, pay cash, enjoy low insurance rates, and smile all the way to an exotic vacation with the savings!

Bonnie A. Hughes, CFP®
President, A&H Financial Planning and Education, Inc.

New or used? What's the financial impact of this often emotional decision? Consider the difference between buying a new car versus a two-year-old car every four years if you're now 31. By the time you turn 54 you would buy six cars either way. But save the difference in the monthly payments over that time, and you may accumulate the funds to purchase your next six or seven cars! Buy new cars and you'll not only have higher car payments for those 24 years, you'll have to save additional money in order to have the funds to purchase cars in retirement—used or new!

Cheryl A. Moss, CPA/PFS, CFP®, CLU, CDP
Tax Advisor

Try to keep a car 8 to 10 years or longer, if possible. Doing so will save thousands of dollars on financing costs and depreciation. This suggestion assumes ongoing maintenance to reduce the chance of major repair costs in later years. Consider establishing an earmarked savings account for maintenance expenses and funding it regularly (e.g., $50 per month).

Barbara O'Neill, Ph.D., CFP®, AFC, CHC
Author of Saving on a Shoestring

Kelly Blue Book (www.kbb.com). This site will help you find out how much a car is worth.

Inventory items in your pantry that have been there forever. If you look at those items as the piles of money they cost, you'll realize that you've just found a hidden treasure. Stop overbuying groceries that just sit on the shelf and eventually get thrown out. Before you head out to the supermarket, look to see what you can use out of the pantry and buy only what you can consume before the next grocery visit.

Samuel O. Sanders, Jr., CCCC
Director of Education, CCCS of Baton Rouge

Cellular phone costs have gone down dramatically over the past several years. The odds are that if you're still dealing with your original service provider and your original service contract has expired, you're paying too much. Call your present provider and tell them that you're shopping around for lower rates, but want to give them the first opportunity to retain your business. You may be pleasantly surprised!

Michael L. Alberts, M.B.A., CFP®
President, Woodstock Financial Group, LLC

If you are a single parent and find that you are unable to handle unexpected expenses like appliance repairs, consider using a barter system. Let's assume you have a washing machine or clothes dryer in need of repair. Locate someone, perhaps another single parent you know from work, church, or school, who has the training to make these types of repairs. Rather than pay the person, although you will need to pay for needed parts, barter with him or her. Offer to prepare dinner, baby-sit, or teach a skill such as using computers or playing a musical instrument.

Sandra E. Dunaway, CCCC
Director, CCCS of Mobile

A convenient way to reduce your expenses is to take advantage of auto-debit discounts whenever they are offered. For example, many banks will lower your installment loan interest rate by at least one quarter of one percent if you let them take the money out of your account on a prearranged date. Warning: Make sure that you have the funds in the account though; bank overdraft fees will offset your savings if you're caught with a low balance.

Michael L. Alberts, M.B.A., CFP®
President, Woodstock Financial Group, LLC

One of the easiest ways you can reduce your expenses is to share magazine subscriptions with your friends and neighbors. By agreeing to subscribe to the same magazine in alternating years or different magazines each year, you will pocket the savings and significantly reduce your recycling, too!

Michael L. Alberts, M.B.A., CFP®
President, Woodstock Financial Group, LLC

Try giving a Love Coupon when you can't squeeze any more money out of your budget to buy gifts. Collect a list of things this person would appreciate like free babysitting, baked goods, car washing, personal massage, or a home-cooked meal. Get some construction paper and be creative as you make a book of coupons to show this person that your valuable time is a gift. You'll find that creative gifts sometimes generate more satisfaction than the big-ticket items many folks struggle to buy each year.

Samuel O. Sanders, Jr., CCCC
Director of Education, CCCS of Baton Rouge

Want a free safe deposit box? Many banks have vaults filled with small safe deposit boxes that no one wants to rent. Chances are that if you're a good customer of the bank they will seriously consider providing you with free use of a small safe deposit box for one year. All you have to do is ask.

Michael L. Alberts, M.B.A., CFP®
President, Woodstock Financial Group, LLC

Plan your purchases in advance, so that you can take advantage of low prices in the off-season. For example, if you buy swimsuits and lawn-mowers in September, snow blowers in April, or Christmas decorations in January, you will save a bundle!

Raj Pillai, Ph.D., CFP®
NAPFA-Registered Advisor, Financial Fitness Network of Solon

IN MONEY WORDS

If it sounds too good to be true ... Read the fine print

Smoking two packs of cigarettes a day can cost you $2,100 to $3,300 per year or more depending on which part of the country you live in. This means that you would have to earn $3,000 to $4,500 before taxes to afford this addiction. The question is: Did you go on a vacation this year? If the answer is no, it is because you smoked it. See your doctor and start planning that vacation.

Samuel O. Sanders, Jr., CCCC
Director of Education, CCCS of Baton Rouge

MIND OVER MONEY

Money is like time—you don't have too little, you have what you have and need to use it wisely. The trick is making what you have enough and that is mostly a matter of attitude.

Lesley J. Brey, M.B.A., CFA®, CFP®
President, L.J. Brey, Inc.

Each dollar you have has the same potential value to you, regardless of where it came from. It is up to you how you use that value to enjoy life, provide for your family and secure your future. Sometimes the little tricks are the most powerful because they add up over time without causing a huge change in how we live.

Take a Tip with You!

We may give advice, but we cannot give conduct.

Benjamin Franklin (Poor Richard's Almanack)

Money comes in, money goes out. How could we have made things so complicated? Every consumer decision you make has so many pieces. Every investment decision has untold variables. How can you know if you are right and if it will all add up to a happy life? You can't start out expecting perfection, but you can make a promise to yourself that you will see your mistakes as opportunities to grow and learn. Pay attention to each choice and how it turns out. Repeat the successes; abandon the failures. Sounds simple, but we are creatures of habit and often are more comfortable repeating decisions that didn't work the first time.

As you pick out tips to try, you may find that they work for you or they don't. If they don't, try others. The most important thing is to try something. Pick a tip. See if it works in your situation. Chances are, it will at least lead you to an awareness of a new opportunity where you can benefit.

I have enjoyed bringing you this collection and hope you have enjoyed testing your financial knowledge against America's Top Money Minds. They worked hard to bring you the concepts they have seen work consistently with their clients. Tell us what worked for you and how we can help you in the future. Visit us at www.topmoneyminds.com.

A

ABOUT THE CONTRIBUTORS

Harvey D. Aaron
VP and Director of Tax Services, Tandem Financial Services, Inc.
1017 Turnpike Street, #35
Canton, MA 02021

E-mail Address: buz@tandemfinancial.com

Certifications: Certified Financial Planner®, Certified Public Accountant/Personal Financial Specialist

Education: B.S. in Accounting, University of North Carolina at Chapel Hill
J.D. Taxation, Emory University

Organizations: American Institute of Certified Public Accountants, The Financial Planning Association, and American Bar Association

I've got the credentials—so do many other practitioners. What makes our practice different is our heart and the level to which we care about our clients. That's why I do what I do. Not because I can say I care, but because my clients feel it. I was just a "tax guy" for 20 years. It's not a bad thing, the world needs tax guys. But financial planning is so much more. It's getting to know your clients as people and helping them with life problems that are important to them. That's why I do what I do—it's the feeling that helping people is important.

Kathy L. Adams-Smith
Director, Credit Counseling, LifeSpan, Inc.
111 Buckeye Street
Hamilton, OH 45011

E-mail Address: TIME@Lifespanohio.org

Education: M.P.A. in Public Administration, Xavier University
B.A. in Sociology, Xavier University

Organizations: National Foundation for Credit Counseling

After 25 years of providing counseling and social services to the residents of Butler County, I began teaching as an adjunct professor for a local college and thoroughly enjoyed it. I took a job with LifeSpan, Inc., to develop and teach a money management course to the families that were transitioning from welfare to work. Now as the director for the past two years, we have expanded the education services to reach adolescents and adults, and into the neighboring county. Financial literacy is the key to financial success and teaching the "nuts and bolts" to build a financial foundation is critical.

Michael L. Alberts
President, Woodstock Financial Group, LLC
203 County Road
P.O. Box 299
East Woodstock, CT 06244

E-mail Address: woodstockfinancialgroup@hotmail.com

Certifications: Certified Financial Planner®

Education: M.B.A in Finance, The University of Connecticut
B.A. in English, The University of Connecticut

Organizations: The Financial Planning Association, National Association of Personal Financial Advisors

I am a fee-only Certified Financial Planner® and Registered Investment Advisor based in Woodstock, Connecticut. I primarily work with middle-income folks who need retirement planning assistance. After 14 years in banking, I founded Woodstock Financial Group, LLC, in 2001 to provide much-needed assistance to a group that I felt was underserved. Individuals or couples located in eastern Connecticut who are interested in addressing retirement planning, investment management, college planning, or any other aspect of their personal finances with a dedicated professional, may contact me. I am actively accepting new clients at this time.

Kent E. Anthony
President, First Group Insurance
136 South Broadway
Box 67
Sterling, KS 67579

E-mail Address: anthonu@insurewithus.net

Website: www.insurewithus.net

Certifications: Certified Financial Planner®, Certified Insurance Counselor, Chartered Mutual Fund Counselor®

Education: B.S. in Business Administration, Northwestern Oklahoma State

Organizations: Independent Insurance Agents & Brokers of America

I'm a Certified Financial Planner® licensee and insurance broker located in a small agricultural community in the heart of America. Working in a small town requires me to wear more than one hat for my clients. I might work on business insurance for a client one day, and then on his retirement plan or his children's education plans the next. Wearing several hats gives me a real understanding of my customers' needs. I'm not only providing my client many services, but

I'm also their neighbor, their children's softball coach, and a fellow parent driving our kids to school activities.

Frank B. Arnold
CPA/PFS, Panfeld, Edelman & Arnold
414 Portland Road, #100
San Antonio, TX 78216

E-mail Address: fabcpa@urdirect.net

Certifications: Certified Public Accountant, Personal Financial Specialist

Education: B.B.A. in Accounting, Southwest Texas State

Organizations: American Institute of Certified Public Accountants, The Financial Planning Association

I find financial planning to be an art and a science. The challenge of determining what a client needs and then developing a road map for reaching the destination is rewarding beyond measure. My wife, Cindy, periodically has to put me on "time out" from my continual study of this subject. What a gift to love your work!

Carolyn Baker
CEO, Minnesota Credit Association
420 Elm Street
Farmington, MN 55024

E-mail Address: Calyn@aol.com

Certifications: Certified Credit Counselor, Paralegal

Education: AA Paralegal Studies

Organizations: National Foundation for Consumer Credit

I have been in the Credit and Debt industry for 11 years now. My husband and I started our own Credit Counseling and Credit Restoration business 8 years ago in our home and have since moved into an office with 20 employees. Helping people reach their financial goals has been one of the most rewarding things I have ever done. Watching a client get out of debt or get their first home—what a feeling.

Reg Baker
CPA/PFS, Reg Baker, CPA
P.O. Box 371267
Las Vegas, NV 89137
E-mail Address: reg@regbaker.com
Website: www.regbaker.com
Certifications: Certified Public Accountant, Personal Financial Specialist Realtor
Education: B.B.A. in Accounting, University of Central Arkansas
Organizations: American Institute of Certified Public Accountants
I am the Regional Director of the Wealth Management Group for Colonial Bank in Nevada. I have over 20 years' experience as a CPA and Financial Specialist. My emphasis is educating and working with families in the financial planning process to ensure their after-tax investment returns are adequate and correlated to their specific risk factors. I pride myself in working with entire families. This complete family involvement ensures financial success even as older family members become less involved, and it helps educate the younger family members to make the right decisions when the time comes.

Elaine E. Bedel
President, Bedel Financial Consulting, Inc.
9190 Priority Way West Drive, Suite 120
Indianapolis, IN 46240
E-mail Address: ebedel@bedelfinancial.com
Website: www.bedelfinancial.com
Certifications: Certified Financial Planner®
Education: M.B.A. in Finance, Butler University
B.S. in Mathematics, Hanover College
Organizations: The Financial Planning Association, National Association of Personal Financial Advisors

I provide fee-only financial planning since 1978. I founded my current company in 1989 to provide fee-only financial planning and active investment management. I was recognized by *Worth* magazine, *Mutual Fund* magazine, and *Medical Economics* magazine as one of the top financial planning professionals in the country. I am active in the financial planning profession on the national level since 1987. I currently serve as Chair of the Certified Financial Planner® Board of Standards, which establishes the criteria for the certification of individuals in the field of financial planning on a global basis.

Kristofor R. Behn
Director of Strategic Planning
Fieldstone Financial Management Group, LLC
101 Federal Street, Suite 1900
Boston, MA 02110

E-mail Address: krbehn@fieldstonefinancial.com

Website: fieldstonefinancial.com

Certifications: Certified Financial Planner®, Certified Tax Consultant

Education: B.S. in Economics & Financial, Boston University

Organizations: National Association of Personal Financial Advisors

I am passionate about providing unparalleled custom-tailored financial advice and investment management services to each of our clients and have built an organization of multidisciplinary advisors to address each aspect of a client's financial life. We operate as fee-only advisors in an effort to maintain an objective perspective when advising clients on important issues. Like any craft, providing quality comprehensive financial planning and investment advisory services requires a commitment to continued education in order to hone our skills and remain on top of the profession. We have made this commitment our mission.

Phyllis J. Bernstein
President, Phyllis Bernstein Consulting, Inc.
7 Penn Plaza, Suite 1600
New York, NY 10001

E-mail Address: phyllis@pbconsults.com

Website: www.pbconsults.com

Certifications: Certified Public Accountant, Personal Financial Specialist

Education: B.B.A. in Public Accounting, Hofstra University

Organizations: American Institute of Certified Public Accountants, The Financial Planning Association

Publications: *Guide to Investment Advisory Services*, Practitioners Publishing, 2002
Financial Planning for CPAs, Second Edition, Wiley, 2000
Managing Client Expectations, AICPA, 2002

I am the industry's leading resource for helping CPAs make the transition from being an accountant to being a financial advisor. I have won many awards for my efforts. *Financial Planning Magazine* (January 2002) named me as one of the four most influential people in our business, and *Accounting Today* recognized me as one of the most influential people in accounting and one of the names to know in financial planning for the past five years. In my free time, I enjoy cultural events, spending time with my husband, gardening, walking my two English dogs (a springer and a setter), and skiing.

Clark M. Blackman II

Exec. Vice President, Managing Director, and Chief Investment Officer
Post Oak Capital Advisors, L.P.
4265 San Felipe, Suite 1250
Houston, TX 77027
E-mail Address: clark@pocaltd.com

Certifications: Chartered Financial Analyst®, Certified Financial Planner®/Accredited Asset Management Specialist, Certified Public Accountant/Personal Financial Specialist, Certified Investment Management Analyst

Education: B.B.A. in Finance and Accounting, University of Iowa
M.A. in Accounting, University of Iowa

Organizations: American Institute of Certified Public Accountants, Association for Investment Management and Research, The Financial Planning Association

Publications: "The Expanding Reach of the Alternative Minimum Tax," *AAII Journal* (April, 2002)

"Withdrawing from Your IRA: A Guide to the Basic Distribution Rules," *AAII Journal* (August, 2002)

"Estate Planning: Should a Trust Be the Beneficiary of Your IRA?" *AAII Journal* (October, 2002)

I believe a great advisor puts his personal attitudes and opinions aside and creates a plan for the individual that works for that person. My goal in creating an outstanding investment strategy for a client is to ensure that the client is completely comfortable with the investment plan being implemented. My clients are looking for peace of mind more than anything else. I have served CEOs of Fortune 500 companies, wealthy families with nine figure portfolios and widows who don't know a stock from a bond and don't want to know the difference. They're all looking for the same thing—peace of mind and someone they can truly trust.

Sidney A. Blum

President, Successful Financial Solutions, Inc.

3100 Dundee Road, Suite 402

Northbrook, IL 60062

E-mail Address: sblum@concert-financial.com

Website: concert-financial.com

Certifications: Accredited Tax Preparer, Chartered Financial Consultant, Certified Financial Planner®, Certified Public Accountant/Personal Financial Specialist

Education: B.S. in Accounting, University of Illinois
A.A.S. in Real Estate, Harper College

Organizations: American Institute of Certified Public Accountants, Society of Financial Service Professionals, The Financial Planning Association, National Association of Personal Financial Advisors

Publications: *Easy Ways to Organize Your Taxes and Money*, New Seasons, 2001
"Bells, Bricks or Clicks," *Insight* magazine, 2001
Everything Money, Adams Media Corporation, 2002

In addition to being the co-founder of Successful Financial Solutions, I have served on the Adjunct Faculty of the College for Financial

Planning and the Financial Planning Section of Roosevelt University in Chicago. I am also active with numerous financial planning and accounting organizations. I have appeared annually on *Worth*'s list of the best financial advisors since 1996 and was also listed by *Medical Economics* as one the best 150 financial advisors for doctors.

Lesley J. Brey
President, L.J. Brey, Inc.
321 Halaki Street
Honolulu, HI 96821

E-mail Address: ljbrey@yahoo.com

Certifications: Chartered Financial Analyst®, Certified Financial Planner®

Education: B.A. in Mathematics, Pomona College
M.S. in Construction Engineering, Stanford University
M.B.A. in Business, Chaminade University

Organizations: Association for Investment Management and Research, The Financial Planning Association, National Association of Personal Financial Advisors, National Association of Tax Professionals

My greatest joy comes when a client, their child, or their grandchild wants to understand how their financial world and personal world interact to form a satisfying whole. The effort to gain and impart that wisdom feeds my soul. My practice aims to build an environment where a client's financial and nonfinancial interests work together toward a quality life. My personal interest in individuals, families, and the profession drives the ongoing exploration necessary to keep up with financial planning issues. Offering planning services contributes to a healthy balance between work, play, family, friends, and community—both for my clients and for myself.

Connie A. Brezik
CPA/PFS, Asset Strategies, Inc.
11000 N. Scottsdale Road, Suite 290
Scottsdale, AZ 85254

E-mail Address: connie@asset-strategies-inc.com

Website: asset-strategies-inc.com

Certifications: Certified Public Accountant/Personal Financial Specialist

Education: B.A. in Accounting, University of Wyoming

Organizations: American Institute of Certified Public Accountants, The Financial Planning Association, National Association of Personal Financial Advisors

At Asset Strategies, Inc., we provide a structured approach to investment advisory and financial planning services. Our objective is to assist clients in successfully managing their finances. We work together with clients to establish specific financial goals for attaining, preserving, and enhancing wealth. As part of the planning process, alternative strategies are evaluated to meet their financial goals, emphasizing the personal and financial trade-offs inherent in each strategy.

We value close client relationships and provide highly individualized planning and investment services. Specific attention is paid to minimizing the tax consequences of investing.

Susan J. Bruno

Principal, Winged Keel Financial Advisors, LLC

105 Rowayton Avenue

Rowayton, CT 06853

E-mail Address: sbruno@wingedkeel.com

Certifications: Certified Financial Planner®, Certified Public Accountant/Personal Financial Specialist

Education: B.S. in Accounting, Fairfield University

Organizations: American Institute of Certified Public Accountants

I begin my engagements by listening to my clients to determine what they expect to achieve as a result of the engagement. I ask them "If we were meeting three years from today, and you were to look back over those three years to today, what has to have happened during that period for you to feel happy about our progress?" Often this discussion helps clients to more clearly define their financial planning priorities, but also helps them to let go of any unrealistic expectations. After building the plan, I focus on full implementation with the client and their advisors.

Jack B. Capron
Director-TLS, PricewaterhouseCoopers, LLP
One Lincoln Center
Syracuse, NY 13202
E-mail Address: jack.capron@us.pwcglobal.com
Certifications: Certified Public Accountant/Personal Financial Specialist
Education: B.S. in Finance, Babson College
J. D. in Law, Syracuse University College of Law
Organizations: American Institute of Certified Public Accountants

Cary Carbonaro
President, Family Financial
614 E. Highway 50, Suite 112
Clermont, FL 34711
E-mail Address: ccarbonaro@cfl.rr.com
Education: M.B.A. in Marketing/Finance, LI University
B.A. in History, SUNY Cortland
Organizations: The Financial Planning Association, National
Association of Personal Financial Advisors
Publications: *Mature Lifestyles*, Lake, 2002 Marian and Sumter Counties,
Monthly Column
"Money Matters Hotline Expert," *Orlando Sentinel*, 2002

I grew up with my father as a banker and my mom raising her children
to be CPAs. I am a second-generation money mind who has a strong
desire to help people. The independence of working for myself and my
clients is in line with my personal convictions and what I'm passionate
about doing. Money is more emotional than most people will admit. I
council my clients about life issues in addition to money issues. Money
is the tip of the iceberg, life is the iceberg.

Melody A. Carlsen
Director of Research
International Foundation of Employee Benefit Plans
18700 W. Bluemound Road
P.O. Box 69
Brookfield, WI 53008-0069
E-mail Address: melodyc@ifebp.org

Certifications: Certified Employee Benefit Specialist

Education: B.S. in French (Summa Cum Laude), Ohio State University

Publications: *New Kid on the Block: Financial Planning as an Employee Benefit*, International Society of Certified Employee Benefit Specialists, 2001
Financial Planning Education, International Foundation of Employee Benefit Plans, 2001
Retiree Health Benefits, International Foundation of Employee Benefit Plans, 2002

In my experience of conducting employee benefits research over the past 23 years, it has become increasingly apparent that helping employees manage their *money*—whether in the form of choosing the most optimal employer-sponsored health care plan, using health plan benefit dollars wisely, participating in and contributing to a 401(k), managing self-directed investments or selecting from among retirement options—is a crucial employee benefit. Financial planning for the workforce is fast becoming a new and exciting dimension of the employee benefits arena and a win-win situation for employers and employees alike.

Jon S. Chernila
Principal, Corbin & Wertz
2603 Main Street, Suite 600
Irvine, CA 92614

E-mail Address: jchernila@cwcpa.com

Website: www.corbinwertz.co

Certifications: Chartered Financial Consultant, Certified Financial Planner®, Certified Public Accountant/Personal Financial Specialist

Education: M.B.T. in Business Taxation, University of Southern California
B.S. in Business Admin. (Accounting), San Diego State University

Organizations: American Institute of Certified Public Accountants, The Financial Planning Association

I truly enjoy teaching my clients to understand and take charge of their financial well-being. I work as a fee-only, hourly financial planner. Additionally, I handle income tax planning and preparation for both corporate and individual clients. I enjoy the diversity of planning that comes from working with a wide range of clients. Of particular interest is planning for closely held business owners as well as employees with stock options. I also teach in the Personal Financial Planning Certificate Program at the University of California Irvine.

Christine M. Cobb
Portfolio Manager, Lighthouse Capital Management
10000 Memorial Drive, Suite 660
Houston, TX 77024

E-mail Address: ccobb@lightkeepers.com

Website: www.lighthousecapital.com

Certifications: Certified Public Accountant/Personal Financial Specialist

Education: B.S.B.A. in Accounting, University of Arkansas

Organizations: American Institute of Certified Public Accountants

For the last 20 years, my career has been focused on assisting others in managing their personal finances and investments. During my 10 years as a CPA in private practice, I honed my skills in the personal financial planning field. I subsequently joined Lighthouse Capital Management as CFO/Portfolio Manager. I believe that providing effective financial advice requires a close working relationship with each client founded upon an in-depth appreciation of his or her personal situations, current financial status, and long-term objectives. At Lighthouse, we combine integrity and expertise with a high level of customized service in helping our clients achieve and maintain financial security.

Cathie E. Cobe
Retirement Education & Income Management Specialist, Nationwide Retirement Solutions
2267 Starleaf Lane
Columbus, OH 43235

E-mail Address: cobec@nationwide.com

Certifications: Certified Public Accountant/Personal Financial Specialist, Chartered Financial Consultant, Certified Financial Planner®, Chartered Life Underwriter, Certified Fund Specialist, Chartered Retirement Counselor

Education: B.S.B.A. in Accounting, Franklin University

Organizations: American Institute of Certified Public Accountants, Society of Financial Service Professionals, The Financial Planning Association, Institute of Business and Finance

I enjoy working with all aspects of financial planning, but have found that I most enjoy the senior market. I've spent the last several years working with individuals who are approaching or in retirement and whose focus has turned to distribution planning and asset preservation. Most recently, I've been working toward becoming a Certified Senior Advisor, which has helped me to understand seniors and the challenges they face.

Preston Cochrane
Executive Director, AAA Fair Credit Foundation
525 East 100 South, Suite 410
Salt Lake City, UT 84102
E-mail Address: pcochrane@aaafaircredit.org
Website: www.debtfreeforlife.com

Certifications: Accredited Financial Counselor

Education: B.S. in Exercise Physiology, University of Utah

Organizations: Association for Financial Counseling and Planning Education, American Association of Debt Management Organizations

John R. Connell
CPA/PFS, Causey, Demgen & Moore
1801 California Street, Suite 4650
Denver, CO 80202
E-mail Address: jconnell@cdmcpa.com
Website: www.cdmcpa.com

Certifications: Certified Public Accountant/Personal Financial Specialist, Certified Valuation Analyst

Education: B.A. in Economics, University of Denver
M.B.A. in Finance, University of Denver
J.D., University of Denver

Organizations: American Institute of Certified Public Accountants

Publications: *Financial Planning for Divorcing Couples*, Harcourt Brace, 1995

I have worked for 24 years with high-net-worth and/or high-income divorcing individuals helping them navigate the many complex financial hurdles and decisions that must be made. It is especially rewarding to see the new, energized individuals that emerge one to two years after this process is completed. I enjoy the letters I have received thanking me for helping them through the "tough times."

James Victor Conrad
Financial Professional, The MONY Group
103 North Meadows Drive, Suite 231
Wexford, PA 15090

E-mail Address: vconrad@mony.com

Website: www.mony.com/site/vconrad

Certifications: Chartered Financial Consultant, Certified Financial Planner®, Certified Public Accountant/Personal Financial Specialist

Education: B.S. in Accounting, Indiana University of Pennsylvania

Organizations: American Institute of Certified Public Accountants, Society of Financial Service Professionals, The Financial Planning Association, National Association of Insurance and Financial Advisors

My passion is best described by my motto: "Do unto others as they want to be done unto." Since everyone is different, with different likes and dislikes, I take the time to truly understand a client's fears, goals, and desires before custom designing a program to help them on their financial journey. My expertise in this field definitely comes from both my heart and my head. At the end of the day, I take comfort in knowing that my clients feel that: "Everything is taken care of by someone they trust."

Charles P. Copeland
CPA-PFS, The Copeland Group
25809 Business Center Drive
Redlands, CA 92374

E-mail Address: chuck@thecopelandgroup.com

Certifications: Certified Public Accountant/Personal Financial Specialist

Education: B.S. in Accounting, Cal Poly Pomona
M.S. in Taxation, Golden Gate

Organizations: American Institute of Certified Public Accountants

Brad R. Cougill
Partner, Deerfield Financial Advisors, Inc.
8440 Woodfield Crossing, Suite 360
Indianapolis, IN 46240

E-mail Address: bcougill@iquest.net

Website: www.deerfieldfa.com

Certifications: Certified Financial Planner®, Chartered Mutual Fund Counselor®

Education: B.S. in Finance, with High Honors, Butler University

Organizations: National Association of Personal Financial Advisors

In my role as a partner of Deerfield Financial Advisors, Inc., I bring to the firm more than 10 years of financial planning and investment experience in the Indianapolis community. Prior to joining the firm in 1997, I focused on retirement and investment planning with the Indiana office of a national employee benefits consulting firm. In addition, I am an active member in the National Association of Personal Financial Advisors (NAPFA). Outside of the office, I enjoy spending time with my wife, Lorrie, and our two young daughters, Sarah and Hannah.

Joan C. Coullahan
President, Divorce Financial Consultants
171 Heather Glen Road
Sterling, VA 20165-5823

E-mail Address: JoanCDFC@aol.com

Website: www.divorcefinancialconsultants.net

Certifications: Certified Divorce Planner

Education: M.B.A. in Business Administration, Shenandoah University
B.S. in Business, University of Maryland

Publications: *Financial Custody: You, Your Money, and Divorce*, Alpha,
2002

A former Registered Investment Advisor, I have been practicing exclusively as a Certified Divorce Planner (CDP) since March 1997. I am a financial analyst, assisting with all the financial aspects of divorce including calculation of child support and spousal maintenance, valuation of appreciation on separate and marital property, valuing the net worth of stock options and the lump-sum value of government and private defined benefit pension, and annuity plans. My clients make educated decisions because they understand the financial implications of issues such as cash flow and basic taxation changes after divorce, and they are able to evaluate different marital asset and debt scenarios.

William M. Cratty
Senior Financial Planner, MetLife Securities
25 Recreation Park Drive
Hingham, MA 02043

E-mail Address: wcratty@metlife.com

Website: www.wcratty.metlife.com

Certifications: Certified Public Accountant/Personal Financial
Specialist

Education: B.S. in Accountancy, Bentley College
M.S. in Finance, Boston College

Organizations: American Institute of Certified Public Accountants, The Financial Planning Association, National Association of Insurance and Financial Advisors

The focus of my practice is to help my clients achieve financial freedom, however they define it. I do this by creating comprehensive financial plans and keeping them up to date through periodic reviews, and by being a constant source of support and information for my clients. For me, long-term relationships are the cornerstone of my practice.

Donna S. Cygan

President, Essential Financial Planning, Inc.
4800 Juan Tabo NE, Suite D
Albuquerque, NM 87111

E-mail Address: dscygan@essentialfinancialplanning.com

Website: www.essentialfinancialplanning.com

Certifications: Certified Financial Planner®

Education: M.B.A. in Management and Strategic Planning, University of New Mexico
B.A. in Psychology, Indiana University

Organizations: The Financial Planning Association, National Association of Personal Financial Advisors

Publications: "Are You 'On Track' for Retirement?" *MD News Magazine*, 2001
"Focus on Things You Control," *Albuquerque Journal*, 2001
"Kids and Money," *MD News Magazine*, 2001

I love the time I spend with my clients. I learn so much from them, and I am rewarded with their friendship and trust. I have built my practice by providing extensive service and spoiling my clients. I earn their trust quickly, and they sleep better at night knowing I am watching their finances closely, have reduced the risk in their portfolios, and am helping them achieve their goals. I am a fee-only financial planner, and I am passionate about having no conflicts of interest. It is very important to me that my clients know I do not have any hidden agendas, and I am focused solely on helping them achieve their goals.

Jennifer L. Delcamp

Director of Operations
Consumer Credit Counseling Service of Central Oklahoma
3230 N. Rockwell
Bethany, OK 73008-1789

E-mail Address: jdelcamp@cccsok.com

Website: www.cccsok.com

Certifications: Certified Consumer Credit Counselor

Education: B.S. in Sociology, Oklahoma City University

Organizations: National Foundation for Credit Counseling

When things become complicated, people easily feel overwhelmed and avoid confronting their money problems. Applying sound financial principles to our daily lives is not something that comes naturally for most of us. Eventually, we all have to take the time to learn the fundamentals of money management—or sharpen those skills, and it doesn't have to be a complex process full of charts and graphs. I show my clients, and often my family and friends, that even a few painless compromises can make all of the difference in establishing a budget and that getting out of debt can be a fairly simple process.

Jonathan S. Dinkins
Senior Consultant, Glass Jacobson Investment Advisors, LLC
10711 Red Run Boulevard, Suite 101
Owings Mills, MD 21117

E-mail Address: jon.dinkins@glassjacobson.com

www.glassjacobson.com

Certifications: Certified Public Accountant/Personal Financial Specialist, Certified Investment Management Analyst, Chartered Mutual Fund Counselor®

Education: B.B.A. in Accounting, Marshall University

Organizations: American Institute of Certified Public Accountants

Publications: "Understanding Stock Options," *The Business Monthly*, 2002 "Saving for College—Comparing Education IRAs and Section 529 Plans," *The Business Monthly*, 2001

They say three's a charm. Having the advantage of being CPAs, Financial Planners, and Investment Advisors, my firm—Glass Jacobson— and I bring a unique set of qualities to our client relationships. We don't just address stand-alone issues. We take a holistic approach, while overseeing and coordinating our clients' complete financial picture, including income and estate tax, as well as financial and investment planning initiatives. Since the client portfolio ultimately becomes the focal point for all planning, our processes induce a discipline that truly manages "risk," while significantly increasing the probability of achieving market returns and client goals.

Peg A. Downey
Partner, Money Plans
8701 Georgia Avenue, Suite 710
Silver Spring, MD 20910

E-mail Address: PegDowney@MoneyPlans.com

Certifications: Certified Financial Planner®

Education: B.A. in English, University of Rochester
M.A. in American Studies, George Washington University

Organizations: National Association of Personal Financial Advisors

I've been helping individuals accomplish their life goals for over 20 years. In my work with people in many different situations—married, unmarried, divorced, recipients of inheritances, facing life-challenging illnesses—I specialize in working with clients' financial and emotional issues around money. I use my background in education and program development to make the work with clients clear, nonthreatening, and jargon-free—and clients tell me that it is even fun!

Stephen A. Drake
Ph.D., CPA/PFS, CFP®, Optima Financial Resources
2345 Oakwood Drive
Prescott, AZ 86305

E-mail Address: sdrake@optimafr.com

Website: www.optimafr.com

Certifications: Certified Financial Planner®, Certified Public Accountant/Personal Financial Specialist, Enrolled Agent

Education: Ph.D. in Taxation, University of Arizona
M.S. in Taxation, University of Arizona
B.S. in Finance and Accounting, University of Arizona

Organizations: American Institute of Certified Public Accountants, The Financial Planning Association

Publications: "Why Asset Protection?" American Podiatry Association, 2002

"Is a Foreign Trust Right for You?" *American QuarterHorse Racing Journal*, 2002
"Estate Planning That You Never Knew Could Be So Good," *American Association of Equine Practitioners Journal*, 2002

I have been a practicing CPA/CFP® for 25 years with extensive experience in solving many types of business, tax, and financial problems for individuals, families, and companies. I have a particular interest in estate planning, asset protection planning, transactions with large capital gains and, uniquely, the equine industry. I have published extensively and have spoken to a myriad of professional and trade groups. I believe that all problems have several possible solutions and I am committed to finding the right one for each client and their individual and family needs.

Sandra E. Dunaway
Director, Consumer Credit Counseling Service of Mobile
705 Oak Circle Drive
Mobile, AL 36609

E-mail Address: dunaway@mobilecan.org

Website: www.cccsmobile.org

Certifications: Certified Consumer Credit Counselor

Education: B.B.A. in Business, Faulkner

Organizations: National Foundation for Credit Counseling

Publications: "The Ghost of Christmas Past," *The Mobile Register,* 2000
"Surviving the Holidays," *The Mobile Register,* 2000
"Freedom and Credit Cards—A Good Mix," *The Mobile Register,* 2000

Having made financial missteps in my youth, I offer a unique perspective from someone who has "been there, done that." Also, my 24 years of experience as a community leader, having served on numerous boards of directors, has broadened my understanding of community needs. As a result, I feel passionate about offering education and counseling to consumers facing financial hardships in an effort to help them avoid costly mistakes. One way I accomplish this mission is by promoting financial counseling and providing consumer education as a regular contributor and expert on Mobile's FOX 10 News, in addition to being a resource for other local media outlets.

Michael M. Eisenberg
CPA/PFS, Michael M. Eisenberg, An Accountancy Corporation
11444 W. Olympic Boulevard, Suite 240
Los Angeles, CA 90064

E-mail Address: mmecpa@iname.com

Certifications: Certified Public Accountant/Personal Financial Specialist

Education: B.S. in Accounting, California State University Northridge J.D., University of West Los Angeles

Organizations: American Institute of Certified Public Accountants, The Financial Planning Association

I have been in practice for over 20 years. I still get that "special feeling" when a client says "thank you for helping me." I am in a people business. I deal with financial issues, not life-and-death issues. I enjoy working with individuals and my clients appreciate the fact that by working together and allowing ample time and a proper thought process, the vast majority of their financial problems can be solved.

Gregory C. Fenton
CFP®, Cambridge Cape Cod Advisors
128 Route 6A
Sandwich, MA 02563
E-mail Address: gcfenton@capecod.net
Website: nvo.com/capecodadvisors
Certifications: Certified Financial Planner®
Education: B.S. in Accounting, Bowling Green
Organizations: National Association of Personal Financial Advisors

My purpose with all my clients is to help them achieve the life they dream about. I concentrate on more than just numbers and really develop an intuitive relationship that energizes the clients to pursue their true goals in life. When their emotions about money switch from fear, anxiety, greed, or worry to excitement, fun, problem-free lifestyle, etc., that is when the "true" financial and life planning can begin. The results are truly fantastic!

John J. Feyche
Manager, Z&W Wealth Management
25500 Hawthorne Boulevard, Suite 2120
Torrance, CA 90505-6833
E-mail Address: jfeyche@zwcpa.com

Website: www.zwcpa.com

Certifications: Certified Public Accountant/Personal Financial Specialist

Education: B.S. in Accounting, Waynesburg College
M.S. in Accounting, Pennsylvania State University
M.B.T. in Taxation, University of Southern California

Organizations: American Institute of Certified Public Accountants, Financial Planning Association

Throughout different phases of my career I have worked as a tax planner, a financial analyst, a stockbroker, and a financial advisor. My training and experience in a variety of financial areas has given me a unique perspective on the planning process. My background enables me to clearly focus on the different disciplines inherent in each sector of the financial planning process. It also helps me to evaluate the myriad of issues involved in a comprehensive financial plan; and is invaluable in explaining to clients the ripple effect one part of their plan has upon another.

Mitchell Freedman
President, MFAC Financial Advisors, Inc.
15260 Ventura Boulevard, Suite 940
Sherman Oaks, CA 91403

E-mail Address: mitchpfs@mfac-bizmgt.com

Website: www.mfac-bizmgt.com

Certifications: Certified Public Accountant/Personal Financial Specialist

Education: B.B.A. in Accounting, Adelphi University

Organizations: American Institute of Certified Public Accountants

Publications: *Guide to Planning for Performing and Creative Artists*, American Institute of Certified Public Accountants
Guide to Planning for Divorce, American Institute of Certified Public Accountants

How does a financial advisor differentiate himself from the crowd, when there are so many providing advice to clients? In my case, I don't promise to make my clients rich. I inform them that they will accumulate the bulk of their wealth from their careers and businesses. What separates me from others is that my investment philosophies will not likely allow my clients to get poor. I aim to have them achieve their goals by obtaining reasonable investment returns while taking risks that they are comfortable with and by reducing portfolio volatility.

Jill I. Gianola
Fee-Only Financial Planner, Gianola Financial Planning
2094 Tremont Center, Suite 4
Columbus, OH 43221

E-mail Address: jill@gianolafinancial.com

Website: www.gianolafinancial.com

Certifications: Certified Financial Planner®

Education: B.A. in Economics, University of Wisconsin
M.S. in Economics, University of Wisconsin
M.B.A., University of Illinois

Organizations: The Financial Planning Association, National Association of Personal Financial Advisors

Publications: *Planning for the Times of Your Life*, self-published (contributor), 1998
Online Financial Expert and Columnist for iVillage.com, 2000–2001

At the time I started my financial planning firm, objective, competent advice was not widely available to middle-income individuals. This is the group I have focused on in my practice. I help my clients articulate their dreams, map out the path to their goals, and stay on course. I am a Certified Financial Planner® certificant and I offer comprehensive advice on a fee-only basis exclusively. I previously worked as an economist and as a small business manager and consultant, but financial planning is the career for me.

Don A. Gomez
President, Momentum Financial Advisors
3475 Lenox Road, Suite 400
Atlanta, GA 30326

E-mail Address: FeeOnlyPlanner@netscape.net

Website: www.Momentumfinancialadvisors.com

Certifications: Certified Financial Planner®

Education: B.S. in Mechanical Engineering, University of Notre Dame

Organizations: The Financial Planning Association, National Association of Personal Financial Advisors

John Grable
Director, Institute of Personal Financial Planning
Kansas State University
School of Family Studies and Human Services
318 Justin Hall
Manhattan, KS 66506

E-mail Address: grable@humec.ksu.edu

Website: www.ksu.edu/ipfp

Certifications: Certified Financial Planner®, Registered Financial Consultant

Education: Ph.D. in Family Financial Planning, Virginia Tech
M.B.A. in Business, Clarkson University
B.S. in Business/Economics, University of Nevada

Organizations: Association for Financial Counseling and Planning Education

Publications: "Technique for Calculating the Maximum Withdrawal from Accumulated Savings," *Financial Planning Monthly*, 2002
"A Further Examination of Financial Help-Seeking Behavior," *Financial Counseling and Planning*, 2002
"A Subsequent Study of the Relationships Between Self-Worth and Financial Beliefs, Behavior, and Satisfaction," *Journal of Family and Consumer Sciences*, 2001

My academic passion involves understanding the knowledge, attitudes, and behaviors of individual investors. I use an eclectic research approach, including psychology of investing theories, money management techniques, and financial planning practice approaches, to better understand why and how investors make decisions. A risk tolerance scale I developed with a colleague is currently used by university researchers and financial planning firms. I enjoy writing and teaching. I currently serve as the editor for the *Journal of Personal Finance*, and I am active in several national financial planning and counseling organizations.

Sherman D. Hanna
Professor, The Ohio State University
1787 Neil Avenue
Campbell Hall 262
Columbus, OH 43210-1290

E-mail Address: hanna.1@osu.edu

Education: Ph.D. in Consumer Economics, Cornell University
B.S. in Economics, Massachusetts Institute of Technology

Organizations: Association for Financial Counseling and Planning Education

Publications: Hanna, S. & Chen, P. (1999, July). "Small Stocks Versus Large: It's How Long You Hold That Counts." *AAII Journal, XXI* (6), 26-27.

Yuh, Y., Hanna, S., & Montalto, C. P. (1998). "Mean and Pessimistic Projections of Retirement Adequacy." *Financial Services Review*, 7(3), 175-193.

Hanna, S. (2000). "Financial statements and budgeting." In Garman, E. T. & Xiao, J. J. (eds.) *The Mathematics of Personal Financial Planning*, Second edition, 122-145.

Patrick T. Hanratty
Managing Director, Capital Advisors, Ltd.
626 Terminal Tower
50 Public Square
Cleveland, OH 44113

E-mail Address: phanratty@capitaladvisorsltd.com

Website: capitaladvisorsltd.com

Certifications: Certified Financial Planner®, Certified Public Accountant/Personal Financial Specialist

Education: B.A. in Accounting, Cleveland State University
M.B.A. in Finance, Cleveland State University

Organizations: American Institute of Certified Public Accountants, The Financial Planning Association, NFLPA Registered Player Financial Advisor

My training and experience allows me to bring perspective and vision to the field of financial planning. I combine a strong educational background and a professorial mentality with a passion for excellence, service, and helping people. My technical expertise allows me to identify complex issues and explain them in a way clients understand. Simply stated, I educate my clients so they can make informed financial decisions. I coordinate activities with other advisors to ensure all facets of my clients financial lives are being addressed. My best attributes are that I am innately qualified to do a job I truly enjoy.

Joe Harper
CFP®, Harper Associates, Inc.
1620 Zollinger Road
Columbus, OH 43221

E-mail Address: harps@jadeinc.com

Website: www.JoeHarper.com

Certifications: Certified Financial Planner®

Education: B.S. in Education, The Ohio State University

Organizations: The Financial Planning Association, National Association of Personal Financial Advisors

I have had the unique experience of knowing two salespeople who "went bad"; embezzling from clients and winding up in jail. My resulting conversion from commission to Fee-Only compensation has served both clients and myself well. I am highly suspicious of the financial industry and have used that screen as an asset in helping clients avoid most problem transactions. With small businesses on both sides of my family, I have been able to provide guidance to clients who face various intra-family issues. Our clients tend to be conservative, down to earth folks who would rather miss a boat than catch one that sinks.

Timothy M. Hayes
President, Landmark Financial Advisory Services, LLC
16 Landmark Lane
Pittsford, NY 14534-1623

E-mail Address: lfas@rochester.rr.com

Website: www.landmarkfas.com

Certifications: Chartered Mutual Fund Counselor®, Registered Financial Consultant

Education: M.B.A. in Finance, St. John Fisher College
B.S. in Management, St. John Fisher College

Organizations: The Financial Planning Association, National Association of Personal Financial Advisors

I think financial planning is among the noblest and most rewarding careers a person could choose. It's a demanding discipline that comes with real responsibilities. Clients place a very high degree of trust in our ability to help them make sense of their financial situation. I consider it a privilege to be able to use the knowledge I've acquired in service to my clients and their families. I get tremendous satisfaction from knowing that I am able to help people from all walks of life to achieve their most cherished financial objectives. It's why I do what I do.

Bruce R. Heling
President, Heling Associates, Inc.
P.O. Box 1385
Brookfield, WI 53008-1385

E-mail Address: bheling@heling.com

Certifications: Certified Financial Planner®, Certified Public Accountant/Personal Financial Specialist

Education: B.B.A. in Accounting, University of Wisconsin–Oshkosh

Organizations: American Institute of Certified Public Accountants, The Financial Planning Association

Publications: "Needs-Based Asset Allocation: Five Ways to Figure Out How Much Risk a Client Should Manage," *Wisconsin CPA*, 1998
"Asset Allocation: A Primer for Qualified Plan Sponsors," *Journal of Pension Benefits*, 1994

I love what I do … helping people to become successful financially by teaching them the fundamentals of financial management and how to keep things as simple as possible and only as sophisticated as necessary. And while others focus on building a "business," I love having a "practice." It's just me, my office manager, and my clients. The close relationship we have and the high degree of trust that develops allows us to almost be part of our clients' families, and I like that (as long as they don't all show up for Thanksgiving dinner!).

David O. Hogan
Principal, Hogan & Slovacek, PC
6120 South Yale, Suite 350
Tulsa, OK 74136

Certifications: Certified Public Accountant/Personal Financial Specialist, Certified Financial Planner®

Education: B.S. Accounting, University of Central Oklahoma

Organizations: American Institute of Certified Public Accountants

I have specialized as a tax consultant during my entire business career. In recent years I have had considerable experience in retirement, estate, and personal financial planning. I serve as a frequent speaker at pre-retirement planning seminars provided by various companies to their employees. My clients include many closely held businesses for which I provide income and estate-tax planning services to the companies and their shareholders.

Angie H. Hollerich
Professional Speaker, Brass Ring Productions, Ltd.
P.O. Box 307318
Gahanna, OH 43230-7318

E-mail Address: angieh@brassringpro.com

Website: www.brassringpro.com

Certifications: Certified Educational Planner

Organizations: Association for Financial Counseling and Planning Education

Publications: *Grab the Brass Ring of Financial Security*, self-published, 1995
The Weight and Wealth Factors, self-published, 2000
The Weight and Wealth Factors Strategy Boxes, self-published, 2000

Because I speak from my unique life experiences, I am able to communicate financial strategies, information, and solutions to my audiences on a level that is easily understood by people from all economic, social, and professional backgrounds. I identify, in layman's terms, simple solutions to seemingly complex financial problems. I break down "industry" terminology to user-friendly vocabulary that everyone can understand. I believe my professional background, my personal experiences, and my successes with my former financial clients combines to bring powerful messages to my audiences.

Dennis N. Houlihan, CFP®
Managing Director, Houlihan Asset Management, LLC
203 E. Berry Street, Suite 1211
Fort Wayne, IN 46802

E-mail Address: dhoulihan@fwi.com

Certifications: Certified Financial Planner®

Education: B.S. in Finance, Indiana University
M.S. in Financial Planning and Portfolio, College For Financial Planning

Organizations: National Association of Personal Financial Advisors

Bonnie A. Hughes
President, A&H Financial Planning and Education, Inc.
30 Forest Meadow Drive SW
P.O. Box 743
Rome, GA 30165

E-mail Address: ashbyandhughes@comcast.net

Website: www.ashbyandhughes.com

Certifications: Certified Financial Planner®

Education: B.S. in Family Economics and Management, Southern Illinois University
M.S. in Financial Planning, College of Financial Planning

Organizations: The Financial Planning Association, National Association of Personal Financial Advisors, National Association of Tax Professionals, Association of Financial Counseling and Planning Education

As an Hourly As-Needed financial coach, I have the best job in the world. I take a personal interest in empowering each client with the knowledge they need to improve in all aspects of their financial lives. It is truly rewarding to see them develop confidence and peace of mind as they build the brightest futures based on a solid foundation of financial knowledge. Half the fun is sharing my insights on spending, saving, investing, and so forth. But the real fun begins as clients get tuned in to a higher level of financial thinking—and come up with great ideas themselves!

Henrietta O. Humphreys

Principal, The Henrietta Humphreys Group
3401 Clay Street, Suite #703
San Francisco, CA 94118

E-mail Address: henri@humphreysgroup.com

Website: www.humphreysgroup.com

Certifications: Certified Financial Planner®

Education: M.B.A. in Graduate School of Business, Stanford University
B.A. in Philosophy, Converse College

Organizations: The Financial Planning Association, National
Association of Personal Financial Advisors

I suppose that the single most important thing in my working relationship is that I really like people. Not just the easy ones, the ones whose
problems are easily solved, but even the difficult ones, people you
wouldn't normally choose to associate with. I seem to have a knack for
building a rapport with all people and they open up to me, so it makes
my job that much easier. And in the end I usually find that I've made a
friend as well as a satisfied client.

Alexis M. Jensen

President, Z&W Wealth Management
25500 Hawthorne Boulevard, Suite 2120
Torrance, CA 90505-6833

E-mail Address: ajensen@zwcpa.com

Website: www.zwcpa.com

Certifications: Certified Public Accountant/Personal Financial Specialist

Education: B.S. in Accounting, California State University Long Beach

Organizations: American Institute of Certified Public Accountants, The
Financial Planning Association

My success is entirely due to each and every one of my clients, all of
whom I consider my extended family. I'm there 24/7 for them and I will
always go the extra mile. I truly and sincerely care and want to help. I
listen to clients' situations and concerns not with the intent to sell them

a product or service, but with a deep passion to find the absolute finest solution for them. Anyone can obtain financial knowledge and run a computer, but I firmly believe my achievements are rooted in my passion, energy, commitment, and enthusiasm I have for my clients' best interest, just as I would for any family member.

Ann D. Jevne
Partner, Schwartz & Hofflich LLP, CPA
37 North Avenue
Norwalk, CT 06851

E-mail Address: ajevne@shcpa.com

Certifications: Certified Financial Planner®, Certified Public Accountant/Personal Financial Specialist

Education: B.S.B. in Accounting (Cum Laude), Sacred Heart University

Organizations: American Institute of Certified Public Accountants, The Financial Planning Association

Steve J. Johnson
Financial Planner, Steven J. Johnson CPA/PFS, CFP®
3525 N. Causeway Boulevard, Suite 600
Metairie, LA 70002

E-mail Address: johnson@acadiacom.net

Certifications: Certified Financial Planner®, Certified Public Accountant/Personal Financial Specialist

Education: B.S. in Accounting, University of Illinois–Chicago

Organizations: American Institute of Certified Public Accountants, The Financial Planning Association

I believe that teaching clients about investing and other financial planning matters makes them better informed and better able to make good financial decisions. My goal is to treat every client with the respect they deserve and to make them feel that they are my most important client. This is the foundation of a relationship that can weather any financial storm.

Raymond C. Julian

Executive Vice President, Compass Capital Corporation
One Gateway Center
Newton, MA 02458

E-mail Address: ray@CompassSecurities.com

Website: www.compasssecurities.com

Certifications: Certified Financial Planner®

Education: B.S. in Management & Communications, Boston College

Organizations: The Financial Planning Association

Publications: Host, *Today's Millionaire*, personal financial radio program, network/station

It's not hard to draw an analogy between my love of sailing and philosophy of financial planning. I liken my role as a Certified Financial Planner® to that of a ship's captain, where the primary responsibility is being in charge of the overall safety and welfare of everyone. When a client comes onboard and places their unquestionable trust in my abilities, I accept the responsibility to be fully focused on helping them to achieve their financial goals. I tell my clients, "When you have financial gains, you should also plan to enjoy them." I relish the challenges that come with making my clients happy with their lives.

William K. Kaiser

CPA/PFS, Howard Financial Services, Inc.
8350 Meadow Road, Suite 286
Dallas, TX 75287

E-mail Address: bill@jhcpa.com

Website: www.howardfinancialservices.com

Certifications: Certified Financial Planner®, Certified Public Accountant/Personal Financial Specialist

Education: B.B.A. in Accounting, University of Texas at San Antonio

Organizations: National Association of Personal Financial Advisors

I bring to my clients experience obtained from some of the top firms in the financial industry including Ernst & Young, Fidelity Investments, and Northern Trust. Since 1987, I have specialized in providing investment management services, and helped clients with asset allocation and selecting money managers. I identify and monitor alternative investment strategies and help clients analyze and evaluate other investment opportunities, including cost/benefit analysis of insurance products. I currently work for Howard Financial Services, a private financial planning firm comprised solely of CPAs who provide fee-only services.

James S. Kantowski
Advisor, RSM McGladrey, Inc.
6701 Democracy Boulevard
Bethesda, MD 20817

E-mail Address: jim_kantowski@rsmi.com

Certifications: Certified Financial Planner®, Certified Public Accountant

Education: B.S. in Accounting, East Tennessee State

Organizations: American Institute of Certified Public Accountants

I believe that diversification, tax planning, low expenses, passive investments, and a long-term strategy are the keys to having a positive investment experience. My experience as a CPA, a fee-based investment approach, and the use of low-cost, passively managed institutional mutual funds gives me the tools to help clients meet their long-term investment goals.

Stuart Kessler
Co-chair, Personal Financial Planning Group, American Express Tax & Business Services, Inc.
1185 Avenue of the Americas, 4th Floor
New York, NY 10036

E-mail Address: stuart.i.kessler@aexp.com

Certifications: Certified Public Accountant/Personal Financial Specialist, Accredited Estate Planner

Education: B.A. in Economics, Brooklyn College
M.B.A. in Taxes, CUNY
J.D., Brooklyn Law
L.L.M. in Taxes, NYU

Organizations: American Institute of Certified Public Accountants

I am more than a money man. I am part psychiatrist and clergyman and a good listener, leaving enough space for clients to tell me things they might not impart to others. I am often the lightening rod. Long-suppressed thoughts pass from one spouse to the other through me. In this manner, I provide advice and solutions to people who live very hectic lives and do not have or wish to spend their time on financial matters. Discussions on values, the client's intellectual interests, and extracurricular work activities are key to my discussions of overall personal financial planning.

Paul D. Knott
Financial Consultant, Smith Barney
4301 Chart House Drive
Wilmington, NC 28405-7404

E-mail Address: pjpjknott@ec.rr.com

Certifications: Certified Financial Planner®, Certified Public Accountant/Personal Financial Specialist

Education: B.S. in Accountancy, University of North Carolina at Wilmington

Organizations: American Institute of Certified Public Accountants, The Financial Planning Association

Randall Kratz
CFP®, Kratz Investment Advisory Network
3730 Kirby Drive, Suite 1200
Houston, TX 77098

E-mail Address: randallkratz@msn.com

Website: www.kianonline.com

Certifications: Certified Financial Planner®

Education: B.S. in Communications, University of Texas

Organizations: National Association of Personal Financial Advisors

I also work with people who don't have a sizeable enough portfolio to work with firms that specialize in asset management. My "a la carte services" help those clients who have specific questions or concerns, so they can build large enough assets to manage.

Marsha G. LePhew
President, LePhew Financial Services, Inc.
452 Lakeshore Parkway, Suite 115
Rock Hill, SC 29730

E-mail Address: marsha@lephew.com

Certifications: Chartered Financial Consultant, Certified Financial Planner®, Certified Public Accountant/Personal Financial Specialist

Education: B.S. in Business Administration, Concord College

Organizations: American Institute of Certified Public Accountants, The Financial Planning Association, National Association of Personal Financial Advisors

I focus on growing client relationships by helping clients blend their financial and life objectives into written plans and by helping them to make wise decisions and to be diligent in remaining focused on their goals. Expertise in tax and accounting, combined with financial planning and investment advisory skills, allow me to provide my clients with one key individual to function as their family's personal controller. Achievements include recognition by *Worth* magazine as one of the top 250 financial advisors in the nation in the July/August 2002 edition.

Randall L. Leshin
Executive Director, Express Consolidation, Inc.
413 NE 3rd Street
Delray Beach, FL 33483

E-mail Address: rleshin@expressconsolidation.com

Education: J.D., Nova Southeastern
B.S. in English, University of Wisconsin–Madison

Organizations: American Association of Debt Management Organizations

Believe it or not, like most lawyers, I entered the profession to help people. But practicing law does not always provide fulfillment. Clients may not appreciate it when you win, and can turn really ugly when you lose. No matter how much you win for the client, it is never enough. So while I still practice law, the greatest satisfaction I get these days is from counseling people regarding their debt and credit management.

You have no idea how a little shared knowledge, that seems so familiar to me, can bring a thank you that makes me blush.

Deborah O. Levine
Financial Planner, AFP Group
11835 W. Olympic Boulevard, Suite 1150E
Los Angeles, CA 90064

E-mail Address: Deborah@d-blevine.com

Certifications: Certified Financial Planner®, Certified Public Accountant/Personal Financial Specialist

Education: M.B.A. in Business, Harvard University
M.S.T. in Taxation, DePaul University
B.A. in Liberal Arts, Northwestern University

Organizations: American Institute of Certified Public Accountants

Publications: "Retirement Savings," *California Accountant*

Financial planning is my passion. When I work with a client, my only concern is the financial well-being of that client. My extensive experience and strong academic background allow me to work seamlessly with all clients regardless of the complexity of their situation. The pleasure I receive from helping a young couple with a plan for financial independence is no less than what I experience when I develop a multi-faceted program for an established entity. I am pleased to say that the excitement from participating with the client in executing the plan has not diminished over the years.

John Henry and Constanza Low
President and Vice President, Knickerbocker Advisors Inc.
P.O. Box 312
Pine Plains, NY 12567

E-mail Address: jhlow@knick.com

Website: www.knick.com

John Henry Low:

Education: M.B.A. in Executive Program, Management, Wharton School, University of Pennsylvania
B.S.E. in Electrical Engineering & Computer Science, Princeton University

Constanza Low:

Education: M.I.M. in International Finance, American Graduate School of International Management
B.S. in Economics, University of Michigan

Organizations: Association for Investment Management and Research, The Financial Planning Association, National Association of Personal Financial Advisors

Publications: *The Lawyer's Guide to Retirement*, 3rd Ed., ABA Press, 1998
Best of ABA Sections, ABA Press, 1997
The Savvy Investor, quarterly column, *Experience*, 1996–1998

We believe that money should not make you worry and there is an appropriate way for each person or for each family to invest. These two tenets of our practice make all the difference for our clients. By preparing a financial plan, implementing a solid and sensible investment strategy, and monitoring investments and their performance, we put our clients well on the road to meeting their financial goals. Better yet, our clients no longer have to worry about short-term market fluctuations, or if they are saving enough, or if they are invested in the right things. And that is the most rewarding of all!

Judith D. Ludwig
CPA, Tandem Financial Services, Inc.
1017 Turnpike Street
Canton, MA 02021

E-mail Address: jdludwig@yahoo.com

Certifications: Chartered Financial Consultant, Certified Financial Planner®, Certified Public Accountant/Personal Financial Specialist, Accredited Estate Planner

Education: B.A. in Mathematics, Douglass College, Rutgers

Organizations: American Institute of Certified Public Accountants, The Financial Planning Association

I think that what makes me a "special" Money Mind is that I truly care about my clients. I am very selective about the clients I work with because this is such a personal relationship that we have. I do quite a bit of estate and retirement planning, and in that capacity I learn very intimate details about my clients' lives. In the course of my work, I try very hard to bring shattered families together again. I am fortunate that I do not "have" to work but do so because I love what I do and I love helping other people.

Paul D. Lyons
Manager, KPMG
8200 Brookriver Drive, Suite 200
Dallas, TX 75247

E-mail Address: pdlyons@kpmg.com

Certifications: Certified Financial Planner®, Certified Public Accountant/Personal Financial Specialist

Education: B.B.A. in Accounting and Finance, Baylor University

Organizations: American Institute of Certified Public Accountants, The Financial Planning Association

I am a manager in the personal financial planning practice of an international accounting firm. My primary focus is fee-based, comprehensive planning. I enjoy working with clients from all ends of the spectrum, whether its a high-net-worth business owner or a struggling middle-class family of four. My twelve years of experience includes investment analysis, estate planning, tax preparation and strategizing, and retirement planning. I believe the three most important roles of an advisor are educating their clients, providing them with real solutions, and encouraging them in the implementation of their plan.

Suzi Marsh
LCSW, Behavioral Solutions, Inc.
951 Gordon Street
Stone Mountain, GA 30083

E-mail Address: suzimarsh@mindspring.com

Education: B.S.B.A. in Marketing, Univ. of Alabama, Tuscaloosa
M.S.W. in Mental Health, The Ohio State University

I am a psychotherapist who is a recovering addict of twenty years and also living with learning disabilities (ADHD and dyscalculia—a math comprehension problem). I have both first-hand and professional experience in creating ways to stay sane with money. I help my clients manage their urges to spend and offer nontraditional methods to coping with finances. I am also a host of a public affairs show called "Choosing Life: Addictions, Mental Health & Recovery."

Judi Martindale
Certified Financial Planner®, Martindale & Associates
1076 Pacific Street
San Luis Obispo, CA 93401

E-mail Address: jm@judimartindale.com

Website: www.judimartindale.com

Certifications: Certified Financial Planner®, Enrolled Agent

Education: B.S. in Education, University of Cincinnati
M.Ed. in Education, Miami (of Ohio) University

Organizations: National Association of Enrolled Agents, National
Association of Personal Financial Advisors

Publications: *No More Baglady Fears: A Woman's Guide to Retirement
Planning*, iUniverse.com, 1999
Simple Ways to Manage Your Money, iUniverse.com

I have lived what I recommend. I divorced after years of being a first
grade teacher, faced with making financial decisions with no experience
nor much money. I have lived through years of being on my own, self-
employment, purchasing a home, remarriage, life-threatening illness
(breast cancer), parents' death, and unexpected early death of a niece.
As a student, I take cutting-edge courses to understand and work sensi-
tively with people, knowing that financial issues are never just about
the money.

Jeffrey N. Mehler
Principal, Jeffrey N. Mehler, CFP®
90 Main Street, Suite 105
Centerbrook, CT 06409

E-mail Address: jeff@jnmehler.com

Website: www.jnmehler.com

Certifications: Certified Financial Planner®

Education: B.S. in Industrial, Fairleigh Dickinson University
M.B.A. in Finance/Information Systems, New York University

Organizations: The Financial Planning Association, National
Association of Personal Financial Advisors

I founded my firm in 1992 *to provide clients with the practical, unbiased advice they need to make informed financial decisions.* The firm is listed with all required government regulatory agencies. All financial planning and investment advisory services are performed on a fee-only basis. I have been quoted in the *Wall Street Journal* and have appeared on the Dow Jones Television Network for my expertise in college planning. I also lead seminars on IRA Distributions and College Planning.

Jeff W. Michael

Director of Education, Springboard Non-Profit Consumer Credit Management
6370 Magnolia Avenue, 2nd Floor
Riverside, CA 92506

E-mail Address: jeff.michael@credit.org

Website: www.credit.org

Education: B.A. in Humanities, College of the Ozarks

Organizations: National Foundation for Credit Counseling

Helen L. Modly

VP & Director of Planning, Focus Financial Consultants, Ltd.
201 East Washington Street
P.O. Box 1613
Middleburg, VA 20118

E-mail Address: hmodly@focusfinancialconsultants.com

Website: www.focusfinancialconsult

Certifications: Chartered Financial Consultant, Certified Financial Planner®, Chartered Life Underwriter, Certified Divorce Planner

Education: B.S. in Nursing, George Mason University

Organizations: The Financial Planning Association, The Institute for Certified Divorce Planners

Publications: Various articles published on MorningstarAdvisor.com, 2001-2002

I love my work! It is so rewarding when my clients tell me that they feel in control of their financial destiny for the first time in their lives. The incredible resources a firm such as ours can bring to the table enables us to bring clarity to chaos. I take personal pride in the comprehensive nature of our planning work and the fact that we don't just tell clients what they should do, we get it done!

Steven B. Morris
Owner, Steven B. Morris, CPA, PFS, CFP®
1770 Indian Trail Road, Suite 275
Norcross, GA 30093

E-mail Address: sbmcpa@mindspring.com

Website: www.sbmcpa.com

Certifications: Certified Financial Planner®, Certified Public Accountant/Personal Financial Specialist

Education: M.B.A. in Taxation, Long Island University
B.B.A. in Accountancy, Baruch College

Organizations: American Institute of Certified Public Accountants, The Financial Planning Association

I am more than a bean counter. I earn my clients' trust by listening to them and offering them solutions to their financial problems and by providing them with information and advice to protect and increase their wealth. I believe in providing services beyond the traditional accounting firm services. I consider primary services to be business consulting and financial services. I take the time to advise my clients on how they can reach their financial goals. I believe that my practice has successfully grown because I go the extra mile for my clients by listening to their problems and concerns and by consulting with them on a regular basis.

Cheryl A. Moss
Tax Advisor, Cheryl A. Moss, CPA/PFS, CFP®, CLU
340 N. Wisconsin Street
DePere, WI 54115

E-mail Address: mossfamily1@msn.com

Certifications: Certified Financial Planner®, Chartered Life Underwriter, Certified Public Accountant/Personal Financial Specialist, Certified Divorce Planner

Education: B.A. in Accounting & Business, Carthage College

Organizations: American Institute of Certified Public Accountants, Society of Financial Service Professionals, The Financial Planning Association, National Association of Insurance and Financial Advisors

Early in my career as a CPA, I discovered a passion for helping clients solve problems and make wise financial choices. Using a unique planning methodology called The Legacy Wealth Optimization System®, I help clients integrate their values, vision, mission, and goals with appropriate strategies, tactics, and tools. The resulting clarity clients gain about their financial independence status gives them the confidence they need to craft family and charitable legacy plans that truly fulfill their deepest values. I provide these fee-based financial planning services as a registered investment advisory associate of Midwest Professional Planners, Ltd.

Craig J. Olson

Partner, Parrott Partnership, LLP
12725 SW 66th Avenue, #202
Portland, OR 97223

E-mail Address: craigo@parrottpartnership.com

Certifications: Certified Public Accountant/Personal Financial Specialist

Education: B.S. in Accounting, California State University Hayward

Organizations: American Institute of Certified Public Accountants

As my clients work toward financial independence, I work to define and help them achieve their tax and financial objectives. I do this by creating comprehensive financial plans that provide customized wealth navigation solutions. I have written financial articles for national and local publications and was featured on the cover of a national magazine. I also am a frequent lecturer on financial planning to national audiences.

Barbara M. O'Neill
Professor, Rutgers University
Rutgers Cooperative Extension
3 High Street, First Floor
Newton, NJ 07860

E-mail Address: oneill@aesop.rutgers.edu

Website: rce.rutgers.edu/money2000

Certifications: Accredited Financial Counselor, Certified Financial Planner®, Certified Housing Counselor

Education: Ph.D. in Family Financial Management, Virginia Tech
M.S. in Consumer Economics, Cornell University
B.S. in Home Economics Education, SUNY at Oneonta

Organizations: Association for Financial Counseling and Planning Education, The Financial Planning Association, National Association of Personal Financial Advisors

Publications: *Investing for Your Future* (Project Director and Co-Author), Natural Resource, Agriculture, and Engineering Service, Ithaca, NY, 2002
Investing on a Shoestring, Dearborn Financial Publishing, 1999
Saving on a Shoestring, Dearborn Financial Publishing, 1995

My strength as a university professor, financial journalist, and author is making complex concepts understandable to middle- and lower-income individuals, many with limited financial knowledge and experience. In 24 years of adult education, I've consistently organized information into "bite-sized pieces." My two books, *Saving on a Shoestring* and *Investing on a Shoestring*, target readers with small amounts of discretionary income and describe how to grow wealthy over time by making regular deposits. I teach thousands of people annually in a variety of formats including classes and conferences, newsletters, a weekly newspaper column in *The New Jersey Herald*, and the website www.rce. rutgers.edu/money2000.

Lloyd E. Painter

President, Painter Financial
3610 Lexington Road
Louisville, KY 40207

E-mail Address: painter@painterfinancial.com

Website: painterfinancial.com

Certifications: Chartered Financial Consultant, Certified Financial Planner®, Chartered Life Underwriter, Certified Public Accountant/Personal Financial Specialist, Certified Funds Specialist

Education: B.S. in Business Administration, Tusculum College

Organizations: American Institute of Certified Public Accountants, Society of Financial Service Professionals, The Financial Planning Association

My background as a CPA has been such a positive element in my success as a financial planner. Not only did it give me a background in taxation, but it taught me to listen. As a CPA, I constantly ask questions to help solve a problem. As a financial planner, that same process takes place. I love my business and the opportunity it affords me to continue increasing my education and income while being a positive force in my clients' lives. The feedback I receive from my staff and clients should keep me interested and enthused for a long time.

Raj P. Pillai

President, Financial Fitness Network, Inc.
6175 SOM Center Road, Suite 210
Solon, OH 44139

E-mail Address: advisor@unbiased.com

Website: www.unbiased.com

Certifications: Certified Financial Planner®

Education: Ph.D. in Chemistry, Penn State University

Organizations: The Financial Planning Association, National Association of Personal Financial Advisors

My relationship with my clients is built on a foundation of the three Cs: character, caring, and competence. The bedrock of this relationship is integrity—for a financial advisor, nothing is more important. I care deeply about my clients, and I enjoy being a coach, cheerleader, and trusted advisor, helping them achieve their cherished goals. My previous career as a research scientist has given me the analytical tools I need to be an innovative problem-solver.

William R. Pomeroy
Executive Vice President, The Shobe Financial Group
One Oak Square
8280 YMCA Plaza Drive
Baton Rouge, LA 70810

E-mail Address: bpomeroy@shobe.com

Website: www.shobe.com

Certifications: Certified Financial Planner®, Certified Retirement Counselor

Education: B.S. in General Business, Louisiana State University
M.S. in Marketing, Louisiana State University

Organizations: Society of Financial Service Professionals, The Financial Planning Association, National Association of Insurance and Financial Advisors

Publications: "Evolution of Financial Education," *Personal Finances and Worker Productivity*, 2000
"The Benefits to Employers from Workplace Financial Education," *Personal Finances and Worker Productivity*, 1999

Ever since I started in business in 1983, I've approached things from a financial planning perspective. I chose to join The Shobe Financial Group (SFG), one of the elite financial planning firms in the country. Acceptance into the Registry of Financial Planning Practitioners was a hallmark of the best of the best. By 1991, I had developed a passion for another area—workplace financial education. Today Ed Shobe, CFP®, CLU, our good friend Floyd Green, CFP®, and I also own one of the nation's top workplace financial education companies—The EDSA Group, Inc.—and it is still a lot of fun to come to work every day!

Barbara J. Raasch

Partner, Ernst & Young, LLP
5 Times Square
New York, NY 10036

E-mail Address: barbara.raasch@ey.com

Certifications: Certified Financial Analyst®, Certified Public
Accountant/Personal Financial Specialist

Education: B.B.A. in Accounting, University of Wisconsin–Milwaukee

Organizations: American Institute of Certified Public Accountants,
Association for Investment Management and Research

Publications: *Ernst & Young's Financial Planning for Women*, Wiley
Ernst & Young's Personal Financial Planning Guide, Wiley
Former personal financial planning columnist, *The Milwaukee Journal*
and *The Dallas Times Herald*

I have consistently set my bar very high for both excellent client service and the breadth and depth of my knowledge. The people I have
been fortunate to surround myself with have enabled me to be the best
I can be. The success I have enjoyed in my career is directly related to
the guidance I've received from my wonderful parents and mentor, the
assistance I receive from outstanding Ernst & Young professionals, and
the support I've received from my husband and children. Moreover, as
a Personal Financial Specialist, my clients have always trusted my
advice—compelling me to be the best.

Gregory M. Railsback

President & Majority Shareholder, Railsback & Associates, P.C.
1970 Rhododendron Drive
Woodland, WA 98674

E-mail Address: cpataxes@pacifier.com

Certifications: Certified Financial Planner®, Certified Public
Accountant/Personal Financial Specialist

Education: B.B.A. in Finance, University of Portland

Organizations: American Institute of Certified Public Accountants

In addition to having my own tax and accounting practice, I work with a financial planning firm in the strategic design of comprehensive financial plans. The tax implications of planning decisions are ignored by many financial services firms. Being a CPA allows our team to address the tax considerations and provides the client with the information they need to make informed decisions. The best thing I can do for clients is deliver the message they need to hear and not the one they want to hear.

Kathleen M. Rehl

Certified Financial Planner®, Rehl Financial Advisors
21502 Woodstork Lane
Lutz, FL 33549

E-mail Address: rehlmoney@earthlink.net

Website: www.rehlmoney.com

Certifications: Certified Financial Planner®

Education: Ph.D. in Education, University of Illinois
M.S. in Education, University of Wisconsin
B.S. in Education, University of Wisconsin

Organizations: The Financial Planning Association, National Association of Personal Financial Advisors

Publications: *Planning for the Times of Your Life: 45 Great Financial Planning Ideas*, Cambridge Advisors

New clients usually come to me with some specific question, such as "Do I have enough money to retire?" Or they might ask, "Where's the best place to put my money these days?" It doesn't take long before we start talking about what they really value in life and what their goals are. Together we develop strategies that balance decisions related to money, family, work, health, social relationships, leisure, spirituality, and personal growth and education. I'm blessed to enjoy a wonderful opportunity to positively impact clients' lives as I help them to enjoy a better life that's richer in all respects.

Paul S. Richard

Executive Director, Institute of Consumer Financial Education
2512 Horton Avenue, 2nd floor, West
San Diego, CA 92101-1350

E-mail Address: icfe@cox.net

Website: www.icfe.info

Certifications: Registered Financial Consultant

Organizations: Association for Financial Counseling and Planning
Education

Publications: *The Money Instruction Book*, ICFE, 2002
Do-It-Yourself Credit File Correction Guide—English, ICFE, 2002
Do-It-Yourself Credit File Correction Guide—Spanish, ICFE, 2002

I am a recognized personal finance authority, a bankruptcy reform
advocate, a published author of books and articles, an educator, a savings advocate, a public speaker, a seminar leader, and often a quoted
authority on personal finance issues in a wide variety of print and
broadcast medias. I am the creator of the ICFE's "Money Instruction
Book." The course is made available through community colleges, adult
education programs, credit unions, etc. In 1996, I was the technical
consultant to the producers of ABC's Schoolhouse Rock's Emmy-
nominated "Money Rock" video, featuring seven songs about money.

Howard G. Safer

Executive Vice President, Regions Morgan Keegan Trust Co.
150 Fourth Avenue North, Suite 1500
Nashville, TN 37219-2434

E-mail Address: howard.safer@regions.com

Website: www.thesafergroup.mkadvisor.com

Certifications: Certified Public Accountant/Personal Financial
Specialist

Education: B.A. in Economics, Vanderbilt University
M.B.A. in Accounting, Tulane University

Organizations: American Institute of Certified Public Accountants

Our group at Regions Morgan Keegan Trust is particularly passionate
about helping our clients enjoy life and their families while leaving the

right resources for future generations. Using my 30 years of experience in financial services and accounting, my approach to servicing clients is holistic and multi-generational. I was included in the original 1996 *Worth* magazine list of the Best Advisors. Editors asked advisors who they would send their mothers to for service and my name kept popping up. After six years of similar honors, I am pleased to note that my own mother is now using my services!

Samuel O. Sanders, Jr.
Director of Education, Consumer Credit Counseling Services–Baton Rouge, LA
615 Chevelle Court
Baton Rouge, LA 70816

E-mail Address: samuel.sanders@realhelp.org

Certifications: Certified Consumer Credit Counselor

Education: B.A. in English, Christopher Newport University

Organizations: National Foundation for Credit Counseling

I have a passion for working with people in search of a resolution to financial problems. My professional goal is to help consumers see that while they think their situation is hopeless, I have hope and they, too, can have hope. Many times, people are angry and embarrassed about needing to seek help. When we are finished working together, they are appreciative and inspired to do what needs to be done to remedy their situation. I love my job and people who encounter me in the workplace know that I love my job, because they see it!

Michael D. Schulman
Principal, Schulman Co. CPA P.C.
203 Summit Avenue
P.O. Box 158
Central Valley, NY 10917

E-mail Address: michael@schulmancpa.com

Certifications: Certified Public Accountant/Personal Financial Specialist

Education: B.S. in Mathematics, Massachusetts Institute of Technology
M.A. in Mathematics, University of California Berkeley
M.B.A. in Finance, Fordham University

Organizations: American Institute of Certified Public Accountants

I have been providing personal financial planning services for over 20 years. I am an active member of both the American Institute of Certified Public Accountants and the New York State Society of Certified Public Accountants. I am a member of the AICPA's Personal Financial Planning Executive Committee where I serve as the committee's liaison to the Elder Care Task Force.

Robert J. Schumann
President, Cambridge Financial Advisors, LLC
1451 Harrison Pond Drive
New Albany, OH 43054

E-mail Address: SchumannR@prodigy.net

Certifications: Chartered Financial Consultant, Certified Financial Planner®, Enrolled Agent

Education: M.A. in Hebrew & Semitic Studies, University of Wisconsin
M.Div. in Theology & Ministry, Wisconsin Lutheran Seminary
M.B.A. in Corporate Finance & Capital Markets, The Ohio State University
B.A. in History, Northwestern College

Organizations: National Association of Enrolled Agents, National Association of Personal Financial Advisors, National Association of Tax Professionals

My training in the behavioral sciences and my background in counseling probably differentiate my practice from many others. I try to listen to my clients and ask questions that will help them discover their conflicting values or money messages that are the human side of their perceived "numbers" or money problems. It's an enjoyable and rewarding process which offers both financial and personal satisfaction.

Joseph E. Sedita
Owner, Joseph E. Sedita and Company
802 W. Martin Luther King Jr.
Plant City, FL 33566

E-mail Address: joe@sedita.com

Website: www.sedita.com

Certifications: Certified Financial Planner®, Certified Public Accountant/Personal Financial Specialist

Education: B.A. in Accounting, University of South Florida

Organizations: American Institute of Certified Public Accountants, The Financial Planning Association

I believe that life is an adventure and that money is a tool to help us live that adventure. My passion lies in helping both businesses and individuals define their vision of success and then helping them create a plan for achieving it. My motto is: Don't Let Your Fears Get in the Way of Your Dreams!

Robert S. Seltzer
CPA/PFS
9595 Wilshire Boulevard, Suite 1020
Beverly Hills, CA 90212

E-mail Address: rsscpa@earthlink.net

Certifications: Certified Public Accountant/Personal Financial Specialist

Education: B.A. in Business Economics, University of California at Santa Barbara

Organizations: American Institute of Certified Public Accountants

My goal in financial planning is to get to know my clients as well as I can to enable them to reach their life and financial goals. In taking this approach, I am able to learn their priorities and help them get where they want to go. I am not in the business of trying to make people rich. I assemble portfolios that are in concert with clients' risk tolerances. I will inform clients if their goals are realistic based on their income and current net worth. Finally, I think it is equally important to help clients keep what they have.

John Sestina
President, John E. Sestina and Company
1161 Bethel Road, Suite 201
Columbus, OH 43220

E-mail Address: jsestina@sestina.com

Website: www.sestina.com

Certifications: Chartered Financial Consultant, Certified Financial Planner® of Fee-Only Financial Planning

Education: M.S.F.S. in Financial Services, American College
B.S., University of Dayton

Organizations: The Financial Planning Association, National Association of Personal Financial Advisors

Publications: *Managing to Be Wealthy*, Dearborn, 2000
Fee-Only Financial Planning, JK Lasser, 2000

As someone who trained to be a teacher, I must have chalk dust still circulating in my blood, because I love to help individuals become better educated about financial matters. When clients tell me how much more organized they are and how much more confidence they have in making financial decisions, my "teacher eyes" light up. When young advisors make the successful transition to fee-only financial planning by following the advice that I've shared along the way, I'm delighted to have donned my "counselor hat." And when readers apply the practical pointers in *Tips from the Top*, education wins again.

Martin J. Sickles
President, Financial Planning Partners
2878 Redding Road
Atlanta, GA 30319

E-mail Address: martin@paracleteplanning.com

Website: www.paracleteplanning.com

Certifications: Certified Financial Planner®, Certified Public Accountant/Personal Financial Specialist Realtor

Education: B.B.A. in Accounting, University of Georgia

Organizations: American Institute of Certified Public Accountants

I ask my clients: Do you lead a balanced life? Have you designed the life you want to live? Have you determined Who and What are important to you? Financial Planning Partners takes Comprehensive Financial Planning to another level and integrates their Life Plan with their Financial Plan while solving these problems: Estate and Income Tax Minimization, Business Succession Planning, Retirement, and Education Planning. While some planners are looking for their next transaction, Financial Planning Partners establishes long-term relationships. My clients appreciate and benefit from the synergy of our full-service approach to Personal Strategic Planning.

Louis P. Stanasolovich
CFP®, CEO and President, Legend Financial Advisors, Inc.
5700 Corporate Drive, Suite 350
Pittsburgh, PA 15237

E-mail Address: legend@legend-financial.com

Website: www.legend-financial.com

Certifications: Certified Financial Planner®

Education: B.S. in Accounting, Pennsylvania State University

Organizations: The Financial Planning Association, National Association of Personal Financial Advisors

I have been the Chief Executive Officer and President of Legend Financial Advisors, Inc. since its inception in January of 1994. My philosophy is to achieve an unequaled standard of excellence in my profession by providing personalized value-added services and to become indispensable to our clients by assisting them in making educated, intelligent financial decisions. I am a firm believer in taking care of the clients' every need and consistently striving to go beyond their expectations. Always being open to new and innovative procedures has attributed much to the financial success of my clients.

Loyd J. Stegent
Director of Financial Planning, Cornelius, Stegent & Price, LLP
24 Greenway Plaza, Suite 515
Houston, TX 77046

E-mail Address: loyd@cpadvisers.com

Website: www.cpadvisers.com

Certifications: Certified Financial Planner®, Certified Public Accountant/Personal Financial Specialist

Education: B.B.S. in Accounting, University of Houston

Organizations: American Institute of Certified Public Accountants, The Financial Planning Association

Confucius said, "The superior man understands what is right; the inferior man understands what will sell." I feel very fortunate to make my living helping others see their choices clearly enough to understand what is right. Such understanding empowers them to create a relationship with me built on trust. With trust, there is belief in the advice given. I believe the financial advice-giving industry should be about two things: people and their futures. My business objective is to create lifelong client relationships with people who are willing to trust me with their future peace of mind, because I know that my financial success is directly related to my clients' financial peace of mind.

Judy A. Stewart
Owner, Stewart Financial Services
2755 Jefferson Street, Suite 203
Carlsbad, CA 92008

E-mail Address: lstewart@cts.com

Website: www.sfsplanning.net

Certifications: Certified Financial Planner®, Enrolled Agent

Education: M.B.A. in Business, University of San Diego
B.A. in Sociology, San Diego State University

Organizations: National Association of Enrolled Agents, National Association of Personal Financial Advisors

I have a passion for helping middle-income clients achieve financial freedom. Life has become way too complicated for this group of hard-working people, and there is precious little time for the really important areas in one's life, such as faith, family, friendships, and fulfillment in their jobs. If I can demystify the financial planning process and help empower folks to be in control of their finances and make smart decisions, then I can "free them up" to discover why they were put on earth and what their life purpose is.

Parke Stratford Teal
Principal, Dreggors, Rigsby and Teal, P.A.
106 N. Woodland Boulevard
DeLand, FL 32720

E-mail Address: drtcpa@bellsouth.net

Certifications: Certified Public Accountant/Personal Financial Specialist

Education: B.S. in Business Administration, University of Alabama

Organizations: American Institute of Certified Public Accountants, Financial Planning Association

The public accounting profession has time and time again exposed me to the life lessons of the value of a dollar saved, and the value of a dollar spent. My exposure has come directly from my clients. I am driven by a genuine concern for my clients' well-being. Investment advising is not about rates of return. Investment advising is about preservation and growth of investments to achieve realistic life goals. As in public accounting, I must continually educate my clients throughout the trusted advisory relationship.

Timothy P. Thaney
Principal, DeJoy, Knauf & Blood, LLP
39 State Street, Suite 600
Rochester, NY 14614

E-mail Address: tthaney@teamdkb.com

Website: www.teamdkb.com

Certifications: Certified Public Accountant/Personal Financial Specialist

Education: B.A. in Economics/Accounting, College of the Holy Cross

Organizations: American Institute of Certified Public Accountants, National Association of Personal Financial Advisors

I am a CPA and a Personal Financial Specialist who believes that my clients deserve objective and experienced counsel from someone whom they trust. With over 20 years of collective experience in public accounting, banking, investments, and financial planning, I provide my clients with comprehensive wealth management services as a service of a mid-sized CPA firm. I assist the firm's clients in developing and implementing a financial plan on a "fee-only" basis. In addition, I provide individual tax planning and return preparation and assistance in the evaluation and design of small business retirement plans.

Lindsey Torbett
CPA/PFS, CFP®, Wealth Development Group
5615 L Jackson Street
Alexandria, LA 71303

E-mail Address: lt@wealthdev.com

Website: www.wealthdev.com

Certifications: Certified Financial Planner®, Certified Public Accountant/Personal Financial Specialist

Education: B.S. in Accounting, Northwestern State University

Organizations: American Institute of Certified Public Accountants

I am a Wealth Coach in Alexandria, Louisiana. I have practiced life planning by selling my CPA practice, securing my financial independence, forming a family partnership, and becoming a tri-athlete. In addition to assisting my clients on wealth and life planning, I am working on running a half-marathon and spending more time flying my family. I founded the Wealth Development Group, LLC, where I along with my partner Jay Pearson, CFP, work to build financial independence for our clients. I am also very active in civic and financial affairs, and am a board member and founder of Red River Bank and the Central Louisiana Community Foundation, and have served on the Alexandria City Council.

Chad P. Tramp

Wealth Management Advisor, RSM McGladrey, Inc
400 Locust Street, Suite 640
Des Moines, IA 50309

E-mail Address: chad_tramp@rsmi.com

Website: www.rsmmcgladrey.com

Certifications: Certified Financial Planner®, Personal Financial Specialist

Education: B.S. in Accounting, Mount Marty College

Organizations: American Institute of Certified Public Accountants, Financial Planning Association

I am one of those fortunate individuals who gets paid to do what he loves. I work for RSM McGladrey, a national consulting and accounting firm. We are a fee-only, comprehensive financial planning shop working with high-net-worth and high-net-income individuals. As a fee-only advisor, we are able to maintain our independence and objectivity. I believe proper financial planning is a process and is relationship-based. As part of this process, I am in constant contact with clients to assist them with any and all financial issues facing them.

Linda L. Tucker
Director of Education, Family Service Agency—CCCS of Little Rock
4504 Burrow Drive
North Little Rock, AR 72116

E-mail Address: ltucker@fsainc.org

Certifications: Certified Homeowner & Educator Counselor, Certified in Family and Consumer Sciences

Education: B.S. in Vocational Home Economics, Tennessee Technological National Foundation for Credit Counseling

Richard A. Vera
CPA & Financial Services, LLC
971 Leonardville Road
Atlantic Highlands, NJ 07716

E-mail Address: CPA@cpafs.com

Website: www.cpafs.com

Certifications: Certified Public Accountant/Personal Financial Specialist, Certified Divorce Planner, Certified Senior Advisor

Education: M.B.A. in Business Administration, Monmouth University
B.S.B.A. in Business Administration, Thomas Edison State College
A.A. in Economics, Brookdale Community College
A.A. in Accounting, Brookdale Community College

Organizations: American Institute of Certified Public Accountants

Publications: "Refinance Your Mortgage and Invest the Difference,"
Atlantic Highlands Herald, 2001
"Test Your Social Security IQ," *Atlantic Highlands Herald*, 2001
"Dollar Cost Averaging," *Atlantic Highlands Herald*, 2001

Holistic personal financial planning allows me to combine my lifelong love of numbers with investing for the benefit of my clients. Many times, while assisting my clients in identifying their financial objectives, I am afforded a glimpse into their dreams, such as financing their children's college education, a comfortable retirement, or perhaps the purchase of a vacation home. I show my clients how to crystallize their dreams into reality by formulating and executing a series of intermediate investment actions that will enable them to bridge the gap between where they stand today and their dreams of tomorrow.

Jim C. Wagenmann
Member, Watkins, Meegan, Drury & Co., LLC
4800 Hampden Lane, 9th Floor
Bethesda, MD 20814

E-mail Address: jwagenmann@wmdco.com

Certifications: Certified Public Accountant/Personal Financial
Specialist

Education: A.A. in Business, Bucks County Community College
B.S. in Accounting, University of Maryland

Organizations: American Institute of Certified Public Accountants,
The Financial Planning Association

I am a member of Watkins, Meegan, Drury & Co., LLC, located in
Bethesda, Maryland. I have over 30 years of experience in the areas of
taxation, estate and trust planning, employee benefits, and financial
planning. I am the resource for the firm on issues dealing with wealth
preservation and all areas dealing with employee benefits such as
health insurance, disability insurance, retirement funding, education
funding, life insurance, and long-term care insurance. I am a Certified
Public Accountant and a Personal Financial Specialist. My practice
covers individuals and businesses of all sizes and markets.

Robert B. Walsh
President, Lighthouse Financial Advisors, Inc.
75 Montgomery Street, Suite 200
Jersey City, NJ 07302

E-mail Address: Robert@lfadvisors.com

Website: www.lfadvisors.com

Certifications: Certified Financial Planner®, Certified Public
Accountant/Personal Financial Specialist

Education: B.S. in Accounting, St. Francis University

Organizations: American Institute of Certified Public Accountants,
The Financial Planning Association, National Association of Personal
Financial Advisors

As the founder of Lighthouse Financial Advisors, Inc. (Jersey City,
New Jersey), I am relentless in my quest to keep us in the forefront

of financial planning. That is why we have aligned ourselves with Cambridge Advisors. Cambridge Advisors is a thriving community of like-minded fee-only financial advisors who share and leverage their knowledge, resources, and experience and are recognized as being at the forefront of holistic financial planning. Our number one goal is to provide our clients with an education about their finances. We equip them with the tools to make their financial and life goals reality.

Frank L. Washelesky
Director, Ostrow Resin Berk & Abrams, Ltd.
455 N. Cityfront Plaza Drive, Suite 2600
Chicago, IL 60611-5555

E-mail Address: washelesky@orba.com

Website: www.orba.com

Certifications: Certified Public Accountant/Personal Financial Specialist, Certified Valuation Analyst/Certified in Mergers & Acquisitions

Education: J.D., DePaul University College of Law
B.S. in Accounting, Northern Illinois University

Association: American Institute of Certified Public Accountants

Nate J. Wenner
Personal Financial Counselor
5423 Washburn Avenue South
Minneapolis, MN 55410

E-mail Address: njwenner@yahoo.com

Certifications: Certified Financial Planner®, Certified Public Accountant/Personal Financial Specialist, Certified Investment Management Analyst

Education: B.A. in Economics, Accounting, University of St. Thomas

Organizations: American Institute of Certified Public Accountants, The Financial Planning Association

I am a firm believer in taking the time to help my clients define their true financial and nonfinancial goals in life. This is the only way to actually help them achieve their dreams. Financial planning can be complex and difficult, but it's truly not rocket science! Once we complete this step together, we can have frank, honest, and educational discussions to describe the recommended options for achievement of the objectives. I've found that most people want a greater understanding of why their financial planner recommends certain tactics—and this approach has proven to be extremely helpful for my clients.

Steven D. Wightman
Principal, Lexington Financial Management
1 Aaron Road
Lexington, MA 02421

E-mail Address: Finance@Secure-plan.com

Website: www.secure-plan.com

Certifications: Certified Financial Planner®

Education: B.S. in Biotechnology, Rivier, Nashua, NH

Organizations: The Financial Planning Association, National Association of Personal Financial Advisors

Publications: *Ear to the Ground* (a weekly web-based newsletter), 2002

Personal Finance by Stephen Leeb (contributor), 2001

Money talk often brings out deep-seated feelings, values—even our meaning in life. I've found that working with people's values is far more interesting than working with valuations of what people own. My passion is coaching clients through barriers that prevent them from reaching their goals and living fuller lives. Often they discover that how much money they have means little compared to how they relate to it. Understanding this, they find, is vital to achieving peace of mind. Money is a means, not an end. Exploring those ends is sometimes difficult, but I know no journey more rewarding.

Mark D. Wilson
Vice President, Tarbox Equity, Inc.
500 Newport Center Drive, Suite 500
Newport Beach, CA 92660

E-mail Address: mark@tarboxequity.com

Website: www.tarboxequity.com

Certifications: Certified Financial Planner®, Accredited Pension Administrator

Education: B.S. in Computer Science, University of California Irvine

Organizations: The Financial Planning Association, National Association of Personal Financial Advisors

I am one of those lucky few who have a great family life and work life! Although financial planning and investment management is very difficult work, I cannot imagine doing anything else. Every day, I get to collaborate with an incredible team of financial advisors (each worthy of being a Top Money Mind) to provide financial advice to our clients. I'm very proud of the work that we accomplish.

Leonard C. Wright
Principal, Strategic Financial Group
888 West Sixth Street, Suite 200
Los Angeles, CA 90017

E-mail Address: wrightplanners@hotmail.com

Certifications: Chartered Financial Consultant, Certified Financial Planner®, Chartered Life Underwriter, Certified Public Accountant/Personal Financial Specialist

Education: B.A. in Business, California State University at Fullerton

Organizations: American Institute of Certified Public Accountants, The Financial Planning Association

Publications: "Life Insurance: Getting Down to Basics," *California CPA Magazine*, 2002

I listen to my clients to craft risk-management and investment-planning strategies that minimize the impact of taxation. What this means to clients is that their insurance and investment planning is fully flexible and can be adapted due to the inevitable changes in family and business circumstances that will occur over the years. The real benefit is that their actions and intentions are in alignment. Business mission: Working together to achieve financial success through understanding, education, and action.

John H. Wyckoff
CPA/PFS, Ron McCallister Financial Advisors, Inc.
10300 SW Greenburg Road, Suite 190
Portland, OR 97223-5414

E-mail Address: jwyckoff@jhw.com

Website: www.feeonlyadvisors.com

Certifications: Certified Financial Planner®, Certified Public
Accountant/Personal Financial Specialist

Education: B.A. in Sociology, University of California
M.B.A. in Accounting, University of California
Master in Taxation, Portland State University

Organizations: American Institute of Certified Public Accountants,
The Financial Planning Association

Susan G. Zimmerman
Financial Planner & Therapist, Zimmerman Financial Group
14530 Pennock Avenue
Apple Valley, MN 55124

E-mail Address: susan@zimmermanfinancial.com

Certifications: Chartered Financial Consultant, Chartered Life
Underwriter, Licensed Marriage & Family Therapist

Education: B.S. in Social Science, University of Minnesota
M.A. in Counseling, Alfred Adler Graduate School

Organizations: Association for Financial Counseling and Planning
Education, The Financial Planning Association, National Association
of Insurance and Financial Advisors

Publications: 2002, *Fiscal Therapy Exercise Book*, Aha Action Team
The Power in Your Money Personality, Beavers Pond Press, 2002
The Money Rascals, Arhymatherapy Press, 1998

I really am a split personality, professionally—and I love teaching positive methods of change and self-discovery. I combine my education and experience in financial planning with Marriage and Family Therapy (LMFT) to create tools that help people achieve healthy psychological habits with money. My books, tapes, and seminars integrate psychotherapeutic techniques and financial concepts that people can use to modify their habits and achieve greater results. Steve Zimmerman, CFP®, ChFC, CLU, and I work as a team with our clients to assess their money personalities and histories so they can be incorporated into their financial plans for lasting and positive wealth-building strategies.

B

ABOUT THE CREDENTIALS

AEP ACCREDITED ESTATE PLANNER

National Association of Estate Planners & Councils
1120 Chester Avenue, Suite 470
Cleveland, OH 44114
866-226-2224
www.naepc.org

Contributor: Judith Ludwig

The National Association of Estate Planners & Councils (NAEPC) has designated The American College as the provider of the education required to earn NAEPC's Accredited Estate Planner (AEP) designation. Applicants for the AEP designation must successfully complete two graduate courses through the Richard D. Irwin Graduate School of The American College.

The NAEPC's particular focus is on:

- Accounting
- Insurance
- Law

- Trust Services
- Financial Planning

A primary goal of the NAEPC is to encourage specialization programs to increase recognition and acceptance of estate planning as a specialty.

Accredited Estate Planner (AEP) is available to individuals in four disciplines. This designation is for individuals who have met the requisite requirements, including estate planning experience and recommendations by colleagues, and currently requires completion of certain graduate estate planning courses. All individuals obtaining the AEP designation demonstrate commitment to the team approach in estate planning.

AFC   ACCREDITED FINANCIAL COUNSELOR

Association for Financial Counseling and Planning Education
2121 Arlington Avenue, Suite 5
Upper Arlington, OH 43221-4339
614-485-9650
www.afcpe.org

Contributors: Preston Cochrane, Barbara O'Neill

Accredited Financial Counselors have certified skills to assist individuals and families in the complex process of financial decision-making, including the ability to:

- Educate clients in sound financial principles
- Assist clients in the process of overcoming their financial indebtedness
- Help clients identify and modify ineffective money management behaviors

- Guide clients in developing successful strategies for achieving their financial goals
- Support clients as they work through their financial challenges
- Help clients develop new perspectives on the dynamics of money in relation to family, friends, and individual's self-esteem

To achieve the designation, a professional must pass two proctored exams, sign a code of ethics, provide three letters of reference, and have two years of counseling experience. Certification is maintained by receiving 30 hours of continuing education every two years.

APA   ACCREDITED PENSION ADMINISTRATOR

National Institute of Pension Administrators
401 N. Michigan Avenue, #2200
Chicago, IL 60611-4267
1-800-999-6472
nipa@sba.com
www.nipa.org

Contributor: Mark Wilson

The Accredited Pension Administrator designation is earned by the successful completion of six study courses and examinations covering all aspects of plan administration. Any person may take APA examinations, but two years of experience in plan administration is required for the designation. The APA is maintained by annually completing 15 hours of continuing education and current NIPA membership. Potential APAs include pension administrators, retirement relationship managers, and ERISA compliance specialists.

ATP   Accredited Tax Preparer

Accreditation Council for Accountancy and Taxation, Inc.
1010 N. Fairfax Street
Alexandria, VA 22314-1574
1-888-289-7763
www.acatcredentials.org

Contributor: Sid Blum

The Accredited Tax Preparer (ATP) designation is a voluntary credential for professionals who have a thorough knowledge behind the existing tax code and tax preparation of individual, corporate, and partnership tax returns.

Individuals seeking this designation must successfully complete coursework administered by Surgent Educational Software and subsequently register with ACAT. Once successfully completed, an individual must meet the three years of work experience in tax preparation and compliance. One year is considered a tax season (i.e., January through April).

The two-course program through Surgent covers critical compliance issues and the mechanics of preparing a variety of tax returns. These courses give a thorough understanding of the concepts behind tax code and how these concepts apply to a wide range of situations.

CCA   Certified Certification Analyst

Women's Business Enterprise National Council
1120 Connecticut Avenue NW, Suite 950
Washington, DC 20036
202-872-5515
www.wbenc.org

Contributor: Angie Hollerich

The Women's Business Enterprise National Council (WBENC, pronounced wee-bank), created in 1997, is dedicated to enhancing opportunities for women's business enterprises in America's major business markets. In partnership with women's business organizations throughout the United States, WBENC provides access to a national standard of certification and provides information on certified women's businesses to purchasing managers through an Internet database—WBENCLink. To achieve the designation, a business must meet the following requirements:

- Fifty-one percent ownership by a woman or women
- Proof of effective management of the business (operating position, by-laws, hire-fire and other decision-making roles)
- Control of the business as evidenced by signature role on loans, leases, and contracts
- U.S. Citizenship or U.S. Resident Alien Status

CCCC CERTIFIED CONSUMER CREDIT COUNSELOR

National Foundation for Credit Counseling
801 Roeder Road, Suite 900
Silver Spring, MD 20910
301-589-5600
www.nfcc.org

Contributors: Samuel Sanders, Jennifer Delcamp, Sandra Dunaway

The National Foundation for Consumer Credit instituted the Counselor Certification Program in 1975. It is designed to demonstrate to clients and the community that NFCC Member counselors have attained a high degree of professional skill and knowledge. Only NFCC Member agency counselors can take the counselor certification exam. Each book contains quizzes and practice tests so that by the time the counselor finishes reviewing the material, the information has been internalized. The exam is administered by an independent third-party organization and is taken online at the agency level. Counselors are able to receive immediate test results at their agency location. The requirements for Counselor Certification include obtaining certification within one year of hire date by passing the first six certification exams. The first six certification manuals are:

- Consumer Rights and Responsibilities
- Spending Plans and Budgeting
- Credit and Borrowing
- Debt Management and Bankruptcy
- Challenging Issues
- Counseling Principals and Process

CDP CERTIFIED DIVORCE PLANNER

Institute For Certified Divorce Planners
24901 Northwestern Highway, Suite 710
Southfield, MI 48075
1-800-875-1760
www.institutecdp.com

Contributors: Joan Coullahan, Cheryl Moss, Richard Vera

Professionals with the CDP designation have been trained in the importance of reviewing each party's claimed expenses and asset inventory. They learn the treatment of various property in divorce settlements, such as pension and retirement accounts, the marital home, and liquid assets. In addition, they cover alimony, child support, Social Security benefits for divorcing clients, and insurance issues, as well as bankruptcy, debt, and credit issues. They also cover material on the tax impact of dividing property, potential tax pitfalls and recapture that can be avoided, and taxation of alimony, and explain in detail how to utilize the personal tax return to find forensic data for divorce cases.

In order to receive the CDP designation from the Institute for Certified Divorce Planners, a professional must complete four separate self-study modules and then successfully pass an exam based on the material for each module. Exams for modules one through three are proctored. The exam for the fourth course, a comprehensive Case Study exam, is an "open book" exam that they take in their own office. Along with module four, they receive the DivPlan software as well as instructions on how to use it to illustrate the short-term and long-term financial impact of proposed divorce settlements.

CEBS CERTIFIED EMPLOYEE BENEFIT SPECIALIST

International Foundation of Employee Benefit Plans
18700 W. Bluemound Road
Brookfield, WI 53008-0069
262-786-6700
www.ifebp.org

Contributor: Melody Carlsen

CEBS is the premier credential in the employee benefits industry. Over 9,000 benefit professionals have earned the designation and thousands more are pursuing it.

The CEBS program consists of a 10-course curriculum designed to help individuals develop a comprehensive understanding of employee benefit principles and concepts. To become a Certified Employee Benefit Specialist (CEBS), a professional needs to successfully complete 10 examinations.

CFA CHARTERED FINANCIAL ANALYST

The Association for Investment Management and Research
560 Ray C. Hunt Drive
Charlottesville, VA 22903-0668
800-247-8132
www.aimr.com

Contributors: Barbara J. Raasch, Lesley J. Brey, Clark M. Blackman II

The *Chartered Financial Analyst (CFA®) Program* is a globally recognized standard for measuring the competence and integrity of financial analysts. Three levels of examination measure a candidate's ability to apply the fundamental knowledge of investment principles at a professional level. The CFA exam is administered annually in more than 70 nations worldwide.

CFCS CERTIFIED IN FAMILY AND CONSUMER SCIENCE

American Association of Family and Consumer Sciences
1555 King Street
Alexandria, VA 22314-2738
1-800-424-8080
www.AAFCS.org

Contributor: Linda Tucker

To become a professional certified in Family and Consumer Science (CFCS), one must meet the educational criteria (B.S. degree), as well as pass the examination requirement. This designation demonstrates ongoing commitment to the pursuit of excellence in the multi-dimensional family and consumer sciences profession. It signifies the professional possesses a broad professional knowledge base; demonstrates involvement in the profession; is growth-oriented and self-directed; remains professionally current and understands and appreciates human well-being from a family and consumer sciences perspective.

To maintain certification, a CFCS is required to earn 75 professional development units (PDUs) every three years by participating in approved professional meetings and workshops, publishing, self-study, academic courses, and noncredit continuing education programs.

CFMC   Chartered Mutual Fund Counselor

Institute of Wealth Management
College for Financial Planning
6161 South Syracuse
Green Wood Village, CO 80111
303-220-1200
www.fp.edu

Contributors: Kent Anthony, John Dinkins

Chartered Mutual Fund Counselor (CMFC®) Professional Education Program provides a thorough knowledge of mutual funds and their various uses as investment vehicles. As investment professionals, CMFC's gain comprehensive knowledge of mutual funds and how to make the most of the opportunities to use them. As a graduate of the program a CMFC can approach mutual funds with a new understanding and confidence, and with the ability to communicate that confidence to clients. The CMFC designation is awarded to students who successfully complete the program, pass the final examination, and sign a code of ethics commitment and declaration form.

CFP   Certified Financial Planner

CFP Board of Standards
1700 Broadway, Suite 2100
Denver, CO 80290-2101
1-800-487-1497
www.CFP.net

Contributors: Jill Gianola, Alexis M. Jensen, John E. Sestina, Brad R. Cougill, Elaine E. Bedel, Kathleen M. Rehl, Cheryl A. Moss, Marsha G. LePhew, Bill Pomeroy, Susan J. Bruno, Lindsey Torbett, Chad P. Tramp, Kent E. Anthony, Gregory M. Railsback, Donna Skeels Cygan, Steve Johnson, Paul D. Knott, Steven B. Morris, Loyd J. Stegent, Ann D. Jevne, J. Victor Conrad, Harvey D. Aaron, Sid Blum, Steve Wightman, Joe Harper, Stephen A. Drake, Peg Downey, James Kantowski, Bruce R. Heling, Clark M. Blackman II, Louis P. Stanasolovich, Judy Ludwig, Michael L. Alberts, Deborah O. Levine, Don A. Gomez, John Grable, Bob Schumann, Gregory C. Fenton, William K. Kaiser, John Henry Wyckoff, Helen L. Modly, Nate Wenner, Randall Kratz, Judy A. Stewart, Cary Carbonaro, Leonard C. Wright, Bonnie A. Hughes, Ray Julian, Judi Martindale, Robert B. Walsh, Mark Wilson, Barbara O'Neill, Raj Pillai, Joseph E. Sedita, Martin J. Sickles, Jeff Mehler, Patrick T. Hanratty, Lesley J. Brey, Jon S. Chernila, Dennis N. Houlihan, Lloyd E. Painter, Paul D. Lyons, Cathie E. Cobe, Henrietta Humphreys, Kristofor R. Behn

The Certified Financial Planner Board of Standards is a nonprofit professional regulatory organization established to benefit the public by fostering professional standards in personal financial planning. The Board owns the following certification marks: CFP®, CERTIFIED FINANCIAL PLANNER®. Individuals who meet initial educational, testing, ethical, and ongoing requirements may use them. You can contact the Board to find out if your planner is certified or has any disciplinary history. You may also file complaints or request free educational brochures.

CFS   CERTIFIED FUND SPECIALIST

Institute of Business and Finance
7911 Herschel Avenue, Suite 201
La Jolla, CA 92037-4413
1-800-848-2029
www.icfs.com

Contributor: Lloyd Painter, Cathie Cobe

Students have 12 months from the date of enrollment to take and pass the CFS final examination. Average completion time is usually within three to five months. The CFS course consists of materials that provide the best mutual fund and annuity education available. It provides a comprehensive, in-depth collection of quantitative and qualitative information.

To provide the most current information available, the core reading materials are regularly reviewed and updated. The courses include Investment Companies, Fixed-Rate and Variable Annuities, Wealth Management & Performance Measurement, The Planning Cycle, Strategies, and Asset Allocation.

CHC CERTIFIED HOUSING COUNSELOR

Association for Financial Counseling and Planning Education
2121 Arlington Avenue, Suite 5
Upper Arlington, OH 43221-4339
614-485-9650
www.afcpe.org

Contributor: Barbara O'Neill

A certified housing counselor objectively assesses the client's current financial situation; identifies problem areas the client may face; recommends appropriate actions to help clients obtain and maintain adequate housing; evaluates the housing and financial status of low-, moderate-, and middle-income families; and understands the essential workings of all aspects of the industry in order to help clients make appropriate housing decisions. Certified Housing Counselors must earn a passing grade (70 percent) on each of three examinations; adhere to the CHC Code of Ethics; submit three letters of reference attesting to professional competence; and have three years of admissible housing counseling experience.

CHEC CERTIFIED HOMEOWNER EDUCATOR AND COUNSELOR

American Homeowner Education & Counseling Training Institute
1156 15th Street, NW, Suite 1220
Washington, DC 20005
1-888-243-2499
www.aheci.org

Contributor: Linda Tucker

To become AHECTI-certified, one must first attend the AHECTI-sponsored homeowner education and counseling training sessions. This is a five-day training course offering a thorough review of the AHECTI Core Curriculum which consists of:

- The Homebuying Process
- Life Long Money Management
- Financing a Home
- Qualifying for a Mortgage
- Shopping for a Home
- The Loan Application Process
- The Closing Process
- Life as a Homeowner
- Getting to Know and Take Care of a Home
- How to Prevent Foreclosure

Once the coursework is complete, there are two exams which must be passed.

To maintain certification, the CHEC must offer eight hours of instruction to consumers, in order to help consumers make informed decision in areas such as budgeting and credit and financial management in order to obtain, maintain, or sustain homeownership.

CHFC   CHARTERED FINANCIAL CONSULTANT

The American College
270 S. Bryn Mawr Avenue
Bryn Mawr, PA 19010
1-888-263-7265
www.amercoll.edu

Contributors: Sid Blum, John E. Sestina, Helen L. Modly, Jon S. Chernila, Susan Zimmerman, Judy Ludwig, J. Victor Conrad, Marsha G. LePhew, Cathie E. Cobe, Leonard C. Wright, Lloyd E. Painter, Bob Schumann

The American College is the nation's oldest and largest institution for higher learning devoted exclusively to distance education for financial services professionals. The Chartered Financial Consultant (ChFC) designation focuses on the comprehensive financial planning process as an organized way to collect and analyze information on a client's total financial situation; to identify and establish specific financial goals; and to formulate, implement, and monitor a comprehensive plan to achieve those goals. The ChFC program provides financial planners and others in the financial services industry with in-depth knowledge of the skills needed to perform comprehensive financial planning for their clients. Since its inception in 1982, more than 32,000 men and women have met the educational, experience, and ethics mandates needed to earn the ChFC designation.

CIC   Certified Insurance Counselor

Society of Certified Insurance Counselors
Box 27027
Austin, TX 78755-2027
1-800-633-2165
www.scic.com

Contributor: Kent Anthony

To receive the CIC designation, a professional must:

- Attend all five CIC institutes, or four CIC institutes and one Certified Risk Manager (CRM) course
- Pass all five of the examinations, or four of the CIC examinations and one CRM examination
- Successfully pass the entire series of CIC examinations within five calendar years after passing the first examination.

To retain the CIC designation, they must attend at least one continuing education course annually.

CIMA   Certified Investment Management Analyst

Investment Management Consultants Association (IMCA)
9101 E. Kenyon Avenue, Suite 3000
Denver, CO 80237
(303) 770-3377
www.imca.org

Contributors: Nate Wenner, Jonathan Dinkins

The mission at IMCA is to ensure quality service to the public by developing and encouraging high standards in the investment consulting profession. The goal of the organization has been to broaden the public's understanding of investment management consulting and to promote and protect the interests of the profession. It also provides forums for ongoing education and information-sharing among our members. IMCA believes these activities build a common purpose among its members, establishing a network of support that makes them more knowledgeable professionals in day-to-day work.

Experience is a mandatory requirement to be eligible for the Certified Investment Management Analyst program. In order to qualify for the certification course, a candidate must have three years of verifiable experience in the field of investment management consulting. This experience may include the following areas:

- Manager search and due diligence
- Performance measurement and monitoring
- Designing investment policies or guidelines
- Structuring asset allocation strategies.

CLU   Chartered Life Underwriter

The American College
270 S. Bryn Mawr Avenue
Bryn Mawr, PA 19010
1-888-263-7265
www.amercoll.edu

Contributors: Lloyd E. Painter, Cathie E. Cobe, Leonard C. Wright, Helen L. Modly, Susan Zimmerman, Cheryl A. Moss

The American College is the nation's oldest and largest institution for higher learning devoted exclusively to distance education for financial services professionals. The Chartered Life Underwriter (CLU) designation is the undisputed professional credential for persons involved in the protection, accumulation, preservation, and distribution of the economic values of human life. Since the first examinations were held in 1928, more than 85,000 men and women have met the educational, experience, and ethics mandates needed to earn the CLU designation. The CLU program provides insights into the life insurance business, its importance to the economy, its operation and distribution systems, and its resurging importance for safe and secure investments. For agents, field managers, home office personnel, and others involved in providing life insurance products to the public, the CLU designation is the common bond for continuing growth and commitment to professionalism.

CPA   Certified Public Accountant

The American Institute of Certified Public Accountants
1211 Avenue of the Americas
New York, NY 10036-8775
1-888-777-7077
www.aicpa.org

Contributors: Sid Blum, Michael David Schulman, Jim Wagenmann, Craig Olson, Cheryl A. Moss, Alexis M. Jensen, Jonathan S. Dinkins, Bill Cratty, Reg Baker, Frank B. Arnold, Steve Johnson, John J. Feyche, Paul D. Knott, Harvey D. Aaron, James Kantowski, Stephen A. Drake, Ann D. Jevne, Loyd J. Stegent, Bruce R. Heling, Clark M. Blackman II, Chris Cobb, Steven B. Morris, Gregory M. Railsback, Richard A. Vera II, J. Victor Conrad, Robert S. Seltzer, Stuart Kessler, Nate Wenner, Leonard C. Wright, John R. Connell, Frank L. Washelesky, Deborah O. Levine, Judy Ludwig, John Henry Wyckoff, Howard Safer, Paul D. Lyons, Lloyd E. Painter, Jon S. Chernila, Cathie E. Cobe, Robert B. Walsh, Patrick T. Hanratty, Marsha G. LePhew,

Martin J. Sickles, Joseph E. Sedita, Jack B. Capron, Barbara J. Raasch, Michael M. Eisenberg, Charles P. Copeland, William K. Kaiser, Mitchell Freedman, Connie Brezik, H. Lindsey Torbett, Susan J. Bruno, Timothy P. Thaney, Phyllis Bernstein

To become a CPA, you need to meet the requirements of the state or jurisdiction in which you wish to practice. These requirements, which vary from state to state, are established by law and administered by the state boards of accountancy.

To qualify for certification, you must:

1. Complete a program of study in accounting at a college/university (the AICPA recommends at least 150 semester hours of college to study to obtain the common body of knowledge for becoming a CPA.)
2. Pass the Uniform CPA Examination, which is developed and graded by the AICPA
3. Have a certain amount of professional work experience in public accounting (not all states require this).

The Uniform CPA Examination is given over a two-day period twice annually (in May and November). The exam consists of four sections:

- Business Law & Professional Responsibilities
- Auditing
- Accounting & Reporting-Taxation, Managerial, and Governmental and Not-for-Profit Organizations
- Financial Accounting & Reporting-Business Enterprises

The AICPA has produced a brochure with additional details on the exam: the Uniform CPA Examination Candidate Brochure. Once you have become a CPA, most states require you to take specified amounts of continuing professional education courses annually to retain your professional license to practice.

CRC   Certified Retirement Counselor

The International Foundation for Retirement Education
2230 Gallows Road, Suite 380
P.O. Box 125
Dunn Loring, VA 22027-1101
703-934-0941
www.infre.org

Contributors: William Pomeroy, Cathie Cobe

The International Foundation for Retirement Education (InFRE) awards the Certified Retirement Counselor (CRC) certification upon the completion of a comprehensive, four-course program as described below. Enrollees will be required to pass four proctored examinations to demonstrate mastery of the subject matter. The CRC certification also requires:

- A college degree (or equivalent experience)
- A minimum of two years' related professional experience (within the past five years)
- Two professional references

CSA   Certified Senior Advisor

Society of Certified Senior Advisors
1777 S. Bellaire Street, #230
Denver, CO 80222
303-757-2323
800-653-1785
www.society-csa.com

Contributor: Richard Vera

The Society of Certified Senior Advisors grants the Certified Senior Advisor (CSA) designation. They are an educational organization that provides in-depth training on senior issues to professionals who work with seniors.

The Society of Certified Senior Advisors was founded in 1996 by a group of forward-thinking geriatric MDs, gerontologists, elder law attorneys, CPAs, financial planners, and other qualified professionals. Senior citizens prefer to use professionals who are well trained and specifically educated in the issues that are most important to seniors.

More than 8,000 professionals from 50 states and the District of Columbia have enrolled in the CSA training. CSAs represent the following disciplines: accountants, attorneys, business executives, clergy, doctors, nurses, pharmacists, financial planners, geriatric care professionals, home health professionals, insurance agents, long-term care consultants, reverse mortgage lenders, senior housing professionals, and social workers.

The Society of CSAs offers its designation training in two formats:

- Live Class. An intensive $3^{1}/_{2}$ day educational program taught live by faculty members flown in for the class. The class ends with a closed-book, multiple-choice exam administered the morning of the fourth day.

- Correspondence Course. Correspondence course participants receive a comprehensive study guide and audiocassettes of 22 live class presentations, which average 50 minutes in length. The correspondence course is self-paced; the student completes it by taking a monitored examination and doing a brief writing assignment.

CVA   CERTIFIED VALUATION ANALYST

National Association of Certified Valuation Analysts
1111 Brickyard Road, Suite 200
Salt Lake City, UT 84106-5401
1-801-486-0600
www.nacva.com

Contributors: Frank Washelesky, John Connell

The Certified Valuation Analyst is the National Association of Certified Valuation Analyst's (NACVA) original business valuation certification. A primary requirement for becoming a CVA is to hold a valid license as a Certified Public Accountant (CPA). Professionals must complete a five-day training program as prescribed by the Association, submit three personal and three business references; and then pass a comprehensive two-part examination. Part One is a half-day proctored exam. Part Two is a take-home/in-office exam incorporating a standardized case study (provided by NACVA) that requires performing a complete business valuation.

EA   Enrolled Agent

National Association of Enrolled Agents
200 Orchard Ridge Drive, Suite 302
Gaithersburg, MD 20878-1978
301-212-9608
www.naea.org

Contributors: Judy A. Stewart, Bob Schumann, Stephen A. Drake, Judi Martindale

An enrolled agent is a person who has earned the privilege of practicing, that is, representing taxpayers, before the Internal Revenue Service. Enrolled agents, like attorneys and certified public accountants (CPAs), are generally unrestricted as to which taxpayers they can represent, what types of tax matters they can handle, and which IRS offices they can practice before. In contrast, practice before the IRS is much more limited for other individuals such as unenrolled tax return preparers, family members, full-time employees, partners, and corporate officers.

LMFT   Licensed Marriage and Family Therapist

American Association of Marriage and Family Therapists
112 South Alfred Street
Alexandria, VA 22314-3061
703-838-9808
www.aamft.org

Contributors: Susan Zimmerman

Marriage and family therapy is a distinct professional discipline with graduate and postgraduate programs. Three options are available for those interested in becoming a marriage and family therapist: Master's degree (two to three years), doctoral program (three to five years), or postgraduate clinical training programs (three to four) years. Historically, marriage and family therapists have come from a wide variety of educational backgrounds including psychology, psychiatry, social work, nursing, pastoral counseling, and education.

The Federal government has designated marriage and family therapy as a core mental health profession along with psychiatry, psychology, social work, and psychiatric nursing. Currently, 42 states also support and regulate the profession by licensing or certifying marriage and family therapists, with many other states considering licensing bills.

The regulatory requirements in most states are substantially equivalent to the American Association of Marriage and Family Therapists Clinical Membership standards. After graduation from an accredited program, a period—usually two years—of post-degree supervised clinical experience is necessary before licensure or certification. When the supervision period is completed, the therapist can take a state-licensing exam, or the national examination for marriage and family therapists conducted by the AAMFT Regulatory Boards. This exam is used as a licensure requirement in most states.

NAPFA Registered Financial Advisor

National Association of Personal Financial Advisors
355 W. Dundee Road, Suite 200
Buffalo Grove, IL 60089
1-888-333-6659
www.napfa.org

Contributors: Steve Wightman, John E. Sestina, Brad R. Cougill, Elaine E. Bedel, Kathleen M. Rehl, Marsha G. LePhew, Donna Skeels Cygan, Gregory C. Fenton, Sid Blum, Jill Gianola, Robert B. Walsh, Joe Harper, Kristofor R. Behn, Jeff Mehler, Timothy M. Hayes, Randall Kratz, Judy A. Stewart, Bonnie A. Hughes, Cary Carbonaro, Connie Brezik, John Henry Low, Timothy P. Thaney, Bob Schumann, Don A. Gomez, Lesley J. Brey, Judi Martindale, Dennis N. Houlihan, Raj Pillai, Mark Wilson, William K. Kaiser, Henrietta Humphreys, Peg Downey, Louis P. Stanasolovich

In order to belong to NAPFA, a financial planner must have three years' experience in comprehensive fee-only planning, have a college degree or its equivalent, have formal financial planning training, be in compliance with registration laws, and submit a financial plan for approval. The planner may not receive any economic benefit when a client implements that planner's recommendations including (but not limited to) commissions, rebates, awards, finders' fees, and bonuses. NAPFA members also must avoid any circumstances that could create a possible conflict of interest.

There are three categories of membership in NAPFA: NAPFA-Registered Financial Advisor, Provisional Member, and Sustaining Member. An individual is eligible to become a NAPFA-Registered Financial Advisor if he or she agrees to be bound by the NAPFA Code of Ethics, Fiduciary Oath, and Standards of Membership and Affiliation, and meets all of the educational, training, and experience requirements. Only NAPFA-Registered Financial Advisors have voting rights in NAPFA issues and business.

PFS   CPA/Personal Financial Specialists

The American Institute of Certified Public Accountants
1211 Avenue of the Americas
New York, NY 10036-8775
1-888-777-7077
www.aicpa.org

Contributors: Sid Blum, Michael David Schulman, Jim Wagenmann, Craig Olson, Cheryl A. Moss, Jonathan S. Dinkins, Bill Cratty, Reg Baker, Frank B. Arnold, Steve Johnson, John J. Feyche, Paul D. Knott, Harvey D. Aaron, Stephen A. Drake, Ann D. Jevne, Loyd J. Stegent, Bruce R. Heling, Clark M. Blackman II, Chris Cobb, Steven B. Morris, Gregory M. Railsback, Richard A. Vera II, J. Victor Conrad, Robert S. Seltzer, Stuart Kessler, Nate Wenner, Leonard C. Wright, John R. Connell, Frank L. Washelesky, Deborah O. Levine, Judy Ludwig, John Henry Wyckoff, Howard Safer, Paul D. Lyons, Lloyd E. Painter, Jon S. Chernila, Cathie E. Cobe, Robert B. Walsh, Patrick T. Hanratty, Marsha G. LePhew, Martin J. Sickles, Joseph E. Sedita, Jack B. Capron, Barbara J. Raasch, Michael M. Eisenberg, Charles P. Copeland, William K. Kaiser, Mitchell Freedman, Connie Brezik, H. Lindsey Torbett, Susan J. Bruno, Timothy P. Thaney, Phyllis Bernstein

There are several requirements for becoming a CPA/PFS:

1. Be a member in good standing of the AICPA
2. Hold an unrevoked CPA certificate issued by a state authority
3. Have demonstrated experience in six areas:
   - Personal financial planning process (goal setting)
   - Personal income tax planning

- Risk management planning
- Investment planning
- Retirement planning
- Estate planning

4. Meet lifelong learning and continuing professional education requirements
5. Pass an exam (there are seven eligible exams: CPA/PFS, CFP, ChFC, CFA, and NASD Series 65, 66 and 7)
6. Submit references
7. Agree to apply for re-accreditation every three years.

RFC   REGISTERED FINANCIAL CONSULTANT

International Association of Registered Financial Consultants
P.O. Box 42506
Middletown, OH 45042
1-800-532-9060
www.iarfc.org

Contributors: John Grable, Paul Richard, Timothy Hayes

The Registered Financial Consultant is a professional designation awarded by the International Association of Registered Financial Consultants to those financial advisors who can meet high standards of education, experience, and integrity. Because there are no consistent licensing requirements for the various persons who call themselves "financial planners," the public has a critical need for a method of distinguishing the qualified and dedicated financial advisor. The Registered Financial Consultant has met the qualifications required to serve the public effectively, and moreover, is committed to the essential professional continuing education.

C

ABOUT THE ASSOCIATIONS

AADMO AMERICAN ASSOCIATION OF DEBT MANAGEMENT ORGANIZATIONS

P.O. Box 5579
Houston, TX 77325
281-360-8709
www.AADMO.org

Contributors: Randall L. Leshin, Preston Cochrane

The American Association of Debt Management Organizations is an industry education and advocacy organization whose mission is to provide our members and the consumer public with information about the credit and debt counseling industry. AADMO provides a proactive government affairs and advocacy program that promotes laws, regulations, and policies favorable to the debt management industry and our members. Our process of actively monitoring policy initiatives allows us to respond to legislative and regulatory proposals adverse to the interests of our members and the industry. The central point of our government affairs program is active involvement by our members. The AADMO grassroots network helps to take an active role in the development and formulation of policies that protect the functioning of the debt management industry, the consumers the industry serves, and the strong economic foundation of our nation.

AADMO works to promote the public education and consumer awareness of the credit and debt counseling industry through gathering and publishing statistics, media alerts, consumer brochures, customer newsletters, educational campaigns, technical papers, and proactive media relations.

AADMO members are debt management organizations, consumer counselors, personal finance educators, credit and debt information publishers, debt pooling organizations, debt negotiators, debt adjusters, credit counselors, consumer lawyers, and many, many others.

AFCPE   Association for Financial Counseling and Planning Education

2121 Arlington Avenue, Suite 5
Upper Arlington, OH 43221-4339
614-485-9650
www.afcpe.org

Contributors: John Grable, Barbara O'Neill, Paul S. Richard, Angie Hollerich, Sherman D. Hanna, Susan Zimmerman, Preston Cochrane

AFCPE is a nonprofit, professional organization comprised of researchers, academics, and financial counselors, educators, and planners. The purpose of the organization, as stated in its Bylaws, is to:

- Promote improved personal financial management education
- Promote the education, training, and certification of financial counseling and planning professionals
- Promote research in personal financial management
- Disseminate research findings and program methodologies related to financial counseling and planning education

Our common goal is to improve the quality of life of our end users—families and individuals who, regardless of their incomes, are struggling to get ahead.

AICCCA ASSOCIATION OF INDEPENDENT CONSUMER CREDIT COUNSELING AGENCIES

11350 Randoms Hill Road, Suite 800
Fairfax, VA 22020
703-934-6118
www.aiccca.org

Contributor: Jeff Michael

The Association of Independent Consumer Credit Counseling Agencies (AICCCA) is a national membership organization of 48 credit counseling agencies established to promote quality and consistent delivery of credit counseling services. The Association, founded in 1993, fulfills its mission by establishing a consensus among consumer professionals regarding service standards and professional industry conduct, as well as by establishing and maintaining strong relationships with credit management professionals and consumers.

AICPA THE AMERICAN INSTITUTE OF CERTIFIED PUBLIC ACCOUNTANTS

1211 Avenue of the Americas
New York, NY 10036-8775
1-888-777-7077
www.aicpa.org

Contributors: Sid Blum, Michael David Schulman, Jim Wagenmann, Craig Olson, Cheryl A. Moss, Alexis M. Jensen, Jonathan S. Dinkins, Bill Cratty, Reg Baker, Frank B. Arnold, Steve Johnson, John J. Feyche, Paul D. Knott, Harvey D. Aaron, James Kantowski, Stephen A. Drake, Ann D. Jevne, Loyd J. Stegent, Bruce R. Heling, Clark M. Blackman II, Chris Cobb, Steven B. Morris, Gregory M. Railsback, Richard A. Vera II, J. Victor Conrad, Robert S. Seltzer, Stuart Kessler, Nate Wenner, Leonard C. Wright, John R. Connell, Frank L. Washelesky, Deborah O. Levine, Judy Ludwig, John Henry Wyckoff, Howard Safer, Paul D. Lyons, Lloyd E. Painter, Jon S. Chernila, Cathie E. Cobe, Robert B. Walsh, Patrick T. Hanratty, Marsha G. LePhew, Martin J. Sickles, Joseph E. Sedita, Jack B. Capron, Barbara J. Raasch, Michael M. Eisenberg, Charles P. Copeland, Mitchell Freedman, Connie Brezik, H. Lindsey Torbett, Susan J. Bruno, Timothy P. Thaney, Phyllis Bernstein, Chad P. Tramp

The American Institute of Certified Public Accountants is the ISO 9001- certified national professional organization that represents roughly 340,000 member CPAs in business and industry, public practice, government, and education. The AICPA's staff of 650, which supports the membership and its activities, is divided between the national headquarters in New York City and offices in Washington, DC; Jersey City, New Jersey; and Lewisville, Texas. The AICPA represents the profession nationally in dealing with rule-making, standard-setting, and legislative bodies, public interest groups, state CPA societies, and other professional organizations. The AICPA's proactive communications program is designed to inform regulators, legislators, the public, and others of the varied roles and functions of CPAs in society. The AICPA develops standards for audit and other services by CPAs, provides educational guidance materials to its members, prepares and administers the Uniform CPA Examination, and monitors and enforces compliance with the profession's technical and ethical standards. The AICPA's founding in 1887

established accountancy as a profession distinguished by rigorous educational requirements, high professional standards, a strict code of professional ethics, a licensing status, and a commitment
to serving the public interest.

AIMR ASSOCIATION FOR INVESTMENT MANAGEMENT AND RESEARCH

560 Ray C. Hunt Drive
Charlottesville, VA 22903-0668
1-800-247-8132
www.aimr.org

Contributors: Lesley J. Brey, Constanza and John Henry Low, Clark M. Blackman II, Barbara J. Raasch

The Association for Investment Management and Research (AIMR) is an international, nonprofit organization of more than 50,000 investment practitioners and educators in over 100 countries.

Founded in January 1990, AIMR was created from the merger of the Financial Analysts Federation (FAF) and the Institute of Chartered Financial Analysts (ICFA). The FAF was originally established in 1947 as a service organization for investment professionals in its societies and chapters. The ICFA was founded in 1959 to examine candidates and award the Chartered Financial Analyst (CFA) designation.

AIMR's mission is to serve its members and investors as a global leader in educating and examining investment managers and analysts and sustaining high standards of professional conduct. AIMR's membership is global in scope, and its activities are worldwide.

The Research Foundation of the AIMR sponsors practitioner-oriented research through funding and publishing a diverse assortment of monographs, tutorials, and research papers to broaden investment professionals' knowledge and understanding of their field.

AIMR offers services in three broad categories: Education through seminars and publications; Professional Conduct and Ethics; and Standards of Practice and Advocacy.

AIMR's members are employed as securities analysts, portfolio managers, strategists, consultants, educators, and other investment specialists.

These professionals practice in a variety of fields, including investment counseling and management, banking, insurance, and investment banking and brokerage firms.

FEI FINANCIAL EXECUTIVES INTERNATIONAL

973-898-4625

http://www.fei.org/

FEI is the preeminent professional association for senior level financial executives, representing 15,000 individuals. Membership driven, FEI provides peer networking opportunities, emerging issues alerts, personal and professional development and advocacy services to Chief Financial Officers, VPs or Finance, Controllers, Treasurers, Tax Executives, Finance and Accounting Professors in academia. We do this principally through our strong Internet community, our 86 chapters, and our 9 technical committees. Membership is limited to individuals holding senior management positions similar to those listed above, but we allow other finance professionals to join if they meet certain criteria. We also have a special rate and status for academics. Other typical titles held by FEI members include Assistant Controller, Subsidiary CFO or Controller, Assistant Treasurer, and Director of Tax.

Financial Executives International was founded in 1931. Over time, the role of the financial executive expanded and the Institute adopted its broader present name in 1962. As the global economy developed, we were the driving force in forming the International Association of Financial Executives Institutes in 1969. We proactively helped design the CFO Act, and have a history of supporting legislation that enhances the business climate.

FPA FINANCIAL PLANNING ASSOCIATION

3801 E. Florida Avenue, Suite 708

Denver, CO 80210

1-800-322-4237

www.fpanet.org

Contributors: Bill Cratty, Donna Skeels Cygan, Jim Wagenmann, Cheryl A. Moss, Henrietta Humphreys, Frank B. Arnold, Sid Blum, Steve Wightman, Alexis M. Jensen, Bill Pomeroy, Elaine E. Bedel,

Kathleen M. Rehl, Constanza and John Henry Low, J. Victor Conrad, Loyd J. Stegent, Steven B. Morris, Louis P. Stanasolovich, Steve Johnson, Bruce R. Heling, Nate Wenner, Ann D. Jevne, Stephen A. Drake, Paul D. Knott, Harvey D. Aaron, John E. Sestina, Leonard C. Wright, Susan Zimmerman, Clark M. Blackman II, Raj Pillai, Helen L. Modly, Judy Ludwig, Paul D. Lyons, Lloyd E. Painter, Timothy M. Hayes, John Henry Wyckoff, Jon S. Chernila, Michael L. Alberts, Ray Julian, Phyllis Bernstein, Patrick T. Hanratty, Jeff Mehler, Marsha G. LePhew, Joseph E. Sedita, Jill Gianola, Dr. Barbara O'Neill, Mark Wilson, Deborah O. Levine, Michael M. Eisenberg, Don A. Gomez, Cary Carbonaro, Bonnie A. Hughes, Connie Brezik, Chad P. Tramp, Joe Harper, Robert B. Walsh, Lesley J. Brey, Cathie E. Cobe

The Financial Planning Association is the membership organization for the financial planning community. It was created when the Institute of Certified Financial Planners (ICFP) and the International Association for Financial Planning (IAFP) unified on January 1, 2000. Members include individuals and companies who have contributed to building the financial planning profession and all those who champion the financial planning process. FPA members are dedicated to supporting the financial planning process in order to help people achieve their goals and dreams. The FPA believes that everyone needs objective advice to make smart financial decisions, and that when seeking the advice of a financial planner, the planner should be a CFP® professional.

A nationwide network of local chapters is the backbone of the FPA. Each one promotes the advancement of knowledge in financial planning, supporting programs and projects that enable members to better serve their clients.

The FPA's official publication is the *Journal of Financial Planning*. This award-winning publication features prominent writers who cover all aspects of financial planning including news that shapes the community. FPA's web presence includes articles, forums, online networking, and substantive information of interest to those who support the financial planning process.

The FPA offers services and resources designed to help the public understand the importance of the financial planning process and the value of objective advice from a CFP® professional. Resources include issue-based campaigns designed to educate consumers about specific personal finance issues, a service to connect consumers with local CFP® professionals, web-based consumer information and brochures.

IARFC INTERNATIONAL ASSOCIATION FOR REGISTERED FINANCIAL CONSULTANTS

The Financial Planning Building
2507 North Verity Parkway
Middletown, OH 45042
1-800-532 9060
www.iarfc.org

Contributors: John Grable, Timothy M. Hayes

Since 1993, the IARFC has grown into an organization of approximately 1000 proven financial professionals formed to foster public confidence in the financial planning profession, assist the public in locating quality advisors, help financial advisors exchange planning techniques, and give deserved recognition to those practitioners who are truly qualified and committed to professional education.

There are seven requirements for membership: education, examination, experience, licensing, business integrity, adherence to a strict code of ethics, and maintenance of proficiency with a minimum of 40 hours per year of continuing education in the field of financial planning.

In a society that grows more complex every day, consumers are presented with the need to balance personal financial security with the constant pressures of family, career, community responsibilities, and personal enrichment. The financial marketplace is ever-changing with new laws, regulations, products, and conflicting media messages. Making the right moves at the right time is critical to accomplishing personal objectives.

A professional advisor guides the financial planner process: goal identification, data organization, analysis, problem identification, recommendations, and most important—plan implementation and results monitoring. IARFC sponsors learning seminars and has a computer bank of members and their website links and provides them with the names, addresses, and phone numbers of the nearest Registered Financial Consultant. You can also confirm the RFC's standing by e-mail at director@iarfc.org.

IIABA INDEPENDENT INSURANCE AGENTS & BROKERS OF AMERICA

127 South Peyton Street
Alexandria, VA 22314
1-800-221-7917
www.iiaa.com

Contributor: Kent Anthony

The Independent Insurance Agents & Brokers of America (IIABA), the nation's oldest and largest independent agent association, is both a highly regarded consumer advocacy organization and a powerful force within the insurance industry, on Capitol Hill, and in the media. Founded in 1896 by a small group of local fire agents, the association today represents 300,000 agents and their employees.

Now in its second century, IIABA's activities have expanded to address the many challenges and opportunities that independent insurance agents and brokers face. Through its federation of 51 state associations, as well as its headquarters and Capitol Hill offices, IIABA provides advocacy, business tools, and media visibility to its members.

IIABA represents more than half of all the independent insurance agencies and brokerage firms in the country. Its members range from small rural agencies selling personal lines to large commercial brokers handling major national accounts.

IMCA INVESTMENT MANAGEMENT CONSULTANTS ASSOCIATION

9101 Kenyon Avenue, Suite 3000
Denver, CO 80237
303-770-3377

Contributors: Jonathan Dinkins, Clark M. Blackman II, Nate Wenner

A nonprofit organization with members in the United States, Canada, Britain, and Australia, the Investment Management Consultants Association (IMCA) has promoted education, ethics, and standards for the investment consulting profession for 17 years. The association's 5,000 members benefit from peer networking opportunities, information sharing, and cutting-edge forums on risk management, portfolio construction, and practice management. IMCA's Certified Investment Management Analyst designation assures clients of a consultant's expertise and commitment to professional ethics. IMCA Practice Standards, Performance Reporting Standards, and Questionnaires for Investment Managers offer practical guidelines to members seeking to enhance their client relationships. The semiannual *Journal of Investment Consulting* publishes original research and in-depth articles on investment agent theory and practice, and *The Monitor*, a bimonthly membership publication, informs members of the latest news on industry trends and investment strategies. IMCA members also receive regular updates on important legislation and regulatory developments in Washington and the 50 states through the association's Legislative Network.

NAEA NATIONAL ASSOCIATION OF ENROLLED AGENTS

200 Orchard Ridge Drive, Suite 302
Gaithersburg, MD 20878
1-800-424-4339
www.naea.org

Contributors: Judi Martindale, Judy A. Stewart, Bob Schumann

The National Association of Enrolled Agents (NAEA) is a national association of over 10,000 independent, licensed tax professionals called Enrolled Agents (EA). The association is dedicated to helping its members maintain the highest level of knowledge, skills, and professionalism in all areas of taxation, so that their members may most effectively represent the needs of their clients.

Members of NAEA are required to complete a minimum of 30 hours of continuing professional education each year in the interpretation, application, and administration of federal and state tax laws in order to maintain membership in the organization. This requirement surpasses the IRS-required minimum of 16 hours per year.

The mission of NAEA is to:

- Foster the professionalism and growth of its Members;
- Be an advocate of taxpayer rights;
- Protect the interests of its Members; and
- Enhance the role of the Enrolled Agent among government agencies, other professions, and the public at large.

NAEPC   National Association of Estate Planners and Councils

1120 Chester Avenue, Suite 470
Cleveland, OH 44114
866-226-2224
www.naepc.org

The NAEPC's particular focus is on:

- Accounting
- Insurance
- Law
- Trust Services
- Financial Planning

A primary goal of the NAEPC is to encourage specialization programs to increase recognition and acceptance of estate planning as a specialty. NAEPC has two separate and distinct specialization programs: Accredited Estate Planner (AEP) and the Estate Planning Law Specialist.

NAEPC serves to assist its individual members and their Local Councils by providing a forum to maintain and strengthen:

- Their cutting-edge awareness of the continually changing and expanding opportunities
- Communication and development of a common language between the four disciplines
- A unified point-of-approach

NAIFA   National Association of Insurance and Financial Advisors

1922 F Street, NW
Washington, DC 20006-4387
703-770-8116
www.naifa.org

Contributors: J. Victor Conrad, Bill Pomeroy, Bill Cratty, Susan Zimmerman, Cheryl A. Moss

The National Association of Insurance and Financial Advisors (NAIFA) is a national nonprofit association representing the interests of 80,000 life and health insurance agents and financial advisors nationwide, through its federation of 900 state and local associations. One of the oldest and largest nonprofit trade organizations in the insurance and financial field, NAIFA plays a vital role in encouraging legislation and regulation at the federal and state levels to protect policyholders and maintain a healthy and well-regulated marketplace. NAIFA also provides its members with education, training, and resources to help them maintain and grow their practices. Additionally, NAIFA includes a Division of Financial Advisors and three specialty conferences: the Association for Advanced Life Underwriting (AALU), the Association of Health Insurance Advisors (AHIA), and GAMA International.

The mission of NAIFA is to improve the business environment, and enhance the professional skills and promote the ethical conduct of agents and others engaged in insurance and related financial services who assist the public in achieving financial security and independence.

An advocate for insurance agents, financial advisors, and consumers, NAIFA was founded on June 18, 1890, in Boston as the National Association of Life Underwriters (NALU). In 1951, NALU created the General Agents and Managers Association (GAMA) to enhance the quality and capability of the insurance industry's field management. In 1957, NALU formed the Association for Advanced Life Underwriting (AALU) to support advanced life insurance underwriters, agents engaged in complex areas of life insurance such as business continuation planning, estate planning, retirement planning, deferred compensation, and employee benefits planning. In 1990, a third conference of NALU, the Association of Health Insurance Agents (AHIA), was formed to sustain and enhance the business environment for health insurance agents and to improve the financing and delivery of health care in the United States. In 1999, the organization changed its name to the National Association of Insurance and Financial Advisors to more accurately describe its membership and to attract professionals from the broad spectrum of financial services.

NAPFA National Association of Personal Financial Advisors

355 W. Dundee Road, Suite 200
Buffalo Grove, IL 60089
1-888-333-6659
www.napfa.org

The idea for the National Association of Personal Financial Advisors, a nonprofit organization that advances the practice of fee-only financial planning, grew from a Society of Independent Financial Advisors meeting at Emory University in Atlanta, Georgia, in 1982.

A discussion among several fee-only financial advisors centered on helping prospective planners who asked for assistance in starting their practices. These veteran planners were certainly interested in encouraging new fee-only financial advisors. However, the experienced planners discovered they were overwhelmed by requests to visit their offices.

A meeting to provide information to anyone interested in fee-only financial planning was scheduled in Atlanta for February 1983. More than 125 people attended that first meeting and NAPFA was born. Richard W. Whitehead, Atlanta, Georgia, one of the members of the first board of directors, suggested that the name "National Association of Personal Financial Advisors" best represented what the infant organization was all about.

Strict standards were set for membership, which remain intact today. In order to belong to NAPFA, a financial planner must have three years' experience in comprehensive fee-only planning, have a college degree or its equivalent, have formal financial planning training, be in compliance with registration laws, and submit a financial plan for approval. The planner may not receive any economic benefit when a client implements that planner's recommendations including (but not limited to) commissions, rebates, awards, finders' fees, and bonuses. NAPFA members also must avoid any circumstances which could create a possible conflict of interest.

NATP National Association of Tax Professionals

720 Association Drive
Appleton, WI 54914
920-749-1040
www.natptax.com

Contributors: Jill Gianola, Bonnie A. Hughes, Bob Schumann

The National Association of Tax Professionals (NATP), founded in 1979, is a nonprofit association dedicated to excellence in taxation and related financial services. Our national office is located in Appleton, Wisconsin, and employs 38 professionals.

NATP was formed to serve professionals who work in all areas of tax practice. The approximately 15,000 members include Enrolled Agents, Certified Public Accountants, individual practitioners, accountants, attorneys, and financial planners.

Through NATP's Tax Research Center, staff experts annually assist members with more than 40,000 federal tax-related questions. State assistance volunteers also assist fellow members with state taxation questions. As the leading continuing professional education provider for tax professionals, NATP presents more than 20 workshops each year on topics that include partnerships, corporations, estates, and trusts. NATP also sponsors the Enrolled Agents Training Workshop and more than 80 Famous 1040 and 1040 Extra Workshops.

NATP members participate in an Annual National Conference and Exposition and network with colleagues through various State Chapters. Member services include access to the Tax Store catalog, TAXPRO Monthly Newsletter, TAXPRO Weekly E-Mail, the TAXPRO Quarterly Journal, plus much more.

NIPA National Institute of Pension Administrators

401 North Michigan Avenue, #2200
Chicago, IL 60611-4267
1-800-999-NIPA (6472)
www.nipa.org

Contributor: Mark Wilson

The National Institute of Pension Administrators (NIPA) is a nationwide educational association whose mission is to enhance professionalism in the retirement and employee plan administration industry. It was founded in 1983 to foster the highest standard of ethical and professional conduct by bringing together professional benefit administrators and other interested parties to encourage greater dialogue, cooperation, and educational opportunities. To this end, NIPA offers a variety of educational pursuits and programs focusing on the various aspects of plan administration.

NIPA works for the benefit of its 850 members—and the entire industry as a whole—to increase the general and technical level of knowledge about retirement and other employee benefit plans and their administration. A cornerstone of NIPA education are its two professional designation programs: the Accredited Pension Administrator (APA), covering all aspects of plan administration; and the Accredited Pension Representative (APR), dedicated to defined contribution plans and investment philosophy.

NIPA prides itself on the opportunities it provides for advancing knowledge in the pension and retirement plan industry as a whole. The organization designs, implements, and administers comprehensive educational forums focusing on the various aspects of plan administration. Two industry conferences each year provide the opportunity to enhance your business by strengthening existing relationships, establishing new ties, and garnering a wealth of information on our industry's future direction. Local NIPA chapters foster self-improvement to all members and interested parties.

NFCC   National Foundation for Credit Counseling

801 Roeder Road, Suite 900
Silver Spring, MD 20910
301-589-5600
www.nfcc.org

Contributors: Kathy Adams-Smith, Jennifer Delcamp, Jeff Michael, Sandra E. Dunaway, Linda L. Tucker, Samuel O. Sanders, Jr., Carolyn Baker

The National Foundation for Credit Counseling, Inc., (NFCC)®, founded in 1951, is the nation's largest and longest-serving national nonprofit network providing premier consumer money management, credit, and debt counseling and educational services. With more than 1,300 community-based offices nationwide, NFCC members help more than 1.5 million households annually. NFCC members, mostly known as Consumer Credit Counseling Service (CCCS)® and other names, can be identified by the NFCC member seal. This seal signifies high standards for agency accreditation, counselor certification, and policies that ensure free or low-cost confidential services.

NSA   National Speakers Association

1500 S. Priest Drive
Tempe, AZ 85281
480-968-2552
www.nsaspeaker.org

Contributors: Angie Hollerich, Joseph Sedita, Judi Martindale

The National Speakers Association (NSA) is the leading organization for experts who speak professionally. NSA's 4,000 members include experts in a variety of industries and disciplines, who reach audiences as trainers, educators, humorists, motivators, consultants, authors, and more. Since 1973, NSA has provided resources and education designed to advance the skills, integrity, and value of its members and the speaking profession.

PAN   Philanthropic Advisors Network

1828 L Street, NW
Washington, DC 20036
202-466-6512
www.cof.org
202-466-6612

Contributor: Cary Carbonaro

The Philanthropic Advisors Network (PAN) is a network of 230 legal and financial advisors that provides subscribers with the opportunity to discuss charitable issues, assist their clients, and learn from one another. Since 1999, the network has focused on the complex areas of foundation and giving program creation and growth, tax issues, and governance.

PAN is an ideal professional development resource for high-net-worth advisors. It allows subscribers to network in an exclusive and collegial setting while having access to the Council on Foundations, which has a 54-year history as leaders in organized philanthropy. The Council's staff of experts in the field is available to assist advisors with legal questions as well as issues specific to family, community, and corporate philanthropy. In addition, the Network keeps subscribers fully informed on emerging issues in the field and breaking legislative developments in Washington, D.C.

SFSP   Society of Professional Service Professionals

270 S. Bryn Mawr Avenue
Bryn Mawr, PA 19010-2195
1-888-243-2258
www.financialpro.org

Contributors: Lloyd E. Painter, Sid Blum, J. Victor Conrad, Cheryl A. Moss, Bill Pomeroy, Cathie E. Cobe

The Society of Professional Service Professionals is the professional association that insurance and financial advisors turn to for high-quality professional development and continuing education programs. The Society keeps its members informed on developments in the industry and offers a multitude of career advancement tools to position its members most favorably in the marketplace. Our strong commitment to ethics forms a firm foundation upon which our reputation is built. Local, national, and online networking opportunities bring additional value to our members.

The members of the Society of Financial Service Professionals have earned one or more highly respected professional designations and are dedicated to high standards of professionalism in serving the needs of their clients effectively. To that end, they adhere to strict requirements in the areas of continuing education and ethical conduct.

INDEX